ASYLUM, MIGRATION AND COMMUNITY

D0497049

tial R
0196

ASYLUM, MIGRATION AND COMMUNITY

Maggie O'Neill

This edition published in Great Britain in 2010 by

The Policy Press
University of Bristol
Fourth Floor
Beacon House
Queen's Road
Bristol BS8 1QU
UK

t: +44 (0)117 331 4054
f: +44 (0)117 331 4093
tpp-info@bristol.ac.uk
www.policypress.co.uk

North American office:
The Policy Press
c/o International Specialized Books Services (ISBS)
920 NE 58th Avenue, Suite 300
Portland, OR 97213-3786, USA
t: +1 503 287 3093
f: +1 503 280 8832
info@isbs.com

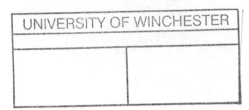

British Library Cataloguing in Publication Data
A catalogue record for this book is available from the British Library.

Library of Congress Cataloging-in-Publication Data
A catalog record for this book has been requested.

ISBN 978 1 84742 222 4 paperback
ISBN 978 1 84742 223 1 hardcover

Cover design by The Policy Press.
Front cover: image kindly supplied by Jeffer M.-Garib.
Printed and bound in Great Britain by Hobbs, Southampton.

The Policy Press uses environmentally responsible print partners.

Contents

List of figures

List of abbreviations

AHRB	Arts and Humanities Research Board
AHRC	Arts and Humanities Research Council
BNP	British National Party
CEAS	common European asylum system
ECHR	European Convention on Human Rights
EMPAF	East Midlands Participatory Arts Forum
ESOL	English for speakers of other languages
EU	European Union
FGM	female genital mutilation
HDHS	Human Dignity and Humiliation Studies
IND	Immigration and Nationality Directorate
NAM	new asylum model
NASS	National Asylum Support Service
NAWEF	Nottingham African Women's Empowerment Forum
NGO	non-governmental organisation
NIACE	National Institute of Adult Continuing Education
PA	participatory arts
PAR	participatory action research
RCO	refugee community organisation
SAEMP	Somali Afro European Media Project
TUC	Trades Union Congress
UDHR	Universal Declaration of Human Rights
UKBA	United Kingdom Border Agency
UN	United Nations
UNCRC	United Nations Convention on the Rights of the Child
UNHCR	United Nations High Commissioner for Refugees
VoT	victims of trafficking

Acknowledgements

Many people have helped and influenced the development of this book. My first thanks must go to the artists and community arts organisations with whom I have had the privilege of working with and learning from. Charnwood Arts, Soft Touch, City Arts Nottingham, Long Journey Home, B Arts, NIACE and Exiled Writers Ink. Maggy Milner, Jennifer Langer, Misha Myers, Bea Tobolewska, Paul and Miriam Gent, Stuart Brown, Gaylan Nazhad, Aria Ahmed, Jasim Ghafur, Obediar Madziva, Emmanuel Changunda, Jeffer M.-Garib, John Perivolaris, Nick Clements, Tove Dalenius, Sally Norman, Gill Gill, Hilary Hughes, Amy Edwards, Sarah Bailey, Gerry Flanagan, Heather Connelly, Rosie Hobbs, Kate Duncan, Alma Cunliffe, Kevin Ryan, Chris Sabanda, Coco Kalenga, Les Elus, Bruno Ngumbwe, Karina Martin, Senkal Yaami, Jamie Bird, Ljaja Sterland, Jane Watts, Lawrence Chester, Alex Kamanga, Faith Gakanje, François Matarasso, Mariwan Dara Aeziz, and Nabil Musa – it is such a pleasure working with you.

Jeffer M.-Garib's painting 'Stone Age' was adapted for the cover design. Jeffer can be contacted at jeffer.garib@yahoo.co.uk and more of his work can be found at: http://longjourneyhome.org.uk/artists.html

Readers will see Aria Ahmed's photographs throughout this text. More of Aria's work can be found at www.threedotsdesign.co.uk and she can be contacted at threedotsdesign@hotmail.com

Heather Connelly's photographs of the creative work conducted with City Arts Nottingham and a women's group supported by Refugee Action can be found on pages 155-9. More of Heather's work can be found at: www-staff.lboro.ac.uk/~achc/pages/homepage.html

Paul Gent's work with the Dreamers youth group on page ii is inspirational, blending stories, storytelling and art making. Paul is based at Charnwood Arts in Loughborough; he can be contacted on pablogent@yahoo.com and some of his work can be seen at: www.linkpalestine.org

Heartfelt thanks to the people who took part in the various projects as participants and researchers, people who are living in the asylum-migration-community nexus. Thanks for your generosity and warmth in telling your stories and making art. And to Steve, Patrick and James for putting up with my absences and the long periods 'at the computer'!

Thanks to my colleagues for stimulating conversations, support and the opportunity to present work at various symposia, conferences and research seminars, Brian Roberts, Laurie Cohen, Ruth Lister, Jenny Pearce, Roger Bromley, Gen Doy, Martin Brown, Marsha

Mcskimmon, Iris Wigger, Sarah Pink, Karen O'Reilly, Steve Brown, Phil Hubbard, John Arnold, Mark Webster, Christine Gledhill, Barbara Kennedy, Helmut Kuzmics, Heaven Crawley, Rodanthi Tzanelli, Alice Bloch, Eugene McLaughlin, Jan Haaken, Robert Miller, John Given, Jo Phoenix, Olga Bailey, Ramaswami Harindranath; and colleagues at Durham University and colleagues in the ESA European Biographies Network and the HDHS global network, especially Evelin Lindner and Linda Hartling. Thanks to Kim Knott and the Arts and Humanities Research Council (AHRC) for funding our various projects and to The Policy Press, anonymous reviewers, and Karen Bowler and Laura Greaves for excellent support.

My final thanks go to the very special youth organisation, Dreamers and my inspirational friends Andrew Lake and Kevin Ryan. This book is dedicated to the young people at Dreamers for following their dreams and hopes in the face of fear, destruction, loss, war and suffering.

> 'My mum told us to hide inside a tree with a big hole in it (a hollow tree). She told me and my brother to be quiet as there were bad people outside who would hurt us. She told us a story of a spider who lived in the tree who would spin his web around us to hide from the bad people.' (young person, aged 11, quoted in Lake, 2008, p 27)

> 'The police tied me upside down and fastened me to a metal bar that spanned the room. They put electricity through my body. I thought I was going to die.' (young person, aged 17, quoted in Lake, 2008, p 31)

The young people at Dreamers support group chose the name 'Dreamers' collectively. They also adopted a sleeping person as a logo, to symbolise the safety and security of having somewhere to sleep.

> 'We are all dreamers. When we travelled and when things got tough it was our dreams that kept us going. We dreamed of freedom and safety.' (Lake, 2008, p 13)

Copyright acknowledgements

Grateful thanks to the individuals and organisations listed below for permission to use their photographs. Every reasonable effort has been made to identify the holders of copyright material and to obtain permission for use. The publisher apologises for any errors or omissions in the list and would be grateful to be notified of any corrections that should be incorporated in future reprints or editions of this book.

Figure 1: Archive of the Irish in Britain, London Metropolitan University; Figure 2: Reuters/Pascal Rossignol, Figure 3: Houston Conwill; Figure 4: Karen Fraser, Nottingham City Arts; Figure 5: Soft Touch Arts (www.soft-touch.org.uk/); Figures 6, 7, 8: Article 19 (www.article19.org/); Figure 9: Somali Afro European Media Project (www.saemp.org.uk/); Figure 10: Phil Hubbard; Figures 11, 12: Kevin Ryan; Figures 13, 14, 21, 23, 24, 25, 26, 29, 30, 31, 32, 33: Aria Ahmed; Figures 15, 16, 17, 18, 19, 20: Heather Connelly; Figures 27, 28: Tove Dalenius; Figures, 34, 35: Paul Gent; Figure 36, 37, 38, 39, 40: Dreamers youth organisation/Kevin Ryan.

Preface

Many scholars working in the field of migration are inspired to do so from their own biographical histories and experiences. The humanities and social sciences have a rich range of writings that give voice to the emergence of transcultural communities, the experience of mobilities and migration, of displacement, diaspora, hybridity and belonging. A growing body of literature is available, also in fictive texts, telling stories of colonialism, post-colonialism, migration, mobility, cosmopolitanism and the search for belonging in a glocalised world.

I was personally inspired to engage with the broad field of refugee and migration studies as a consequence of the impact of the Bosnian war and the break up of the Yugoslavian federation on my sociological and criminological imagination. Engaging first with newly arrived Bosnian refugee communities in Nottingham and three waves of Afghan refugees in London, I went on to work with newly arrived migrants seeking safety and liveable lives from the Middle East and the global South. This book emerges from my experience of doing research with asylum seekers, refugees, undocumented people and communities funded largely by the AHRC as well as local authorities and the Home Office via Government Offices in the East and West Midlands.

My own biography includes a family history embedded in the migration of Irish grandparents and the impact of poverty and unbelonging on their lives and my family's internal migration from the North East to the Midlands. My socialisation was rooted in socialism, trade unionism, Irish literature and gendered politics that in turn led to a deeply political attitude to social and sexual inequalities and a commitment to Marx's dictum that people 'make history but not in conditions of their own choosing'. And, that we should not only seek to understand our social worlds but to change them. Thus the importance of critical theory and 'praxis' (purposeful knowledge), of gaining knowledge from below, the vital importance of social justice, citizenship and processes and practices of inclusion in our theory, research and social policy with refugees and asylum seekers.

This book is written within a trajectory of more than two decades of research with marginalised groups and communities using critical theory, participatory action research (PAR) and participatory arts (PA)-based methods. It is also written at a particular moment in history which is peculiarly Kafkaesque, constituted by liquid modernity, globalisation, the increasing power of supranational bodies and the disembedding of state power, the increasing instrumentalism and bureaucratisation of the major institutions that make up society and the tightening of borders and border controls. The latter includes the withdrawal of humanising practices, a lack of welcome to people seeking asylum and a heightening of the adversarial approach to those who seek to make their lives in the UK. At the same time there is a significant lack of accountability and responsibility by governments and states for their part in the production of the world's refugees.

As an interdisciplinary endeavour the text is written from my immersion in sociology and criminology and it engages with the refugee and migration studies literature, community-based interventions and practice, biographical and arts-based research as well as social policy.[1] It builds on previous interdisciplinary work and seeks to better understand lived experiences of exile and belonging, to feed in to policy and praxis and to challenge and change sexual and social inequalities.

The book stresses the importance of dialogue and debate on these crucial issues; of keeping open critical spaces for resisting and challenging exclusionary discourses; the vital inclusion of migrants, refugees and asylum seekers in discussion and debate; the important role of critical and cultural theory/criminology for imagining a radical democratic future; and the importance of renewing methodologies through interdisciplinary research (ethno-mimesis) to interpret (forced) migration and to facilitate production of new knowledge and counter-hegemonic texts to counter exclusionary processes and offer representational challenges. In the process such research and praxis is committed to fostering an interpretive role that includes facilitating spaces for the marginalised/subaltern to speak for themselves using PAR/PA. Inspired by the critical theory of the Frankfurt School, critical and cultural criminology, the empirical and theoretical work captured in this text seeks to contribute to the development of a sociology of forced migration.[2]

Maggie O'Neill
Durham, March 2010

Notes

[1] Situated at the intersections of western Marxism, critical theory, feminisms, ethnographic and participatory research and policy-oriented praxis this book emerges from interdisciplinary engagement with the lives of asylum seekers, refugees and undocumented people.

[2] The British Sociological Association Conference convened by my colleague Tony Spybey and myself in 2002 was, as Castles (2003, p 14) remarked, a timely event, which, we hoped, would encourage research in this area as well encourage sociologists and criminologists to engage with the development of a sociology of forced migration.

Figure 1: 'No Irish, no Blacks, no dogs'
(sign from a house offering bed and breakfast)

Introduction

That the oft-worked working through of the past has to this day been unsuccessful and has degenerated into its own caricature, and empty and cold forgetting, is due to the fact that the objective conditions of society that engendered fascism continue to exist. (Adorno, 1998, p 98)

Migrants to Britain, including refugees, are being made to suffer in unprecedented ways. They are being stigmatised, pauperised and forced into illegality by the policies of the Labour government, which is engaged in a shameful competition with the Tories to demonstrate that it is 'tougher' than they are towards asylum seekers. In the process asylum seekers, and anybody else who looks foreign, have become targets of racism which is worryingly on the increase. (Hayter, 2001, p 149)

Issues of asylum, migration, humanitarian protection and belonging/integration are of growing interest to scholars, practitioners and policy makers beyond the disciplinary areas of refugee and migration studies. Rooted in more than a decade of research using participatory, biographical and arts-based methods with asylum seekers, refugees and undocumented people as well as new and emerging communities, this book explores the dynamics of the asylum-migration-community nexus. It argues that interdisciplinary analysis is required to deal with the complexity of the issues involved, and offers understanding as praxis (purposeful knowledge), drawing on innovative, participatory, performative and policy-oriented research.

Following Lindner (2006) and Smith (2006), I argue that the concept of humiliation as an act, a process and an experience has a significant role to play in understanding the production of the world's refugees, the phenomenon of forced migration and the asylum-migration-community nexus. Moreover, drawing on a number of scholars, I argue that there is an urgent need for dialogue and debate towards the possibilities for a radical democratic future based on principles of recognition, respect, justice, dignity and redistribution.

The first quotation from Adorno (above) invites us to think about a point running through much of his work, that 'the objective conditions of society that engendered fascism continue to exist' (Adorno, 1998, p 98) and indeed, the notion of 'working through the past', a reference to the psychosocial processes of dealing with the Holocaust, has, in fact, become 'empty and cold forgetting' (Adorno, 1998, p 98). Social theory since the 1950s has developed a strong analysis of modernity as being constituted through totalitarianism and the destructive impact of rationalisation and bureaucratisation (Arendt, 1958; Adorno, 1973, 1980; Adorno and Horkheimer, 1995). The second quotation from Hayter provides some evidence for this point given current responses to asylum seekers and refugees in the UK and representations of asylum seekers in the mainstream media (see Chapter Four, this volume).

In Adorno's analysis of the socioeconomic and cultural dimensions of capitalism, he argues that the spectre of fascism lives on in the conditions of society that engendered fascism, stressing that it cannot be derived from subjective dispositions, but rather the 'danger is objective, not primarily located in human beings' (1998, p 99). The economic order and economic organisation 'renders the majority of people dependent upon conditions beyond their control and thus maintains them in a state of political immaturity' (1998, p 98). This point can be illustrated by the contemporary rise of far-right parties across Europe in the 21st century.[1]

In response to the spectre of fascism, Adorno raised the importance of working 'against forgetfulness of the past', that is, against social amnesia of the Holocaust and national socialism. The role of universities, of pedagogy, was highlighted as important to such a process. 'Whatever aims at the more humanly decent organisation of the whole be it theoretically or practically-politically, is at once also resistance against relapse' (Adorno, 1998, p 343). Smith (1998), in her articulation of Laclau and Mouffe's work on democracy and citizenship, suggests that radical democracy is the best route towards social change for the Left today. Quoting Laclau and Mouffe (1990, p 128), Smith writes that their thesis stresses: 'that egalitarian discourses and discourses on rights play a fundamental role in the reconstruction of collective identities' (Smith, 1998, p 7).

Taking up this challenge, epistemologically and methodologically, this book focuses on the radical potential of critical theory, participatory and arts-based research in reconstructing 'collective identities' through intersubjective recognition. It also introduces the work of a global network of scholars and practitioners, a community of people on a planetary level, working for justice, democracy and human dignity against the forces of humiliation.[2] As Smith says (1998), in contrast to liberal pluralism, which 'reduces democratic participation to voting in a market-like political system…. Radical democratic pluralism

... envisions participatory mechanisms through which rigid and antagonistic subject positions might be transformed by their democratic interaction with other subject positions' (1998, p 147).

This book identifies processes and practices of social exclusion and inclusion, cultural segmentalism and tensions in and between communities as one outcome of responses to the asylum-migration-community nexus. Giddens (1994, p 126) outlines the dangers of increasing cultural segmentalism where local communities 'function through exclusion, a differentiating of insiders and outsiders'.[3] For Bauman (2001, p 74), the vision of a just society that characterised early modernity has given way to a 'human rights rule/standard/measurement'. The current more 'liquid' version of modernity acts as a catalyst that perpetuates the production of difference that leads to 'intense community building-in, digging trenches ... barring intruders from entry, but also insiders from getting out; in short, in a keen control over entry and exit visas' (Bauman, 2001, p 76). Later modernity or liquid modernity is also marked by increasing mobility (Urry, 2007).

A significant amount of research shows that most migration takes place either within countries or between developing countries (Crawley, 2001; Marfleet, 2006); that immigration controls are largely effective and the costs of border control measures are high in both human and financial terms; moreover, that increased immigration will continue to be a reality of 21st-century life (Castles, 2003; Smith, 2006; Marfleet, 2006). Yet, in a world of constant movement, of glocalisation, global mobility, migration and what Castles (2003) calls the 'asylum-migration nexus', an enormous amount of energy, time and money is spent on securing the borders of western states, of erecting stronger and stronger barriers to entry.

Forced migration grew dramatically in the post-Cold War period. 'The global refugee population grew from 2.4 million in 1975 to 10.5 million in 1985 and 14.9 million in 1990. A peak was reached after the end of the Cold War with 18.2 million in 1993. By 2000, the global refugee population had declined to 12.1 million' (Castles, 2003, p 14). At the end of 2008 the number of people forcibly uprooted by conflict and persecution worldwide stood at 42 million. This total includes 16 million refugees and asylum seekers[4] and 26 million people uprooted within their own countries. In the first half of 2009 asylum applications to industrialised countries rose by 10 per cent, with a total number of 185,000 asylum applications filed in the first half of the year. Applications were received by '38 European countries, the United States, Canada, Japan, Australia, New Zealand, and The Republic of

Korea', with the top countries of asylum being Iraq, Afghanistan and Somalia (UNHCR, 2009). High Commissioner António Guterres said:

> These statistics show that ongoing violence and instability in some parts of the world force increasing numbers of people to flee and seek protection in safe countries.... There is an acute need for countries to keep their asylum doors wide open to those who are in genuine need of international protection. (quoted in UNHCR, 2009)[5]

Castles (2003) and other authors; Black, 1998; Cernea and McDowell, 2000) show that there are many other forms of forced migration that are difficult to quantify:

> Millions of people are displaced every year by development projects such as dams, airports, roads, luxury housing, conservation areas and game parks. The World Bank puts their number at 10 million a year. Some are able to rebuild their livelihood, but many experience permanent impoverishment and marginalization.... In addition, many people have to migrate because of environmental degradation, natural disasters and industrial accidents or pollution. A final form of forced migration is the trafficking of people across international boundaries for purposes of exploitation. (Castles, 2003, p 15)

Asylum-migration nexus

The asylum-migration nexus is the complex relationship between migration (the movement of people, usually across borders) and forced migration (forced movement due to civil war, natural disasters or decolonisation). The distinction between forced and economic migration has become blurred and there are complex factors and outcomes operating that link the global with the local. Some of these are documented below.

Research shows there are multiple reasons for mobility. Forced migration is not 'the result of a string of unconnected emergencies, but an integral part of North–South relations' (Castles, 2003, p 9). Post–Cold War processes of globalisation speeded up and cross-border flows of people from the South and East to the North increased, in part as a result of global inequalities (Spybey, 1995; Bloch, 2002a; Dunkerly et al, 2002; Castles, 2003; Marfleet, 2006; Castles and Miller, 2009).

Moreover, at the level of communities, transnational communities emerge who have affiliations in more than one country; this phenomenon can also be defined through the concepts of 'diaspora' and 'hybridity'. Interrelationships between new arrivals (asylum seekers, refugees and economic migrants) and established communities can lead to conflict in and between communities. Following the 'race' riots in northern towns and the Cantle report on community cohesion (Cantle, 2002), communitarian discourses have had an impact on the development of research and practice aimed at resolving differences and supporting community cohesion initiatives, such as the Resolving Differences, Neighbourhood Renewal and Civic Renewal programmes. Funded by central and regional Government Offices such programmes reflect a focus on increased community consultation, bridge building and fostering community capacity and leadership. Related to this is the impact of dispersal on local authorities, services and communities, where asylum seekers and refugees are housed, and the concomitant processes of community formation, as well as the re-invigorating and re-imagining of communities.

Certainly many scholars see the active and participative development of refugee communities and community organisations as important to processes of integration. A key theme in this literature is the duality of fostering refugee community organisations (RCOs) using principles of community development, and fostering routes across diversity such as the Cantle report recommends. Increases emerge in the social and cultural diversity of populations. There is also the impact of legislation and the tightening of border controls.

One response to the increases in forced migration is the development of entry restrictions in the North and containment measures in the South. The plethora of asylum and immigration acts produced in the last decade make it very difficult to gain asylum in the UK. The use of detention and containment has increased, as has the number of removals. The impact of government immigration and asylum policy and the ways that this is interpreted by the general public and represented in the mass media has an important bearing on the reception of asylum seekers and migrants at all levels of society. The Immigration and Nationality Directorate (IND) has been renamed the UK Border Agency (UKBA). The Labour government's approach to refugee policy can be read off from asylum policy as offering 'faster, fairer, firmer' solutions to border control. Liam Byrne MP and ex-Home Office Minister espouses communitarian principles of shared values and responsibilities, that 'individuals do best when they are part of a community' (Byrne, 2009), at the same time as marshalling support for the exclusion and othering of asylum seekers. In a press release in October 2007 he said:

> We have secured our borders as never before, stopping nearly 180,000 people boarding planes to the UK in the last 5 years – that's around 2 jumbo jets a week. In the last 12 months we oversaw removal of over 16,000 illegal immigrants who tried to abuse the asylum system – that's one every half hour. As a result of both measures we saw asylum applications fall to their lowest levels not just since 1997, but since 1993…. In the next year, I will oversee, if I last, the biggest shake-up of the immigration system in its history. In 12 months time our immigration system will have changed out of all recognition. In 140 days time a points based system, shaped by the success of Australia, will begin to make sure that only people Britain needs can come here to work and study. (Home Office, 2009)

Legal context to the asylum-migration nexus

It is useful to look at the processes involved in seeking safety in the UK as well as the anomalies, as not everyone seeking asylum can be processed under the terms of the international legislation.

An asylum seeker is someone who has made a claim to be considered for refugee status under the 1951 United Nations (UN) *Convention and protocol relating to the status of refugees*, the 1967 *Protocol relating to the status of refugees* and/or Article 14 of the Universal Declaration of Human Rights (UDHR) (individuals have a 'right to seek and enjoy asylum from persecution'). The 1951 Convention emerged in the aftermath of the Second World War and, as discussed in Chapter One, is useful for some but not for all of those seeking refuge.

The 1951 Convention states that a refugee (refugee status is not conferred until a successful asylum application has been made) is someone who

> as a result of events occurring before 1 January 1951 and owing to well-founded fear of being persecuted for reasons of race, religion, nationality, membership of a particular social group or political opinion, is outside the country of his nationality and is unable, or owing to such fear, is unwilling to avail himself of the protection of that country; or who, not having a nationality and being outside the

country of his former habitual residence as a result of such events, is unable or, owing to such fear, is unwilling to return to it. (UNHCR, 2007)

There are no internationally agreed standards and procedures for defining refugee status and not all states have signed up to the Convention. The 1967 Protocol extended the Convention to those who had become refugees after 1951. At European level the Council of Europe has adopted several instruments concerning refugees. These include: the European Agreement on the Abolition of Visas for Refugees (1959); Resolution 14 (1967) on Asylum to Persons in Danger of Persecution; the European Agreement on Transfer of Responsibility for Refugees (1980); the Recommendation on the Harmonisation of National Procedures Relating to Asylum (1981); the Recommendation on the Protection of Persons Satisfying the Criteria in the Geneva Convention who are not Formally Refugees (1984); and the Dublin Convention (1990), which lays down criteria for determining which member state is responsible for examining an asylum request when the applicant has filed an application for asylum with one or more member states of the European Community.

Thus, the bottom line is that refugee law protects people when their own state has failed to do so. Human rights law protects the fundamental human rights of people such as the right to life, prohibition of torture, prohibition of slavery and forced labour, the right to liberty and security, to a fair trial, to respect for private and family life and to freedom of religion, thought and conscience. A focus on humanitarian protection and rights-based humanitarian action (in contrast to humanitarian assistance) is a prominent discourse, and indeed, as Lindner (2006) argues, rights-based discourses, together with resistance and response to humiliation and conflict, can give rise to forced migration as well as further conflict.

In the UK asylum and immigration legislation has evolved since the Aliens Act 1905 that excluded 'undesirable' aliens from entering the UK, with most rejected on the basis of being a burden on public funds. Sales (2007, pp 131-7) documents three phases of immigration control: control of mainly Jewish immigration from the 1905 Act until after the Second World War; controls on new (black) Commonwealth immigration from the 1960s onwards; and the current focus on 'managed migration' that includes selectivity regarding labour migration and strict controls on asylum, from 2000 onwards.[6]

The third period began in 1993 with the Asylum and Immigration Appeals Act, when the 1951 Convention and 1967 Protocol were incorporated into domestic law (the Act also withdrew rights of appeal for visitors and students); the Human Rights Act 1998 gave legal effect in the UK to certain fundamental rights and freedoms contained in the European Convention on Human Rights (ECHR).

Asylum applications were previously dealt with under the Immigration Act 1971. Indeed, the UK experienced a noisy period of asylum and immigration legislation from the mid-1990s. The Asylum and Immigration Appeals Act 1993 was followed in 1996 by the Asylum and Immigration Act, and a raft of legislation passed by the Labour government ensued: the Immigration and Asylum Act 1999, the Nationality, Immigration and Asylum Act 2002, the Asylum and Immigration (Treatment of Claimants, etc) Act 2004 and the Immigration, Asylum and Nationality Act 2006.

The Nationality, Immigration and Asylum Act 2002 'introduced the legal basis for citizenship tests and a compulsory citizenship ceremony involving an oath of allegiance and pledge to the UK, as well as a citizenship test, to be taken by applicants for naturalisation in the UK' (Rutter et al, 2007, p 24). From 2005 onwards all applicants had to 'sit and pass a "Life in the UK" citizenship test, or pass an ESOL [English for speakers of other languages] course with a citizenship component in the teaching' (Rutter et al, 2007, p 24). In a response to the report on citizenship by Lord Goldsmith (2007), the Refugee Council said:

> Refugees are unique in that they have come to the UK not out of choice but to seek a place of safety. Despite this they show massive resilience and are determined to contribute, with many volunteering and playing an active role in their new communities. Whether they become citizens or not, refugees make a huge contribution to this country, and we hope this is recognised within the context of the ongoing debate around citizenship. (www.refugeecouncil.org.uk/news/archive/press/2008/march/20080312_b)

In 2005 the government also announced the new asylum model (NAM) as part of a five-year strategy. From 2005 the period of settlement to those granted refugee status was limited to five years.[7] The 2006 Act aimed to improve and speed up the asylum system and administrative processes in the UK. In 2007 the UK Borders Act was enacted as part of a response by the then Labour government to strengthen and secure the UK's borders, controlling migration, increasing the powers of immigration officers as well as supporting the NAM. The main points of the NAM are:

- no quota system for admitting refugees;
- the government will not withdraw from the 1951 Refugee Convention;
- refugees will initially be given temporary status for five years;[8]
- more failed asylum seekers will be detained and electronic tagging will be used;
- new visa requirements will be implemented if the government is concerned about immigration abuses by certain nationalities.

The recent Borders, Citizenship and Immigration Act (September 2009) focuses on citizenship, the welfare of children, changes to judicial review and short-term holding facilities. Commencing in 2011, sections 39 and 41 of the Act introduce a new 'path to citizenship' for refugees that 'imposes additional periods of temporary leave as probationary citizens before they get a permanent right to stay'. There is a qualifying period of eight years, possibly reduced to five years if evidence is shown of 'active citizenship'.[9] Section 55 requires all immigration staff to safeguard and promote the welfare of children who are in the UK. Section 25 changes the definition of the places where detainees can be held in the short term and allows some to be held there for unspecified periods. The Refugee Council argue that the 'new definition allows for immigration detainees to be held in facilities where they are with people held on criminal matters' (Refugee Council, 2009); that 'the duty to safeguard children should apply to all UKBA staff wherever they are not just in the UK' (Refugee Council, 2009); and 'Refugees whose need for protection is recognised by the UKBA should immediately be given permanent rights of settlement so they can rebuild their lives' (Refugee Council, 2009) without having to jump through additional hurdles.

Harmonisation of asylum policies across Europe is being conducted within the framework of a common European asylum system (CEAS). Ward (2003, p 8) states that

> there are two stages to this process, the first being the harmonisation of asylum policies in the member states and comprises four directives (on minimum standards for reception, establishing which country is responsible for examining an asylum claim, a common refugee definition, and procedures used for determining claims), and the second

being the establishment of a single asylum system for the whole of the European Union.

As Castles (2003) and others have pointed out, contemporary refugee movements are different from those of the period immediately following the Second World War. Reasons for leaving are often very complex and not always the result of immediate persecution. People flee because of civil conflicts, massive violations of their human rights, foreign aggression and occupation, poverty, famine, disease and ecological disasters. Many do not qualify as refugees on the basis of the UN definition. In order to qualify, the person must be a 'political' refugee. The 1951 Convention emphasises 'fear of persecution' but it does not define the term clearly. Article 33 refers to threats to life and freedom of the individual 'on account of his race, religion, nationality, membership of a particular social group or political opinion'. This definition was drawn up in the context of the postwar years and does not correspond to many of today's refugee situations.

As a result some countries, especially in Africa and Latin America, have expanded the definition of the term 'refugee'. In many other countries, however, the majority of applications for asylum are rejected on a strict reading of the 1951 definition. From a human rights perspective, this situation raises great concern. It will not always be possible to distinguish, with certainty, between a refugee and an economic migrant. It may be argued that if the emphasis is placed on threats to life and freedom, there is little to distinguish between a person facing death through starvation and another threatened with arbitrary execution because of political beliefs.

In the UK there is a huge backlog of applications, with some people waiting years for a decision. Asylum seekers are not allowed to engage in paid work, their basic needs are met and they survive on a fraction of state welfare benefits.

Xhejlane fled from the war in Kosovo in 1999 and is still waiting for a decision on her case:

> 'I have been in this country for almost 10 years and my application is still pending still waiting on a decision. It is difficult you never know where you stand it is wait, wait, wait, you think it will the next day the next morning. My life is just horrible I am not free to look for a job, to study I cannot do anything. Still under restrictions from the Home Office until they resolve my case. I just think people should let me know where I stand, let me stay or deport

me, I just need an answer that's all.' (quoted on www.bbc.
co.uk/learningzone/clips/asylum-three-generations-of-
refugees/6374.html)

These considerations aside, the fact remains that regardless of whether a
person is a refugee or an economic migrant, a citizen or a non-citizen,
whether they are fleeing persecution, armed conflict, threats to life or
abject poverty, that person is entitled to minimum human rights and
minimum standards of treatment.

Asylum-migration-community nexus

What is very clear in any examination of the literature is that migration,
in the context of globalisation and later modernity, is on the increase,
and so is the emergence of transnational identities and communities.
The asylum-migration-community nexus is the complex relationship
between migration, asylum and communities/community formation
and processes of belonging. The migration literature on communities
has focused largely on modes of migrant incorporation (Soysal, 1994)
and the processes involved in integrating refugees into British society
through RCOs (Carey-Wood, 1999; Bloch, 2002a; Griffiths et al, 2005).
Asylum seekers tend to be absent in this literature. Griffiths et al (2005)
explore RCOs in relation to dispersal at a particular point in history,
documenting increasingly restrictive policy measures, leading to the

> social marginalisation of asylum seekers and refugees, both
> in terms of their socio-economic position and in relation
> to their diminishing rights and entitlements ... a sustained
> 'moral panic' around the issue of asylum in general and the
> effects of the current dispersal policy upon local services
> and populations in particular has also taken place. (Griffiths
> et al, 2005, p 2)

Processes of integration, belonging and community formation are
complex and include structural, agentic, relational and psychosocial
aspects. Recent research emphasises the importance of social networks
and transnational connections, but these texts tend not to focus on the
broader concept of community in relation to social networks (Marfleet,
2006; Sales, 2007). The text adds to this literature by addressing the
asylum–migration–community nexus.

1

Community

As Ziller (2004) notes, sociologists have struggled with definitions of community. Ziller prefers to use a set of definitions provided by Peter Willmott (1989) that are also mirrored in Bauman's text on *Community* (2001) and Raymond Williams's (1985) definition of 'community'. Ziller (2004) points out that the word 'community' refers to people who have things in common. What they have in common can be categorised as territory, interests and/or attachments:

- People have territory in common: their street, their state and sometimes much larger territories such as the European Union (EU).
- However, people also have interests in common. An interest community may share ethno-cultural origins, profit motives, religion, politics, sexual preferences, occupation or a common condition or problem. In most urban situations, the distribution of interest communities cuts right across territorial boundaries.
- Willmott's third category of community is people who have attachments, that is, feelings and sentiments in common. It is possible to think of communities of attachment where people do not actually know each other. However, most usage of community in this sense tends to emphasise strongly bonded social relationships based on feelings of belonging and shared daily life.

Research on communities stresses that

> territory-based attachment communities have been on the decline since at least the industrial revolution, if not before, and the trend is continuing. The plethora of commitments and connections between people now rarely coincide with any geographic boundary, much less a local one. Rather, the connections between people, their social, economic, political, religious, cultural, etc affiliations and interests are a diverse and ever shifting kaleidoscope of interrelated layers which cross territorial boundaries with all the ease of electronic communications. These days local ties are weaker than historically they have been, because they overlap much less often than they used to with other ties, of kinship, friendship, work, leisure and other interests. (Willmott, 1989, p 19, cited in Ziller, 2004, pp 467-8)

Community is defined in this book as a multidimensional concept, referring to a sense of place, space, belonging and the togetherness of elective communities bound by shared interests or identity, as well as the intersection or combination of all three aspects. Deeply implicated in experiencing, defining and understanding community are relational dynamics – community involves the connections between people. We live our lives relationally and this involves networks of social relations. Smith (2001) cites what de Tocqueville called 'habits of the heart' in his definition of community, that in the interaction between people something else emerges. 'Feelings and ideas are renewed, the heart enlarged, and the understanding developed, only by the reciprocal action of men one upon another' (de Tocqueville, 1994, p 515, cited in Smith, 2001, p 9). Buber (2004) defines this as the encounter (*Begegnung*) in which relation (*Beziehung*) occurs:

> We can only grow and develop, according to Buber, once we have learned to live in relation to others, to recognise the possibilities of the space between us. The fundamental means is dialogue. 'All real living is meeting' he once wrote.... In the stillness of this 'in-between world' they may encounter what cannot yet be put into words. (Smith, 2001, p 14)

Community is also defined (following Anderson) as symbolic and imagined. Anderson (1983) writes that a nation is an imagined community because

> regardless of the actual inequality and exploitation that may prevail in each, the nation is always conceived as a deep, horizontal comradeship. Ultimately it is this fraternity, that makes it possible, over the past two centuries, for so many millions of people, not so much to kill, as willingly to die for such limited imaginings. (Anderson, 1983, pp 6-7)

The relationship of the individual to the wider collective is a key focus of communitarianism, a philosophy informed by the works of both Buber and de Tocqueville:

> In contrast to conventional 'right' or 'left' approaches to social policy, communitarians emphasize the need for a balance between rights and responsibilities. Communitarians believe that strong rights presume strong responsibilities and that the pendulum of contemporary society has swung too

far in the direction of individual autonomy at the expense of individual and social responsibility. One key to solving contemporary America's social problems is replacing our pervasive 'rights talk' with 'responsibility talk'. (The Communitarian Network, nd)

Beyond a perceived excessive emphasis on liberal individualism and statism communitarians articulate a middle way, 'the powerful "third force" of the community. By reawakening communities and empowering communities to assert their moral standards, communitarians seek to hold individuals accountable for their conduct' (The Communitarian Network, nd).

Etzioni (a student of Buber), who founded The Communitarian Network in North America, wrote in an article for *The Times* in 1995: 'The communitarian call to restore civic virtues, for people to live up to their responsibilities and not merely focus on their entitlements, to shore up the moral foundations of society is said to endanger individual liberties'. He goes on to respond to certain criticisms, such as

community is a vague, fuzzy term and that rebuilding strong communities will curb individual freedoms. As I see it, communities are social webs of people who know one another as persons and have a moral voice. Communities draw on interpersonal bonds to encourage members to abide by shared values, such as, 'Do not throw rubbish out of your window' and 'Mind the children when you drive'. Communities gently chastise those who violate shared moral norms and express approbation for those who abide by them. They turn to the state only when all else fails. Hence, the more viable communities are, the *less* the need for Policing. (The Communitarian Network, 1995)

The core tension at the heart of analysis of community, is, as Bauman identifies, the relationship between freedom and security, that is to say, individualism, a focus on the self and self-interests (liberalism) vis-à-vis collectivism and a focus on the common good (communitarianism):

There is a price to be paid for the privilege of 'being in a community'.... The price can be paid in the currency of freedom, variously called 'autonomy', 'right to self-assertion', 'right to be yourself'. Whatever you choose, you gain some and lose some. Missing community means missing security;

gaining community, if it happens, would soon mean missing
freedom. (Bauman, 2001, p 4)

Majid Yar (2003) provides an excellent account and analysis of
communitarianism, identifying limitations and problems and
developing an alternative approach based on critical theory and the
work of Honneth to develop a concept of community that moves
us beyond the problems and pitfalls of communitariansim towards a
'recognitive critical theory of community' (2003, p 101). Yar writes
about the impossibility of attaining a shared concept of the 'common
good' in modern, complex, differentiated societies – the idea of a
common good reinforces rather than breaks with liberalism and without
a deep understanding of power and inequalities and disadvantage might
simply reinforce hegemonic common conception. Communitarians
see conflict as a deficit of shared norms and values, yet (especially from
an understanding of dialectics) struggles by marginalised and excluded
members of society to attain recognition and rights are 'not driven by
their disinvestment from generalised moral meanings, but conversely
by their attachment to those very meanings' (Yar, 2003, p 112). Social
struggles for rights by marginalised groups around class, gender and
'race' and sexuality, for example, are, as Yar says, a testimony to liberal
culture rather than a breakdown or fragmentation of a 'common moral
framework' (Yar, 2003, p 112).

Yar's position presents communitarianism as evoking a dualism
between atomised individuality and autonomy on the one hand, and
collectivity, solidarity and responsibility on the other, as oppositional.
For communitarians there is too much focus on individualism, the
self, narcissism, to the detriment of the collective, public participation,
possibilities for solidarity. This imbalance in liberalism between rights
(individual, 'self-determination via unfettered and asocial agency')
and responsibilities (collective, 'social determination via culture') is to
be balanced for communitarians by the 'revivication' of community
life. Ultimately for Yar this can serve to close down critique. Yar is not
alone in taking this position; Smith (1998) also argues this, through
her engagement with Laclau and Mouffe.

In a move beyond communitarianism (both Left and Right versions),
drawing on Honneth's work (Honneth, 1996) Yar sees community as
the 'common ground that emerges from the intersubjectively actualised
struggle for recognition ... of community as a ground for an ethical
and political life' (2003, p 114) (see also Chapter Two, this volume).
Yar argues that if we understand community as a social struggle for
recognition, this reconciles autonomy with solidarity. What this means

is that an account of community built on a theory of recognition 'can satisfy the demands of establishing solidarity, preserving singularity (or difference), and keeping open a space for critique' (2003, p 125).

Hanoch Flum's (1998) work in identifying identity construction in the face of dramatic cultural transition experienced by young Ethiopian Jews who migrated to Israel can be utilised to support Yar (and Honneth's positions) through the concept of 'embedded identity'. Fusing narrative interviewing techniques, Flum found that interdependence for young migrants does not necessarily hinder the development of autonomy. First, that 'an individual can operate with a strong sense of self-determination that originates in a sense of embedded identity' and that this 'relational web' is a strong motivator to achieve (Flum, 1998, p 158). Second, integration is associated with complex and continuing processes of exploration that involve internal and social struggle. The young people were engaged in a 'constant effort to accommodate pre and post-transition cultures' (Flum, 1998, p 159). And finally, individuals who do well are those who manage to accommodate both cultures by translating psychological resources and experiences rooted in culture of origin to the post-transition cultural space, and utilise them in identity reconstruction. The 'transformation of these resources and experiences form the material for building blocks that bridge over transition and maintain a sense of continuity' (Flum, 1998, p 159).

This approach to recognition sits well with a focus on possibilities for a 'radical democratic imaginary' (Smith, 1998), utilising the work of Laclau, Mouffe and Smith and what they call 'radical democratic pluralism'. It also resonates with Nancy's (1991, 2000) theories on community as 'being-together' (Nancy, 1991, p 80), 'being-in-common' (Nancy, 1991, p 69), and 'being-with' (Nancy, 1991, p 103) (see Chapter Two, this volume).

Asylum and the 'deviant other'

Europeanisation of restrictive asylum policy, geopolitical changes since September 11 2001, and EU enlargement have heightened security concerns about unregulated migration and porous borders. And, as identified by Schuster and Solomos (1999, p 3), the evolution of a 'race' relations framework has provided a central axis for the development of asylum policy in the UK: 'Anti-immigration rhetoric, short-term electoralism and concerns over mounting welfare budgets are the immediate context for the increased saliency of asylum in the domestic policy agenda' (Griffiths et al, 2005, p 3).

The construction of the asylum seeker as the 'deviant other' is well documented. Marfleet (2006) and Pickering (2005) argue that the state needs to be called into account for responses to asylum and refugee issues. Pickering (2005, p 1) describes the responses of governments as illegitimate and potentially criminal. Indeed, she defines state responses to refugees in the North as embedded in law and order politics and policies that are maintained via hegemonic relations across three levels of society: civil society (identified in media representations); law enforcement (administration of the law); and domestic and international legal mechanisms (the courts and international human rights regimes). The basis of Pickering's argument is that governments in the North have used 'law and order politics in the development and implementation of refugee policy' (p 3), and this relies increasingly on 'unmitigated ideological and coercive force'; most importantly this distances western nations from their complicity in the production of the refugees and in turn provides them with 'justification for unbridled denunciation and violent rejection' (Pickering, 2005, p 21).

Law and order politics and policies rest on neoliberal ideas about the responsibility of the individual for their situation: 'The responsibility of the individual to know what is wrong and to refrain from doing it and the responsibility of the state to administer punishment when the law is contravened' (Pickering, 2005, pp 1-2). With the focus on individual responsibility, the law and order approach does not fully take into account the complex structural, political and social conditions in the production of refugees, nor the experiences of those seeking safety, nor genuine human rights approaches and responses. Most importantly, as Pickering points out, 'when major parties refuse to debate, or only engage in debate on peripheral issues to immigration, then space for questioning and the space for civil society to exert itself are often reduced' (Pickering, 2005, p 5). Negative and racist attitudes to migrants and asylum seekers can go unchallenged and the closing down of debate simply reinforces limited and limiting attitudes in the general population and political responses that simply reinforce the protection of borders and make deviant those who seek entry as 'dangerous outsiders'.

Hence, despite the cultural, social and economic benefits of welcoming new arrivals into our towns, cities and rural economies, the 'immigration' issue is hotly contested and has ultimately supported the British National Party (BNP) into mainstream politics. The BNP leader Nick Griffin was given a slot on prime time television in October 2009 as a panellist on 'Question time', a television programme based on current news and politics where politicians and key political figures

Figure 2: Sangatte Centre queue

face an audience who ask questions that elicit responses and discussion by panellists. *The Guardian* reported that BNP membership increased by a further 3,000 the day after Griffin's participation (Watt, 2009).

Given this backdrop the following section outlines the three points around which the book is organised – theory, methodology and praxis – and the key themes and terms of analysis.

Theory

The conceptual framework for this book is embedded in scholarship that is influenced by the critical social theory of the Frankfurt School, particularly the principle that analysis of specific social phenomena requires awareness of the connectedness and embeddedness of small-scale phenomena in the broader totality. There is a need for research that deals with micrology within the context of historical and comparative research that casts light on broader social structures and processes. Thus, ethnographic, biographical, narrative and participatory research and policy-oriented praxis are used within this epistemological frame of reference.

Theoretical analysis engages with the broader international contexts to the asylum-migration-community nexus and social policy discussions and debates in the context of Europeanisation, globalisation, international conflict *and* processes and practices of humiliation. Discussion focuses on the possibilities for a radical democratic imaginary – drawing on concepts of egalization,[10] recognition, cultural citizenship, human dignity, human rights and recognitive community

– towards a vision of social justice and against exclusionary discourses and practices, thereby challenging the identity thinking embedded in national, European and international responses to the asylum–migration nexus.

Chapter One reflects on processes of globalisation and the international context to the movements of people across borders, the important role of humiliation in the processes leading to migration, both forced and free, and the humiliation experienced in the process of seeking asylum and refuge. Drawing on research and scholarship on globalisation, humiliation and social justice, Chapters One and Two set the scene by outlining the processes of (forced) migration in the context of human rights and the search for social justice in a world marked by conflict, risk and growing discourses of human dignity and human rights. These chapters define the asylum–migration–community nexus.

Smith (2006) and Lindner (2006) argue that globalisation brings with it the issue of resources and resource-based conflicts, that there has been an increase in rights and a decrease in the political autonomy of nation states, and the growing cosmopolitan condition brings with it risks and uncertainties. Increased global dependency involves displacement and resentment. Smith (2006) describes humiliation with the term 'social displacement'; in fact humiliation emerges by 'outrageous displacement', and that displacement leads to conquest, relegation or exclusionary forms of humiliation.

Chapter One also describes and discusses the international network for human dignity and humiliation studies (HDHS) that is gathering force. The HDHS network is made up of a number of scholars and practitioners globally, who want to be involved in building a different way of being and doing research, practice and policy making at global and local levels in a world marked by deeply embedded processes of humiliation as well as the development of human rights, and what Gilroy (2000) has called 'planetary humanism'.

Chapter Two discusses the asylum–migration–community nexus as it is experienced in the UK within the context of globalisation. Concepts and understandings of 'community' are discussed in the context of broader social and historical processes. The asylum–migration–community nexus acknowledges the existence of communities (of interest, belonging, location and imagined) and includes the complex interrelationship between asylum and migration with experiences of community formation and belonging (both here, in exile, and there, in 'home countries', countries of origin). The concept of community is problematised (it is after all a highly contentious and contingent concept), and it is also defined in multiple ways through the experiences of asylum seekers, refugees and migrants in research with communities that includes understandings of 'community' through related terms such as 'diaspora', 'post-national communities', 'contingent communities' and 'transnational communities'. Yar's (2003) recognitive theory of community and Nancy's (1991, 2000) concept of the 'inoperative community' and 'being singular plural' is called into focus when discussing the asylum-migration-community nexus.

Building on Castles' (2003) concept of the 'asylum-migration nexus' the 'asylum-migration-community nexus' is both problematised and discussed in relation to the use and potential of the concept of 'community' in practice, especially at the local level. Globalisation and community formation at the global level are also discussed. What Pearce defines as 'glocal imaginaries'[11] – the relationship between the local, global and the imaginary – are considered with respect to concepts, understandings and practices involved in the asylum-migration-community nexus, including those of transnational communities, social networks and the relevance of social and cultural capital to established and emerging communities (Griffiths et al, 2005).

Hall (2002) argues that in 'a world of constant movement, both forced and free, both at the centre and periphery of the global system, communities and societies are increasingly global in their nature' (2002, p 25). At the same time, Ziller (2004) acknowledges that: 'treating people's social relationships as if they were primarily place based is both empirically inaccurate and, as an aspiration, unrealistic' (p 469). As Ziller (2004) notes, it would appear that our understanding of 'community' has shifted away from 'solid' communities based on shared identifications of social class, shared space, social norms and mores[12] towards more contingent communities based on diversity, mobility – both temporal and spatial – and are less and less tied to place.

Sociological, cultural criminological and social policy approaches are defined in these two chapters as well as the legal, social and cultural dimensions of 'being' an asylum seeker, refugee or economic migrant.

Methodology

Chapter Three focuses on methodological approaches to researching the asylum-migration-community nexus. Research with and for asylum seekers, migrants and refugees is discussed with a particular focus on the use and value of participatory action research[13] and participatory and community arts methods, which also include narrative and biographical methodologies. Epistemologically and methodologically, in exploring the asylum-migration-nexus, this chapter reinforces the need to include asylum seekers, refugees and migrants in research and dialogue that seeks to inform policy and praxis.

I argue that participatory methodologies offer potential research methods that promote recognition, participation and inclusion in the production of knowledge and public policy.[14] Such methodologies are also instrumental in helping to create spaces for these issues to be raised and dialogue to take place. Participatory methodologies help to challenge dominant discourses and hopefully feed into public policy at local, regional, national and international levels. They instantiate a politics of inclusion and representation through a 'radical democratic imaginary' (Smith, 1998, p 6).

In the research documented here PAR makes use of biographical, narrative, arts–based and performative research methods. Fraser (2000) argues that it is important to conceptualise struggles for recognition so that they can be integrated with struggles for redistribution, rather than displacing and undermining them. It also means developing an account of recognition that can accommodate the full complexity of social identities, instead of one that promotes reification and separatism (Fraser, 2000, p 109).

As academics, researchers, practitioners and policy makers – the intended audience for this book – we have a collective responsibility to challenge and change sexual, social and structural inequalities. This is underpinned, for myself, by Fals–Borda's four key principles of PAR:

1. Respect and combine your skills with the knowledge of the researched or grass–roots communities, taking them as full partners and co–researchers, that is, fill in the distance between subject and object.
2. Do not trust elitist versions of history and science that respond to dominant interests, but be receptive to counter–narratives and try to recapture them.
3. Do not depend solely on your culture to interpret facts, but recover local values, traits, beliefs and arts for action by and with the research organisations.
4. Diffuse and share what you have learned together with the people, in a manner that is wholly understandable and even literary and pleasant, for science should not be necessarily a mystery nor a monopoly of experts and intellectuals (Fals–Borda, 1995, p 4).

In recent work, Harindranath and myself explore the use and importance of taking a biographical approach to conducting PAR with asylum seekers and refugees in order to:

- better understand lived experiences of exile and belonging;
- contribute to the important field of biographical sociology;
- provide a safe space for stories to be told;
- feed people's stories into policy and praxis (O'Neill and Harindranath, 2006).

We develop a case for theory building based on lived experience using biographical materials, both narrative and visual, as critical theory in practice towards a vision of social justice that challenges the dominant knowledge/power axis embedded in current governance and media policy relating to forced migration. Our work illustrates that research methodologies that create spaces for the voices and images of the subaltern – refugees and asylum seekers – through biographical/narrative methods can serve not only to raise awareness, challenge stereotypes and hegemonic practices, but can produce critical texts that may mobilise and create 'real' change. My theoretical and methodological concept of ethno-mimesis (a combination of ethnography and arts-based practice) is defined and explored in Chapter Three to relation to research undertaken with forced migrants.

Bromley (2001) writes about the nature of belonging through analysis of fictive texts and, quoting Said (1993, p xiii), he states: 'the power to narrate or to block other narratives from forming and emerging, is very important to culture and imperialism, and constitutes one of the main connections between them' (2001, p 16). Thus, the sharing of collective responsibilities is a moral imperative in current times. There is an urgent need to develop interventionary strategies based on collective responsibility and, what Benhabib has called, a 'civic culture of public participation and the moral quality of enlarged thought' (1992, p 140) in response to what has been called the global refugee crisis.

Recovering and re-telling people's subjectivities, lives and experiences are central to attempts to better understand our social worlds with a view to transforming these worlds. Such work reveals the daily struggles, resistances, strengths and humour of people seeking asylum, the importance of intersubjective social relations and sociality, as well as knowledge and better understanding of the legitimation and rationalisation of power, domination and oppression. Biographical work represented poetically, visually as well as textually, can help illuminate the necessary mediation of autonomous individuality and collective responsibility. Biographies help us to understand social relations, the processes, structures and lived experiences of citizenship and lack of citizenship and the experiences of humiliation, vulnerability and loss (dominant experiences for some asylum seekers/refugees). They highlight the importance of engaging with the subaltern other, creating spaces for voices and narratives to make sense of lived experience, trauma, loss, but also the productive, creative, generative dimension of forging identities and belonging in the new situation, as an 'asylum seeker' or 'refugee'. This productive dimension is articulated well by Roberts as 'the return to nodal points in life where significant meanings are sought as the individual tries to uncover and decipher the coherence of their lives.... Life historical knowledge is reformulated in the re-creation of the self, as both an interpretive and recollective process' (Roberts, 2003, p 21).

Thus, a politics of representation informed by a politics of subalternity and biographical sociology can provide alternative narratives and praxis (purposeful knowledge) that may feed into public policy and ultimately help shift the dominant knowledge/power axis embedded in current governance related to refugees and asylum seekers. Chapter Four engages with an analysis of media representations of asylum seekers and refugees and discusses media representations and the work of scholars who address the alternative media as a means of facilitating refugees and asylum seekers to speak for themselves. A politics of representation must include an analysis of media representations of asylum seekers and refugees.

Thus Chapters Three and Four explore methodological approaches to the asylum-migration-community nexus, including media analysis and discourses of social inclusion/exclusion and the growth of arts-based work to generate knowledge and challenge processes of labelling and stereotyping as well as aid processes of belonging for new arrivals, predominantly refugees and asylum seekers. These chapters also examine research and social policy that engages with the relational and psychosocial dynamics involved.

Performative praxis (purposeful knowledge)

Chapters Five to Nine deal with specific issues and experiences of the asylum-migration-community nexus and include ongoing activities at local, regional, national and international levels that seek to address and foster processes of integration and belonging. These chapters invoke the concept of the performative praxis while also drawing the reader's attention to issues of social justice, cultural citizenship, community and belonging, with particular attention given to experiences of unaccompanied young people, women and refused asylum seekers. Chapter Nine takes a close look at processes and practices of humiliation and the search for human dignity in a world marked by conflict and a mixture of both honour and human rights codes and concludes the book.

Taken together these chapters provide a methodological and epistemological model that supports processes of social justice, recognitive communities and cultural citizenship, which challenge and seek to transform social inequalities at the intersections of the macro, meso and micro processes of globalisation, modernity and humiliation in relation to the asylum-migration-community nexus.

Hence, drawing on interdisciplinary (sociological and cultural criminological) research linking ethnographic and participatory action and arts-based research, this book examines the asylum-migration-community nexus across three interrelated spheres (themes):

- Globalisation and the search for belonging, human dignity and social justice, as a counter to humiliation, exclusion and liminality (across three levels of social justice: affective, imagined and holistic; see O'Neill et al, 2005, pp 75-8).
- Theoretical and methodological approaches that can inform public policy on these matters, including participatory, performative and visual methodologies.
- Performative praxis, constituted by activities at local, regional, national and international levels that focus on asylum, migration and integration/belonging, to include the work of the HDHS global network.

In summary, this book looks at the interrelationships between asylum, migration and community with a specific focus on the theories and methodologies for understanding the asylum-migration-community nexus,[15] and research that engages with praxis (purposeful knowledge, knowledge for) that seeks to challenge and change sexual and social inequalities and exclusionary discourses and representations. Given that there is a small but growing body of sociological and criminological literature on forced migration, it is hoped that this book will also contribute to the developing body of interdisciplinary theoretical and empirical work in the field of migration and refugee studies.

As Castles states (2003), the arrival of migrants to northern countries, the growth of transnational communities and processes of community formation are important areas to study using analysis that links the micro, meso and macro dynamics. I argue that such analysis is necessarily an interdisciplinary undertaking, emerging from cultural, relational social policy and political research and awareness that every social phenomenon be examined from its embeddedness within the social totality. As noted by Castles (2003, p 22), 'Migration is an existential shift which affects every part of human life. No single discipline can adequately describe and analyse this experience on its own.'

Notes

[1] The British National Party's (BNP's) 'Red, White and Blue' annual festival has been held on a farm in Derbyshire since 2007. In August 2009 far-right activists from across Europe joined Nick Griffin, the party leader, including Roberto Fiore from Italy's Forza Nuova party and Marc Abramson from the Swedish National Democrats. *The Guardian* reported as follows:

> … the mood at the event threatened to turn ugly on Saturday as far-right supporters outside the camp gave fascist salutes to protesters and shouted 'Sieg Heil'. … [A resident (aged 70) described an incident from last year where] 'men were goose-stepping down the street in the early hours of the morning and shouting "Heil Hitler". … It really upset my wife. It may seem funny to them but the second world war is something very real to us.' (www.guardian.co.uk/politics/2009/aug/16/bnp-fiore-red-white-blue-protest)

[2] See www.humiliationstudies.org/index.php.

[3] Elias and Scotson's work is important in this respect (1994)(see Chapter Two, this volume).

[4] A *refugee* is someone whose claim for asylum has been found and is given temporary humanitarian protection or indefinite leave to remain in the country where refugee status was sought and granted. An *asylum seeker* is someone who has submitted an application for asylum and whose claim is in process.

[5] 'As a region, Europe received 75 percent of all asylum applications although the United States remained the single largest recipient country with an estimated 13 percent of all applications filed in industrialized nations (23,700). France ranks as the second recipient nation with 10 percent of all claims (19,400), followed by Canada (18,700), the United Kingdom (17,700) and Germany, ranked fifth (12,000)' (UNHCR, 2009).

[6] See Sales (2007, pp 133-4) for a very helpful table documenting British immigration legislation.

[7] 'Before 2005, those with refugee status were granted indefinite leave to remain in the UK at the same time as their grant of refugee status. Refugee organisations have criticised the move to temporary status as it may limit refugees' ability to integrate and make long-term plans for life in the UK' (Rutter et al, 2007, p 27). This point is evidenced by Rutter et al's interviews with 30 refugees as part of their research on integration and citizenship.

[8] Rutter et al (2007, p 193) found that 'the time the time-limited settlement afforded to those who have gained refugee status since 2005 impacted on career choices and acted as a barrier to integration'.

[9] The Refugee Council note that refugees are given five years leave initially and this leave is then reviewed by the UKBA. Under the new law if their refugee status is then confirmed they will no longer be able to apply straight away for permanent settlement in the form of indefinite leave to remain. They will instead be required to apply for probationary citizenship leave for at least a further year at which point they can then apply for naturalisation as a UK citizen as they will have completed the six years qualifying period. If they fail to meet the 'activity condition', they will be required to wait for a further two years before they can then apply for permanent residence (the new term for indefinite leave to remain). This means that for most refugees the time spent waiting for a decision on their asylum claim will be additional to the time they will have to wait for permanent settlement once they are granted status. Refugees will still, in addition, have to meet the entry requirements for probationary citizenship (that is, pass ESOL Entry level 3 and knowledge of life in the UK, or ESOL with citizenship context). If they do not meet these requirements they will not be eligible for citizenship although they would qualify for permanent residence after a total of eight years qualifying period (www.refugeecouncil.org.uk/Resources/Refugee%20Council/downloads/briefings/BCI%20Act%20Revised%20Brief%20Sept%2009.pdf).

[10] Lindner defines 'egalization' as equal dignity. The human rights revolution 'could be described as an attempt to collapse the master–slave gradient to a line of equal dignity and humility' that she defines as 'egalization' (Lindner 2006, p 3).

[11] Pearce organised a conference exploring glocal imaginaries. The conference emerged from her AHRC-funded project examining how the experience of migration has influenced creative writing in Manchester since 1960, especially

how Manchester's writing is inflected by place, both local and global. For more information see www.lancs.ac.uk/fass/projects/movingmanchester/conference.htm.

[12] Raymond Williams defined 'community' through notions of shared identities, shared territory and shared social interests (1983, p 75).

[13] 'The need was felt instead, by many of us in the South, to look for different kinds of explanation, not only to gain a more clear understanding of the conflictual social processes that affected our lives but also to assist in re-channelling collective energies toward a better course of action for justice and equity. And here we stand today, with PAR as one of those resulting alternatives for our work in the South' (Fals-Borda, 1995, p 3).

[14] Participatory methodologies are gaining ground beyond development studies; for more information see the work of Jenny Pearce (www.brad.ac.uk/acad/icps/) and Rachel Pain (www.dur.ac.uk/beacon/socialjustice/).

[15] Developing Stephen Castles' use of the term 'asylum-migration nexus' (Castles, 2003).

ONE

Globalisation, forced migration, humiliation and social justice

Howard Adelman locates the production of refugees and the discourses and policies that have emerged as a response to the movement or flow of refugees, asylum seekers and stateless people across borders to processes of globalisation,[1] modernity and the political system of nation states:

> Refugees are the products of modernity. Their plight became acute when the processes of modernity became globalized, when the political system of nation states first became extended over the whole globe and efforts were made to sort the varied nations of the world into political states. (Adelman, 1999, p 83)

In this chapter I support this argument as many others have done (Castles, 2003; Marfleet, 2006; Sales, 2007), but I also argue for the need to better explain and understand the processes, discourses and policies related to forced migration, the impact of humiliation and human rights (Lindner, 2006; Smith, 2006).

For Marfleet, the key themes or threads of analysis to explore forced migration include: the underpinning theory of globalisation and the 'implications for patterns of forced migration' (2006, p 5); the character and role of the liberal state and the role of politicians and state officials; refugee movement to the West; and the need for an interdisciplinary lens (refugee studies) when studying migration. This chapter takes up these threads, in particular the need for an interdisciplinary lens in order to examine the connections between globalisation, forced migration, humiliation and the possibilities for social justice.

Century of the refugee: processes of inclusion and exclusion

Adelman suggests that refugees characterise the 20th century because it was in this century that 'the total globe was colonized and set on a course of being divided into self governing nation states' (Adelman, 1999, p 90). And, given the twin forces of modernity and globalisation, the nation state epitomises certain contradictions. 'On the one hand each nation state consolidated itself around a sentimental communal and sometimes atavistic sense of a homogenous nation. At the same time, the state was the vehicle of universal citizenship and, in idealist liberal belief, the upholder and defender of individual rights' (Adelman, 1999, p 90).

Reflecting on the history of the movement of people across borders, Adelman argues that the Huguenots, who fled religious persecution in France, were archetypical refugees of modernity. The Huguenots 'stood for the values of modernity – individualism, tolerance, the rule of reason', but in addition, 'they were the products of a state apparatus used to drive out anyone who did not conform to a homogenous identity of the nation (in this case in terms of religion) and the whims of a despot' (Adelman, 1999, p 90). It is clear that migration is a dominant feature of all recorded history, and as Sales (2007) states, contemporary migration processes are shaped by global inequalities of wealth and power as well as the right of inclusion/exclusion.

Modernity and globalisation

Bauman identifies the role of modernity in the production of refugees as intrinsically linked to globalisation – the processes of modernity and globalisation are underpinned by deep social inequalities that lead people to leave home in search of a better life through choice and/or compulsion, or literally, to flee for their lives. For example, in an earlier phase of modernity, in the wake of industrial revolution, the 'turbulent history of creative destruction known under the name of economic progress' (Bauman, 2004, p 36) led to the disintegration of artisans' guilds and small farms that 'drove men into mines and factories' (2004, p 36). Moreover, in order to release the 'pressure on the life conditions of labourers and to improve their living standards ... a thinning out of the crowds besieging the gates of the establishments offering employment' was sought (2004, p 36). Social inequalities 'allowed the modern part of the globe to seek, and find, global solutions to locally produced "overpopulation" problems' (2004, p 6). People from the 'developed' world would migrate to 'developing' countries. The following excerpt from Bauman (2004, pp 36-7) is a quote from Jeffreys (1948):

> Joseph Arch, leader of the Agricultural Worker's Union testified to Her Majesty's Commissioners of Agriculture:
>
> Q. How do you set about ensuring the labourers' getting higher wages?

> *A*. We have reduced the numbers of labourers in the market
> very considerably....We have emigrated 700,000 souls, men,
> women and children, within the last eight or nine years....
> I went over to Canada, and I made arrangements with the
> Canadian government to give them so much and we found
> so much from the trade.

In current times the focus of concern is less on emigration and more
on immigration, especially in relation to the flow of asylum seekers and
migrants who do not conform to the UK points-based system. The
impact of globalisation and a focus on North–South relations is taken
up by theorists of migration, such as Marfleet (2006) and Castles (2003).
Marfleet examines globalisation and migration in relation to histories
of migration, the role of the nation state and patterns of migration to
the West since the 1950s. Like Adelman, he considers:

> how the changing practices of states have presented refugees
> at different times as heroes and villains ... looks at patterns
> of migration – legal and 'illegal' – and the ways in which the
> changing policies of states in North America and Europe
> have affected the status of refugees today. (2006, p 95)

Castles (2003) argues in a similar vein that globalisation provides a
context for understanding both economic and forced migration in
that 'globalization is not a system of equitable participation in a fairly-
structured global economy, society and polity but rather a system of
selective inclusion and exclusion of specific areas and groups, which
maintains and exacerbates inequality' (2003, p 16). For Castles, the most
significant expression of this inequality is the North–South divide, and
increasing inequality leads to conflict and forced migration. Importantly,
the asylum-migration nexus articulates the fact that the distinction
between forced and economic migration is blurring as a result:

> Failed economies generally also mean weak states, predatory
> ruling cliques and human rights abuse. This leads to the
> notion of the 'asylum-migration nexus': many migrants
> and asylum seekers have multiple reasons for mobility
> and it is impossible to completely separate economic and
> human rights motivations – which is a challenge to the
> neat categories that bureaucracies seek to impose. (Castles,
> 2003, p 17)

Hence, understanding that forced migration 'is not the result of a string of unconnected emergencies but rather an integral part of North–South relationships makes it necessary to theorize forced migration and link it to economic migration' (Castles, 2003, p 17). Indeed, for Castles, the task for contemporary sociology is 'to analyse the new characteristics of forced migration in the epoch of globalization' (2003, p 17).

The crucial characteristics of globalisation for Castles (2003) are the growth of cross-border flows and their organisation by means of transnational networks linked to: trade and investment, political cooperation and international organisations. Such flows are linked to the circulation of people, goods and technology and communications networks, and include 'alternative and criminal networks to enable the flow of people from South to North' (2003, p 190).

Castles and Miller's (2009) *The age of migration*, a classic text in the field, defines five key features or trends of contemporary migration: acceleration (rapid increase in migration); globalisation (marked by the increase in migrants worldwide, with the majority of states experiencing emigration and immigration); diversification (the increasing diversity of migrants' motivations for migration (Sales, 2007, p 34); feminisation (the increase in female migration); and politicisation (increased political attention on migration and immigration policy in western nations (Sales, 2007, pp 99-11; Castles and Miller, 2009, pp 277-95). Acceleration involves the increase in international migration with broad trends for migratory flows from countries of the South to the North. Castles and Miller identify complex flows that include most countries of the world in both emigration and immigration. As Sales (2007, p 33) notes, these 'reflect both long-standing inequalities and newly emerging hierarchies of economic and political power'. For example:

> some parts of the Middle East have developed diverse migratory movements as a result of oil wealth and the resulting new manufacturing and technological power, attracting migrants from neighbouring countries and from outside the region. The latter include the two ends of the migratory spectrum. The poorest, mainly from South East Asia, have often been forced out by impoverishment at home and work in low-status occupations such as domestic work, often in conditions of semi-slavery. At the other end of the spectrum are significant ex-patriate communities, mainly from the West, in business and professional occupations, whose skills and privileged national status allow them

mobility and the ability to command high salaries. There are also substantial numbers of refugee populations in the region, largely as a result of the Israel–Palestine conflict. This population increased substantially as a result of the war in Lebanon in 2006. (Sales, 2007, p 34)[2]

Thus globalisation intersects with acceleration and diversification. Diversification includes various types of migration, including labour, lifestyle, student and forced migration, and circuits of migration as well as temporary migration (Wallace, 2002; Marfleet, 2006). Sales (2007) gives an example of contemporary Polish migration to illustrate short-term and circulatory migration. She states 'strategies are aimed at improving or maintaining quality of life at home, with mobility an "alternative to emigration"' (Sales, 2007, p 37). As Bloch states:

> Immigration status, or the fluidity of immigration status, provides another complexity to the research process as people move in and out of different statuses when necessary or in some cases expedient (Jordan and Duvell, 2002). For example, some refugees may become citizens of the country of refuge, some asylum seekers may become undocumented migrants when their asylum claim is refused and others may enter into the asylum system having originally been undocumented migrants or on temporary visas [and inevitably] this makes it difficult to estimate the population parameters. (Bloch, 2007, p 234)

The feminisation of migration has increased. In 2006 nearly half of workers registered with the British Workers Registration Scheme were women (Sales, 2007, p 37). Remittances home that involve social networks and family support are a key trend and theme emerging from the analysis of migration, both forced and free (Bloch, 2002b, 2005). Sales (2007, p 38) documents that in 2005 an estimated US$233 billion in remittances were being delivered to receiving countries, with US$167 billion going to developing countries. 'Remittances are now recognised as an important source of development finance, and by the end of the 1990s they exceeded aid flows' (Sales, 2007, p 38).

An increase in the number of women migrants as workers, including sex workers (both forced and free) and students, is also a key trend which, as Watters (2007) identifies, makes more complex the key migratory trend of 'chain migration' 'that is initiated by a male family member migrating for work who is then followed by his wife and other family members. By contrast, women migrants may form the majority in groups as diverse as those of CapeVerdians to Italy, Filipinos to the Middle East and Thais to Japan' (Castles and Miller, 2009, p 9). Fifty-one per cent of people 'of concern' identified by the UN High Commissioner for Refugees (UNHCR) in 2002 were women. A report to the UNHCR suggests that, while women and men may face the same kind of harm, 'women are often subject to specific forms of gender-related abuse and violence such as rape, abduction, or offers of protection, documents or assistance in exchange for sex' (Watters, 2007b, p 3).

As Sales (2007) and Koffman et al (2000) show, female migration has been identified with domestic service work and 'invisible' labour (Anderson, 1993) as well as a 'commodified racialised identity' as domestic and service workers (Anderson, 1993, p 677). However, there has been an increase in the migration of professionals such as teachers and nurses as well as women working in global multinationals. Women working in the sex industry are also a key feature of migratory flows (Agustin, 2007; Mai, 2009).

Sales argues that the research and analysis on migration 'displays increasing numbers of migrants and increased diversity in relation to areas of origin of migrants and to their motives and strategies for migration' (2007, p 41). This is, of course, marked by the concentration of wealth from global capitalism being concentrated in the global North, global inequalities of wealth and power, and while this, in part, helps to create the conditions for migration, especially from countries of the South, the response from the North including Europe is to increase surveillance, border controls and the regulation of migration. For Sales, this means that 'new hierarchies are developing in relation to the ease of international mobility and the ability to take advantage of these global opportunities' (2007, p 41).

For research and analysis in the field of migration and refugee studies this has led to theorists moving beyond the 'binary categories that have tended to dominate thinking about migration' (Sales, 2007, p 41) such as forced and voluntary, permanent and temporary, regular and irregular. This also includes moving beyond gender-based binaries that reinforce stereotypical thinking about male and female migration and migratory processes as well as challenging the emphasis on structural forces that ignore the agency of migrants. An example of the latter is work on trafficking. There is a tendency, especially in UK government discourse, to define migrant sex workers as trafficked, which tends to obscure research and analysis of wider experiences and processes of migration and to fix those who migrate to sell sex as being trafficked.

This is clearly not always the case as research by Mai (2009) and Agustin (2007) have evidenced in their ethnographic-based research with migrant sex workers. Comparative research and analysis on the inter-related issues of trafficking, smuggling and migration that examines the complexities within an understanding of what Bauman (2007) calls 'negative globalisation' is urgently needed.

In summary, contemporary research on globalisation and modernity in the migration literature emphasises the importance of social networks, transnational connections and interconnections (Bloch and Levy, 1999; Castles, 2003;

Marfleet, 2006), and the complexity and limitations of immigration policy making (Sales, 2007, pp 97-127) that are gender-biased and linked to 'race' relations policy (Solomos, 2003; Sales, 2007). This is indicative of the politicisation of migration (Castles and Miller, 1985; Sales, 2007, pp 7, 23).

Moreover, in a global capitalist economy based around the circulation of capital, finance and labour, international communication, communication technology and the emergence of transnational networks move, the sovereignty of states is challenged and this can be looked at as a crisis of territoriality. As Benhabib states, 'globalization draws the administrative-material functions of the state into increasingly volatile contexts that far exceed any one state's capacities to influence decision and outcomes' (Benhabib, 2004, p 4). Indeed, the irony is that while sovereignty has waned in economic, and technological domains, it has been vigorously asserted, especially at national borders, which although 'porous, are still there to keep out aliens and intruders' (Benhabib, 2004, p 6). Hence, for Castles (2003) and Bauman (2004), globalisation is not a system of equal participation but is marked by processes of inclusion and exclusion. And, given the rolling back of states' claims to sovereignty in the context of supranational powers such as the EU, nation states 'still claim the foundational, constitutive prerogative of sovereignty: their right of exemption' (Bauman, 2004, p 33). Indeed,

> Stripped of a large part of their sovereign prerogatives and capacities by globalization forces which they were impotent to resist, let alone control, governments have no choice but to 'carefully select' targets which they can (conceivably) overpower and against which they can aim their rhetorical salvos and flex their muscles while being heard and seen doing so by the grateful subjects. (Bauman, 2004, p 56)

Bauman calls this 'negative globalisation'.

Negative globalisation

What Bauman refers to as 'negative globalisation' is the selective globalisation of trade, capital, surveillance and information, violence, weapons, crime and terrorism, and it is a cause of injustice, violence and conflict. Negative globalisation is embedded within five key themes and challenges.

First, the *passage from solid to liquid modernity* (social forms – structures and institutions – are no longer solid and 'cannot serve as frames of reference for human actions and long term life strategies' [Bauman, 2007, p 1]). Second, the *disembedding of the nation state's power and sovereignty in a globalised world and global political arena*. The power of the modern nation state is 'now moving away to the politically uncontrollable global space; while politics, the ability to decide the direction and purpose of action, is unable to operate effectively at a planetary level since it remains, therefore, local' (2007, p 2). Hence 'the real powers that shape the conditions under which we all act these days flow in *global* space, while our institutions of political action remain by and large tied to the ground; they are, as before, *local*' (2007, p 82). Then there 'arises the paradox of an increasingly local politics in a world increasingly shaped and reshaped by global processes' (2004, p 83). But the situation is made more complex (drawing on Benhabib, 2004) given the conflict between human rights claims (and the right to have rights) and sovereignty claims, including restrictive and protectionist state policies that bar entry to migrants, refugees and asylum seekers on the basis of 'territorial sovereignty' (Benhabib, 2004, p 7).

Third, the *rolling back of state welfare functions*, the *subsidising or contracting out of functions of the state*, the withdrawal of support and insurance against 'individual failure and ill fortune', tied to the 'vagaries of commodity and labour markets inspires and promotes division' (Bauman, 2007, p 2). Thus individualisation and market-based competition degrades collaboration, and

> team work to the rank of temporary stratagems that need to be suspended or terminated the moment their benefits have been used up. 'Society' is increasingly viewed and treated as a 'network' rather than a 'structure' (let alone a solid 'totality'): it is perceived and treated as a matrix of random connections and disconnections and of an essentially infinite volume of possible permutations. (Bauman, 2007, p 3)

Fourth, the *weakening or loosening of social structures* that lead to long-term thinking, planning and acting inscribed over a long duree. For example, the shift from 'career' to 'short-term projects' and 'portfolios', where success is for now, rather than built on a foundation that develops in time. In this sense Bauman speaks of life fragmented into 'lateral rather than vertical orientations'; we speak of portfolios, no longer careers but a series of jobs (Bauman, 2007, p 3).

Finally, the *responsibility* for such shifts and changes are placed 'onto the shoulders of individuals – who are now expected to be "free choosers" and to *bear in full the consequences* of their choices' (Bauman, 2007, pp 3-4; emphasis added). 'The risks involved in every choice may be produced by forces which transcend the comprehension and capacity to act of the individual, but it is the individual's lot and duty to pay their price' (Bauman, 2007, p 4).

In Bauman's terms, this sociopolitical, cultural and economic context (liquid modernity driven by global consumer capitalism) is responsible for the creation of an excess of 'human waste' (literally, the excess consumption that embodies consumer capitalism leads to enormous quantities of human waste) and 'wasted lives', marked in contemporary times by redundancies, lifelong unemployment *and* asylum seekers and refugees fleeing war, conflict, destruction of homes and livelihoods.

Wasted lives, published in 2004, develops this key theme in Bauman's work. 'The numbers of homeless and stateless victims of globalisation grow too fast for the planning, location and construction of camps to keep up with them' (Bauman, 2007, p 37). Drawing attention to the contemporary regime for dealing with refugees (the setting up of refugee camps) Bauman also points to the deregulation of wars often conducted by non-state entities, an outcome of the erosion of state sovereignty as well as the 'frontier-land conditions in "suprastate" global space' (Bauman, 2007, p 37).

Those who flee find themselves outside the law, in a 'lawless space'. 'They are outcasts and outlaws of a novel kind, the products of globalisation and the fullest epitome and incarnation of its frontier-land spirit', experiencing 'liminal drift' (Bauman, 2007, p 38). They are on a journey that may never be completed. Bauman gives two examples: Palestinian refugees, many of whom have never experienced life outside the camps, and the three camps of Dabaab in the Kenyan Garissa province, developed in 1991/92 which do not yet appear on a map despite their 'temporary' permanence.

> On the way to the camps they are stripped of every single element of their identities except one: that of a stateless, placeless, functionless and 'paperless' refugee. Inside the

fences of the camps, they are pulped into a faceless mass, having been denied access to the elementary amenities from which identities are drawn and the usual yarn from which identities are woven. (Bauman, 2007, pp 39–40)

'Refugees' are, for Bauman, the epitome of 'human waste':

> ... all measures have been taken to assure the permanence of their exclusion....Wherever they go, refugees are unwanted and left in no doubt that they are.... The statesmen of the European Union deploy most of their time and brain capacity in designing ever more sophisticated ways of fortifying borders and the most expedient procedures for getting rid of seekers after bread and shelter who have managed to cross the borders nevertheless. (Bauman, 2007, p 42)

The following section explores in more detail what has been called 'refugee regimes', the trajectory of responses to the flows of people seeking safety in the North in the 20th-21st centuries, and offers, to a degree, a contrast to Bauman by highlighting the agency and identities of those seeking asylum and refuge. What is very clear from any examination of the literature on forced migration is the *humiliation* of those who bear the label, who are processed (often into camps) by successive refugee regimes. Something of this humiliation is captured by Bauman (2004) in *Wasted lives.*

Forced migration, exemption and refugee regimes

The 20th century is described as the 'century of the refugee' (Adelman, 1999; Kushner and Knox, 1999). This is not because the period was particularly extraordinary in forcing people to flee (Kushner and Knox, 1999), but because of the 'division of the globe into nation states in which states were assigned the role of protectors of rights, but also exclusive protectors of their own citizens, including the role of gatekeeper to determine who could become new citizens' (Marfleet, 2006, p 90). Marfleet argues

> that states have taken a calculated and instrumental approach to people who are vulnerable and often defenceless, and that this must be put on the record and challenged. I have proposed that states should not be left with the responsibility

for refugees: a suggestion that for some is at odds with
an international legal regime based upon the duties of
states in relation to those who merit protection. But states
themselves are abandoning their responsibilities: the most
wealthy, powerful and stable states take the most calculating
approach towards refugees, who may be punished again and
again simply because they have been displaced, they are
poor, and they are vulnerable. (2006, p xiii)

Adelman's historical analysis of successive refugee regimes[3] highlights
three different modes/regimes of 'coping with the contradictions
within the nation state' (Adelman, 1999, p 91) that are intrinsically
related to processes of globalisation and modernity. The three regimes
are defined as:

• population exchange and border adjustments
• international humanitarian protection
• the era of regional solutions: the age of the camps.

Population exchange and border adjustments

The first regime emerged in the inter-war years (between the First
and Second World Wars): 'population exchange and border adjustments
became the major model for dealing with a refugee population'
(Adelman, 1999, p 90) linked inextricably to the creation and protection
of nation states. For example, the Greek–Turkish exchanges of 1922-23
are described as a consequence of the formation of nation states out of
the disintegration of the Ottoman Empire. The population exchange
and border adjustment regime in the inter-war years 'endorsed the
right of nation states to exclude those attempting to enter their states
as they fled persecution' (Adelman, 1999, p 91) and prevented 'all but a
token number of Jews from obtaining sanctuary' (p 91) from genocide
and ethnic cleansing.

This regime is identified by Adelman and others (see Feingold, 1970;
Marfleet, 2006) not only as a moral failure on the part of western
countries but also as a failure of the nation state system. Marfleet (2006)
states that the British and US governments, rather than addressing the
Nazi campaigns for the annihilation of an imagined enemy, actually
helped facilitate the discourse of 'alien' and 'other', and in so doing
promoted a 'fundamental ambivalence to Jews and Jewish suffering'
(Marfleet, 2006, p 138).

This analysis supports Arendt's argument (1970, 1973); for her, the modern nation state was transformed into an instrument of the nation alone, and 'national interest' was prioritised over 'law'. For example, Arendt uses a quotation from Hitler to illustrate this point:'right is what is good for the German people' (Arendt, 1970, quoted in Benhabib, 2004, p 54). When states began to practise expulsion of unwanted minorities, creating refugees, aliens and stateless people, they created people without legal status, in a state of limbo, caught between nations, states, territories with no legal status.

It could be argued that the Evian Conference, called by President Roosevelt in July 1938 to address the pressing issue of Jewish refugees on 'humanitarian' grounds, simply reinforced this ideology and cemented discourses of abjection and 'otherness' towards the Jews of Europe. The position taken by the 32 countries represented was that they could do nothing more than they were already doing to help the refugees. Lord Winterton, head of the British delegation, said,

> His Majesty's Government are also carefully surveying the prospects of the admission of refugees to their colonies and overseas territories. The question is not a simple one.... Many overseas territories are already overcrowded, others are wholly or partly unsuitable for European settlement.... No thickly populated country can be expected to accept persons who are deprived of their means of subsistence before they are able to enter it. Nor can the resources of private societies be expected to make good the losses which the emigrants have suffered. (www.cdn-friends-icej.ca/antiholo/evian/chapter2.html)

Similarly the Australian and Swiss delegates reinforced this message. Australia's chief delegate, Colonel White, said 'It will no doubt be appreciated also that, as we have no real racial problem, we are not desirous of importing one'. And, the Swiss delegate, Dr H. Rothmund, Chief of the Police Division of the Swiss Justice and Police Department, said 'Switzerland, which has as little use for these Jews as has Germany, will herself take measure to protect Switzerland from being swamped by Jews with the connivance of the Viennese police' (www.cdn-friends-icej.ca/antiholo/evian/chapter2.html).

The journalist, William Shirer, attended the conference, and wrote 'I doubt if much will be done. The British, French and Americans seem too anxious not to do anything to offend Hitler. It's an absurd situation. They want to appease the man who was responsible for their problem' (www.cdn–friends–icej.ca/antiholo/evian/chapter2.html). No country was willing to offer refuge to large numbers of Jewish refugees and each country simply made their excuses and 'passed the buck'. Martin Gilbert wrote 'It was a neutral stance, not a hostile one, but this neutral stance was to cost a multitude of lives':

> Even though the harassment and killing of German and Austrian Jewry was well known, and caused public outcry, it was still considered an internal affair of the German government. As Adler-Rudel points out, 'The Germans soon realised that no matter how they behaved it did not prevent foreign statesmen from shaking hands or dining with Nazi leaders'. (www.cdn–friends–icej.ca/antiholo/ evian/conclusion.html)

A clear example to illustrate both the failure of this regime for managing what was called the refugee 'problem' and the way that nations became bystanders in the plight of the Jewish refugees is captured in the example of the voyage of the St Louis that took place almost one year after the Evian Conference. In 1939 a German transatlantic liner carrying 937 passengers, mostly Jews fleeing Nazi annihilation, was destined for Cuba, where passengers had secured visas and landing certificates. Constructed as a social problem, and marked by their social and spatial marginality, most 'were German citizens, some were from Eastern Europe, and a few were officially "stateless"' (US Holocaust Memorial Museum, 'The Holocaust', *Holocaust Encyclopaedia*, www.ushmm.org/wlc/en/index. php?ModuleId=10005143).

The voyage of the St Louis, 13 May–17 June 1939

On May 13, 1939, the German transatlantic liner St Louis sailed from Hamburg, Germany, for Havana, Cuba. On the voyage were 937 passengers. Almost all were Jews fleeing from the Third Reich. The German annexation of Austria in March 1938, the increase in personal assaults on Jews during the spring and summer, the nationwide Kristallnacht ('Night of Broken Glass') pogrom in November, and the subsequent seizure of Jewish-owned property had caused a flood of visa applications. The plight of German-Jewish refugees, persecuted at home and unwanted abroad, is illustrated by the voyage of the St Louis.

Cuban officials refused to allow the refugees to land, claiming that the passengers' landing certificates, purchased from a corrupt consular official in Germany, were invalid. Only 28 passengers – among them 22 Jews who had secured valid Cuban visas – were allowed to disembark in Havana.

The rest lingered on the ship for five days as a representative of the American Jewish Joint Distribution Committee negotiated with the Cuban government.

Negotiations failed. The ship was ordered out of Cuban waters, and sailed slowly toward Miami.

Telegrams requesting refuge were sent to the White House and US State Department, but entry was denied. The St Louis turned back toward Europe.

During the return voyage, four western European countries agreed to take the refugees. The passengers disembarked in Antwerp on June 17, 1939, after more than a month at sea.

With the German invasion of western Europe in 1940, many of the St Louis passengers were again trapped under Nazi rule and subsequently perished in the Holocaust.

Source: US Holocaust Memorial Museum, 'The Holocaust', *Holocaust Encyclopaedia* (www.ushmm.org/wlc/en/index.php?ModuleId=10005143)

Gerda Blachmann, aged 15 at the time and born in Breslau, the only child of Jewish parents, looks back at her experience:

> I walked through the city to see the aftermath of a pogrom. The windows of Jewish shops had been shattered. A torched synagogue continued to smoulder. I begged my parents to leave Germany. Months later, they decided we should flee. We got visas to Cuba and left from Hamburg aboard the ship St Louis on May 13, 1939. Arriving in Cuba on the 27th, we were told our visas were invalid. Denied entry, we had to return to Europe.
>
> Well, as you can imagine there was a terrible mood. Everybody was very depressed. A few people committed … tried to commit suicide as I think uh the one man … he, I think he cut his wrists and they, he was the only one who landed because they had to take him to the hospital to … to tend to him. I don't know whether he stayed or not. I think he did. He must have been the only one who stayed. But

you know, humans are always hopeful. You know, we always cling to the hope something is going to happen. They're not going to let us rot on the ocean. I mean, something had to happen to us. Of course, the fear was that we would go back to Germany. That was the big thing you know.

Disguised as farm women, my mother and I drove a hay wagon past the German border patrol to a farm on the French–Swiss border. We walked down a small ravine, crossed a stream and then slipped under a barbed-wire fence that marked the official border. But we were apprehended by Swiss border guards and held overnight. The next day, we were put on a train with other refugees. No one told us where we were going or what was going to happen to us. (US Holocaust Memorial Museum, 'The Holocaust', *Holocaust Encyclopaedia*, www.ushmm.org/wlc/en/media_oi .php?ModuleId=10005267&MediaId=286)

Gerda was interned with her mother in a refugee camp in Switzerland for two years, and then worked in Bern in a blouse factory until the end of the war. Gerda learned that her father had died during deportation. She emigrated to the US in 1949.

International humanitarian protection

The events and experiences of the Jews of Europe led to a second regime that was established after the Second World War with the introduction of an international refugee Convention in 1951 (for European refugees only, followed by the 1967 Protocol that made the Convention universal) that focused on individual rights, and in contrast to the pre-Second World War response of 'moving populations and borders to align nationalities with states.... Borders remained sacrosanct and refugees were recognised as having rights to the protection of some state' (Adelman, 1999, p 95). The development of an international 'global and political humanitarian regime' (Adelman, 1999, p 98) involved either return to the state from which the person had fled, settlement in the country of first asylum or resettlement in other countries.

As Marfleet documents, the first international agreements about the human rights of refugees were written 'against a background of regret for the tragedies of the 1930s but also of continuing fear and rejection of Others' (2006, p 144). The 1951 Convention applied only to those who became refugees in Europe and only those who became refugees as a result of events before 1951. The 1967 Protocol extended the Convention worldwide. 'For Western states it had become a matter of urgency to see refugees contained, as far as possible within their area of origin' (Marfleet, 2006, p 151).

Adelman's analysis stated that access to refugee determination was limited, and increasingly restrictionist policies emerged to respond to refugees from the South seeking entry to countries of the North.

The second regime was based on the rights of individuals within the context of a universal system of law (the 1951 international refugee Convention and the 1967 Protocol), and the protection of those who had a 'well founded fear of persecution' and were outside the borders of their country. At this time 'refugee' referred to those who had crossed the borders of their home country seeking safety, and 'displaced' referred to those who had fled within the borders of their home country and who were 'outside the protection of the international refugee regime' (Adelman, 1999, p 94).

This regime was made up of two systems of protection: 'obligatory', for any state that signed the conventions as in the system defined earlier, and a 'voluntary' system for dealing with large numbers fleeing for reasons other than individual persecution. The flight from oppressive governments in Uganda in 1972, Chile in 1973 and Iran in 1979 are three examples. These people were 'resettled as humanitarian refugees rather than as convention refugees by a voluntary system of resettlement' into countries that were not obliged to take people but did so on humanitarian grounds, 'combined with their self interest in admitting immigrants with skills and talents (particularly when this intake complemented their ideological opposition to the regimes from which refugees fled)' (Adelman, 1999, p 94).

As Adelman and others document, this regime began to falter when the numbers of Convention and humanitarian refugees began to rise (examples given are Iran in 1979 and the 1980s civil wars in Sri Lanka, Lebanon, Afghanistan, Mozambique, Angola, Somalia and Ethiopia), in conjunction with improved access to communication and technology, economic crisis in northern states and the 'legalization of Convention protection within domestic codes of developed states' (Adelman, 1999, p 95).

This situation gave rise to a major contradiction between on the one hand, universal human rights and on the other, restrictionist and protective state policies. What is clear is that 'a series of internal contradictions between universal human rights and territorial sovereignty are built into the logic of the most comprehensive international law documents in our world' (Benhabib, 2004, p 11). The growing paradox between international human rights norms, especially the rights of migrants, refugees and asylum seekers, and 'assertions of territorial sovereignty' (Benhabib, 2004, p 7) marks out the current situation of a 'world of increasingly deterritorialized politics' (Benhabib, 2004, p 11).

For example, while the 1948 UDHR recognises the right of movement across boundaries, the right to enjoy asylum under certain conditions and the right to emigrate, it does not reflect 'states' obligations to grant asylum to immigrants, to uphold the right of asylum, and to permit citizenship to alien residents and denizens' (Benhabib, 2004, p 11). Thus we have a clear contradiction between international human rights norms and the policies and practices of nation states.[4] The 1951 Convention and the Protocol added in 1967 are binding on signatory states alone, and not all states have signed.

The articulation in law of crimes against humanity and the emergence of humanitarian intervention increasingly 'subjects state sovereignty to internationally recognised norms which prohibit genocide, ethnocide, forced labor' (Benhabib, 2004, p 10). At the same time, transnational migration has had an impact on human rights norms. Thus, the conflict between universal human rights and sovereignty claims are, for Benhabib, a paradox 'at the heart of the territorially bounded state-centric international order' (Benhabib, 2004, p 69). And, as argued by Adelman, modernity divided the world into nation states and relied on the sovereignty of states to defend the rights of their members and the nation. Refugees turned out to be the 'Achilles heel of the system' (Adelman, 1999, p 93).

> For if one group of nation states did not provide protection for its own people and instead persecuted them, and if other states would not take them in under the argument that they were responsible only for defending the rights of their own citizens and those who shared the dominant nationality, then individuals were left bereft and unprotected by the system. (Adelman, 1999, p 93)

For Sales, 'the nation state remains the major actor in immigration policy but national sovereignty is challenged from above by international and regional policies and governance and from below by local institutions' (2007, p 97). Measures preventing entry have been introduced in many European countries, alongside tighter visa requirements and sanctions against carriers such as airlines, rail and road transportation companies carrying passengers who lack the correct documentation.

Statelessness and loss of the right to have rights

Arendt (1994) identified 'the twin phenomena of "political evil" and "statelessness" as the most daunting problems of the twentieth and twenty-first century' (Benhabib, 2004, p 50). Statelessness for Arendt meant loss of citizenship and loss of rights, indeed the loss of citizenship meant the loss of rights altogether. Benhabib articulates more closely what the 'right to have rights' means:

> The first use of the term 'right' is addressed to humanity as such and enjoins us to recognise membership in some human group. In this sense this use of the term 'right' evokes a moral imperative 'Treat all human beings as persons belonging to the same human group and entitled to protection of the same'.... The second use of the term 'right' in the phrase 'the right to have rights' is built upon this prior claim of membership ... 'rights' suggest a triangular relationship between the person who is entitled to rights, others upon whom this obligation creates a duty, and the protection of this rights claim and its enforcement through some established legal organ, most commonly the state and its apparatus. (Benhabib, 2004, p 57)

Hence, 'one's status as a rights-bearing person is contingent upon the recognition of one's membership', and 'in Arendtian language the right of humanity entitles us to become a member of civil society such that we can then be entitled to juridico-civil rights' (Benhabib, 2004, p 59). And the right to have rights transcends contingencies of birth. There is a bifurcation between on the one hand, universal human rights and on the other, the right of state protection. Arendt acknowledges that the nation state system carried 'within it the seeds of exclusionary justice at home and aggression abroad' (Benhabib, 2004, p 61). Thus, the conflict between universal human rights and sovereignty claims are 'the root paradox at the heart of the territorially bounded state-centric international order' (Benhabib, 2004, p 69).

The dominance of an exclusionary response to the plight of Convention refugees in European states led to the third refugee regime, defined as the 'era of regional solutions' and the age of the camps. This involved erecting barriers to entry in countries of the North and dealing with the issues that produced refugees by instigating initiatives to resolve the issues in the host countries or regions, largely through the development of camps.

Era of regional solutions: the age of the camps

This third refugee regime emerged in the 1980s and 1990s and sought to deal with refugee issues through 'much greater reliance on the initiatives of refugees and their home and host countries to resolve the refugee issue, and less reliance on the initiatives and organising capacity of the international system' (Adelman, 1999, p 100). '[T]he era of regional solutions', marked by economic globalisation and a focus on 'economic exports and ensuring the country's own people can stay or return home' (Adelman, 1999, p 99), meant greater reliance on refugees and home nations or states to solve their own problems, with humanitarian intervention as the dominant method of support.

Thus, in this third regime, Adelman argues that the universal principle that every individual should have their rights protected will be used by very few as pressure is brought to bear on states to assume proper responsibility for the rights of their own members (Adelman, 1999, p 104).

Indeed, the UNHCR evolved from an agency that sought to protect refugees to being the largest relief agency 'organised to serve refugees and displaced persons' (Adelman, 1999, p 100). Marfleet gives the example of 'safe areas' or 'havens' to illustrate this regime, and states that 'Creation of these zones sometimes reflected a genuine concern among officials of relief organisations to provide protection, but it has often been difficult to distinguish this motive from a more general desire to contain the displaced' (Marfleet, 2006, p 202). For example, the UNHCR claimed safe zones in Sri Lanka improved security for civilians and they were also able to 'limit the scale of refugee outflow to India' (quoted in Marfleet, 2006, p 202). Marfleet also describes the fact that in Bosnia, 'safe zones' were known as 'death zones' because protecting people in a zoned area left people at the 'mercy of attacking forces' (Stubbs, 1999, p 16, quoted in Marfleet, 2006, p 202) when security broke down, as in Bosnia and Rwanda.

Drawing on Rieff's (2002) analysis, Marfleet suggests that in relation to regimes of containment and surveillance, the UNHCR and similar bodies are acting on behalf of states to control and contain the movements of people. In a sense, agencies like the UNHCR 'take on the priorities of states, intervening to control population movements and acting as an alibi of governments disinterested in the real causes of economic breakdown and of conflict' (Marfleet, 2006, p 203). Mass movements of refugees are understood by states as both dangerous and destabilising (Marfleet, 2006, p 203). Dabaab camp in Kenya is a clear example of this third refugee regime and brings to light issues of statelessness, lack of citizenship, the lack of a right to have rights as well as the resistance of the people living in the camp to exclusionary structures, discourses and practices.

Dabaab camp: containment, surveillance and gender-based violence

Arendt's claim that 'one's status as a rights-bearing person is contingent upon the recognition of one's membership' (Behabib 2004, p 59) is documented very clearly in the case of the women of Dabaab camp in Kenya. The 'global realities that stem from the intricate interplay of gender, migration and citizenship, and the inclusions and exclusions that result under specific conditions' (Tastsoglou and Dobrowlesky, 2006, p 4) are expressed very starkly in the 'non-citizen' position of Somali refugee women in the camp.

Mohamed Abdi (2006) explores the 'non-citizen' position of Somali refugee women in Dabaab camp in Kenya (many of which are not temporary but long term, with some of the women interviewed having lived in the camp for 10 years), and their experiences of gender-based violence.

> 'You [refugees] are closed in a trunk [camp]. The journalists don't come to see us; we are not put into the airwaves of the world; nobody takes news from us; and we are not even visible. So what exactly are we? Aren't we human beings? We are not human beings! No, we are not: since the government under whose jurisdiction we have been living for the last ten years has denied us any legal standing, not even simple ID cards which, when needed, we could use to travel, maybe to Nairobi, to try to plead with our people, or to make a phone call. We don't have that.' (Timoro Sugulle, quoted in Abdi, 2006, p 231)

In 1991, at the height of the civil war in Somalia, it is estimated that 400,000 people died from violence and famine, with over a million fleeing to neighbouring countries, as is always the case for those without resources to travel further (Abdi, 2006; Marfleet, 2006). The Dabaab camp was created 100km from the Somali/Kenya border in 1991; 130,000 of the initial 400,000 Somali refugees remain in Dabaab. They are:

> ... prohibited from leaving the area without special permits from the United Nations High Commissioner for Refugees

(UNHCR), the main organization administering the camps. CARE working under UNHCR, is responsible for social service provisions, World Food Program (WFP) for food distribution and Médicins Sans Frontières (MSF) for health. (Abdi, 2006, p 233)

Abdi addresses the increasing personal insecurity of women in the camps since 1993 and through their narratives, explores the intersectionality between forced displacement, gender and citizenship. Abdi concludes that their non-citizenship and existence on the margins of Kenyan society literally and metaphorically is a key factor in understanding the insecurity and fear that women face as well as gender-based violence such as rape, a well-documented and deeply humiliating weapon of war:

> 'At night, the *shiftas* just enter your house. You are sitting among your children and a gunman enters. There is nothing he can't do if he wants to, he will rape you if he pleases, he will rob you of the rations you have collected that day, if he pleases. And the children are without food the next day.' (Anab Ali, quoted in Abdi, 2006, p 238)

> 'There is no security whatsoever here. How many times have we been raped now? We have become grateful that it is only rape. Being only raped by this stranger becomes a luxury. When you have to choose between raped and being killed, you think that it is better to be raped.' (Khadija Ma'alin, quoted in Abdi, 2006, p 238)

At the same time, Abdi also explores women's agency[5] within the constraints they face in the environment of the camps, and their capacity to resist violence and humiliation. Resistance emerges in their focus on the needs and well-being of their families, selling merchandise (clothing, sugar, spices), and cultural resistance in the form of songs and poems about their reality that also condemn the Kenyan government and appeal to the international community. Women represent themselves not as victims but as having the strength to survive rape, violence and humiliation, and to make lives for themselves and their families in the margins of the margins. As Abdi writes:

> Although Kenya is a signatory to both the UN Convention on Human Rights and on refugees, and the OAU Convention on refugees, it has ... taken a hands off approach

to its refugee population. Even after ten years in Kenya, the government still maintains that Somali refugees are aliens in transit thereby refusing to extend legal rights to them. (Abdi, 2006, p 246)

Contemporary forced migration: circuits, time and nodal cities

For those with the resources to pay agents and networks to help them flee beyond the borders of their home countries and beyond the 'regional' responses and the camps, migratory 'transnational networks have the potential to mobilise information and resources which can move migrants quickly over great distances' (Marfleet, 2006, p 221). The reality for many refugees is that these journeys will be circuitous, sometimes involving long stays in countries and cities of transit that Marfleet calls 'waystations' (Marfleet, 1998, p 76). The experience of being a refugee, for Marfleet, is marked by 'circuits of migration' because travel direct to countries of asylum is hampered by restrictions on routes, travel and entry. Like Abdi, Marfleet stresses the agentic nature of the lived experiences of refugees based on in-depth interviews: refugees and asylum seekers, people forced to migrate, make choices albeit in conditions not of their own choosing and often under extreme pressure and fear. In *Refugees in a global era* (2006), Marfleet interviews people about their experiences, their choices, their decisions and their journeys to safety. A refugee living in the Netherlands told him:

> 'I went from Afghanistan to Iran and then to Turkey. We paid a lot of money to go to Germany. With some others we went on a long journey by truck into Eastern Europe. Until now I don't know the route we took. When they let us out they said we were in Germany … we soon knew it was not Germany it was Poland. We went back from Poland to Russia, where we had nothing. Only from there, and after a long time, could we get to Germany.' (quoted in Marfleet, 2006, p 258)

The complexity of contemporary migration and forced migration cannot be reduced to globalisation nor one-dimensional, push-pull factors. Indeed, 'movements of capital, ideas and people which pass across borders, notably those of the nation state, have multiple causes and require new frameworks of understanding' (Marfleet, 2006, p 216). Flux and flow, networks and communities that extend beyond the nation state, and circuits rather than single trajectories or causes are the concepts and processes best used to describe contemporary migration (Castles, 2003; Marfleet, 2006).

'Migrants undertake multiple journeys which may involve repeat, shuttle, orbital, ricochet, and yo-yo migrations, and attempts at settlement and return' (Marfleet, 2006, p 216). Sales (2007) also discusses the role of social networks, 'crucial in facilitating and sustaining migratory flows' (Sales, 2007, p 55). Often linked to established as well as colonial links, the 'existence of networks may be a major encouragement to migrate and to choose a particular destination' (Sales, 2007, p 55).

Social networks and transnational communities operating beyond the jurisdiction of nation states provide important routes to mobility that have emerged in the context of globalisation and modernity/late modernity/post-modernity, the compression of time and space. What we must also be clear about is that nation states in a global era are implicated in the production of refugees, and this is deeply embedded in histories of colonialism and post-colonialism, modernity and globalisation. The final sections of this chapter return to the production of refugees and the role of humiliation and human rights in a global era.

Refugees: humiliation, human dignity and social justice

Lazare (1987) suggests that the experience of humiliation among other things involves feeling stigmatised; feeling reduced in size, that is, feeling belittled, put down or humbled; being found deficient, that is, feeling degraded, dishonoured or devalued; or being attacked, that is, experiencing ridicule, scorn or insult. The dynamics of humiliation are also embedded in the logic of the market and historically in the imperial impulse. The current importance of 'humiliation' is due to the connection with human rights in an era of globalisation (Lindner, 2006, p 173).

Lindner (2006) conducted extensive empirical research that includes fieldwork in Somalia and in Rwanda, and she states that the word 'humiliation' points to an act, second at a feeling and third at a process: I humiliate you, you feel humiliated and the entire process is one of humiliation. Lindner suggests that 'in a globalizing world in which people are increasingly exposed to human rights advocacy, that acts of humiliation and feelings of humiliation emerge as the most significant phenomena to resolve' (2006, p 1). Moreover, that 'all humans share a common ground, namely a yearning for recognition and respect that connects them and draws them into relationships' and 'many of the observable rifts among people may stem from the humiliation that is felt when recognition and respect are lacking' (Lindner, 2006, p 1). Hence, 'only if the human desire for respect is cherished, respected, and nurtured, and if people are attributed equal dignity in this process, can differences turn into valuable diversities and sources of enrichment – both globally and locally – instead of sources of disruption' (Lindner, 2006, p 1).

Lindner founded a global network, Human Dignity and Humiliation Studies, to address, understand and move beyond the experiences of humiliation, non-recognition and lack of respect through transformative social action underpinned by the need for human dignity globally and locally. For Lindner (2004, p 4), there has been a shift (we could call it from modernity to late modernity or post-modernity) in global relations, 'from a world steeped in Honor codes of unequal human worthiness to a world of Human Rights ideals of equal dignity'. Influenced by anthropology, Lindner writes:

> In the new historical context (of equal dignity for all/ human rights legislation), the phenomenon of humiliation[6] (expressed in acts, feelings and institutions), gains significance in two ways: (a) as a result of the new and more relational reality of the world, and (b) through the emergence of human rights ideals. Dynamics of humiliation profoundly change in their nature within the larger historical transition from a world steeped in honour codes of unequal human worthiness to a world of human rights ideals of equal dignity. Dynamics of humiliation move from honour-humiliation to dignity-humiliation, and, they gain more significance. (2004, p 4)

For Lindner, the human rights revolution 'could be described as an attempt to collapse the master-slave gradient to a line of equal dignity and humility' that she defines as 'egalization' (2006, p 3) Lindner writes that feelings of humiliation may lead to (a) depression and apathy, (b) the urge to retaliate with inflicting humiliation (she gives the example of Hitler, genocides, terrorism) or (c) they may lead to constructive social change (she gives the example of Mandela). Lindner is committed to research and action that helps to foster new public policies for driving not only *globalisation* but also *egalization*, and helping to create a peaceful and just world, and she writes that three elements are necessary for this to be progressed.

First, new decent institutions have to be built, both locally and globally, that heal and prevent dynamics of humiliation (see Margalit, 1996).[7]

Second, new attention has to be given to maintaining relationships of equal dignity. Third, new social skills have to be learned in order to maintain relations of equal dignity. We need new types of leaders, who are no longer autocratic dominators and humiliation-entrepreneurs, but knowledgeable, wise facilitators and motivators, who lead towards respectful and dignified inclusion of all humankind as opposed to hateful polarisation. Lindner calls for a moratorium on humiliation to be included into new public policy planning. She would also like to see better institutions and leadership to heal and prevent the dynamics of humiliation, othering, de-humanisation and an examination of governance, both nationally and globally.

Smith (2006) also focuses on humiliation. He argues that unless globalisation changes direction, 'the cost in terms of freedom and human rights will be high' (2006, p 1). He also makes a distinction between what he calls globalisation's 'public agenda', such as market opportunities, business interests, competition for energy resources such as oil and gas, the war on terror and globalisation's 'hidden agenda'. This 'hidden agenda' is shaped by three historical processes that he defines as a 'triple helix': globalisation, the regulation of modernity and the dynamics of humiliation. He suggests that these three socio-historical drivers (and their interrelationships) are shaping the future of global society in the 21st century (2006, p 9).[8] 'Globalisation causes people to be displaced or excluded in ways that make them feel outraged and resentful' (Smith, 2006, p 9).

Globalisation is therefore a cause of humiliation. The two codes of modernity – the human rights code and the honour code – and usually a mixture of the two influence the way humiliation is experienced. Historically the honour code is 'particularistic', it 'values strength: the capacity to maximise your stake in the world and to destroy your enemies' (Smith, 2006, p 13). In contrast, the human rights code is 'universalistic', it respects and recognises 'needs and makes demands that all human beings should be given access to the means of enjoying a decent life' (Smith, 2006, p 13). There is, at the same time, 'the decreasing capacity of the nation state to contain and structure our lives as influence shifts upwards to the global level' (Smith, 2006, p 15). Being humiliated[9] by the experience of forced displacement or exclusion, denied recognition, rights, security, and what you feel is rightfully yours can lead to conquest humiliation, relegation humiliation (being forced downwards in a hierarchy) and exclusion humiliation (being denied membership of a group you feel you belong to). Possible responses involve escape (fear cycles), acceptance (victimisation cycles) and rejection (revenge cycles).

In the three refugee regimes discussed earlier we can see examples of escape and acceptance but also resistance to humiliation. *Humiliation* has become a recent focus for study, particularly at an interdisciplinary level. As Marfleet (2006) outlines, states take a calculated and instrumental approach to people who are vulnerable/defenceless. This must be challenged – they are abandoning their responsibilities, and so states cannot be left with the responsibility for refugees (and this is at odds with international regimes based on the duties of states).[10]

Lindner (2006) and Smith (2006) both focus attention on the role of 'humiliation' in understanding the social processes that give rise to displacement and forced migration that includes analysis of increasing global interdependence. Lindner's (2006) work identifies not only the dynamics of humiliation but through a interdisciplinary approach to understanding humiliation, the global network she is currently leading focuses on human dignity and humiliation to produce research, practice and relationships on a glocal and planetary level that might counter the destructive tendencies emanating from 'the triple helix' of modernity, globalisation and humiliation (Smith, 2006). Lindner's interdisciplinary scholarship entails elements from anthropology, history, social philosophy, social psychology, sociology and political science. She argues that in a globalising world in which people are increasingly exposed to human rights advocacy, acts of humiliation and feelings of humiliation emerge as significant phenomena to resolve.[11] Lindner's PhD was carried out in Somalia, Rwanda and Burundi, addressing their history of genocidal killings. From 1998 to 1999, 216 qualitative interviews were conducted. On the basis of the empirical evidence, she argued that:

> Feelings of humiliation may lead to violent acts of humiliation and spirals of retributive violence. Terrorists are hard to track and difficult to combat; they eclipse traditional warfare methods. Embracing new security strategies that include the mindsets of people in violent conflicts appears one wise alternative. Humiliation-for-humiliation may represent the only real Weapons of Mass Destruction we face. High jacking planes (9-11) or hacking neighbours to death with machetes (genocide in Rwanda 1994) are all 'cost-effective' methods of mayhem that work when leaders manipulate followers into becoming willing perpetrators. Feelings of humiliation can represent the Nuclear Bombs of the Emotions. (Lindner, 2002b, pp 127-9)

She argues that given the shift from the honour code to the human rights code what was once accepted as normal could now be rejected as humiliating (2006, p xv). Using the Hutus as an example, she states that the Hutus lived under a hierarchical system ruled by Tutsi elites for hundreds of years, that this was once regarded as 'normal' and with the shift in moral views and changing power of the Hutus, 'humiliation became a burning wound that that led to a genocidal frenzy against the Tutsi *inyenzi* ("cockroaches")' (Lindner, 2006, p xv). Lindner also describes the ways in which tensions between the honour code and human rights code can elicit feelings of humiliation such as in the case of honour killings. 'a family whose daughter is raped may try to regain its honor by killing the girl; advocates of human rights are appalled ... while defenders of family honor are offended by what they regard as ... the humiliating devaluation of their culture' (2006, p xv).

Smith (2006) further argues that the lack of the following is an indicator that you are in conditions of humiliation: freedom (politics, economic, social, protective security; see Sen, 1999 and also Nussbaum, 2006, quoted in Smith, 2006); agency (Mary Kaldo, 2003); security (Peter Singer, 2004); recognition (Margalit, 1996). Moreover, he argues, global terrorism seems to follow a similar logic, led by humiliation entrepreneurs who instrumentalise feelings of humiliation among the broad masses for violence.

Lindner argues that social change is a process and one must remain mindful of the goal. She tells us that all humans share a common ground, namely a yearning for recognition and respect that connects them and draws them into relationships. Many of the observable rifts among people may stem from the humiliation that is felt when recognition and respect are lacking.

In the foreword to Lindner's (2006) pioneering text on understanding humiliation, Morton Deutsch states that her work enables 'understanding how attacks on one's dignity and the experience of humiliation can foster destructive interactions at the interpersonal and international levels' (2006, p vii). Moreover, for Deutsch, we need to 'enhance knowledge of the conditions which foster dignifying as well as humiliating relationships and, more importantly, which will enhance knowledge of how to transform humiliating relationships to dignifying ones'. The need for dignifying relationships and awareness of the conditions that foster dignifying relationships demand engagement with constructions of social justice, 'community' (especially Yar's notion of a recognitive community), rights and recognition.

Social justice: rights, recognition and community

What does the right to have rights mean?

Arendt stated that the right to have rights was fundamentally a moral claim as well as a political problem for those who did not have the protection of the state, or citizenship, such as Jewish refugees from Germany, discussed earlier in this chapter. Since the Second World War 'the recognition of the universal status of personhood of each and every human being independently of the national citizenship' (Benhabib, 2004, p 68) has developed,[12] and yet the 'challenge ahead is to develop an international regime which decouples the right to have rights from one's nationality' (Benhabib, 2004, p 68). Despite the right to seek asylum being a human right, 'the obligation to grant asylum continues to be jealously guarded by states as a sovereign principle' (Benhabib, 2004, p 69). For the refugee, not having your papers in order, being undocumented, *sans papiers*, is a form of social death (Benhabib, 2004, p 215). And, even in

> the most developed rights regimes of our world, refugees and asylum seekers still find themselves in quasi criminal status. Their human rights are curtailed: they have no civil and political rights of association and representation. The extension of full human rights to these individuals and the decriminalisation of their status is one of the most important tasks of cosmopolitan justice in our world. (Benhabib, 2004, p 168)

Benhabib (2004) argues for a cosmopolitan federalism, that non-territorially based models of democratic representation are possible, that globalisation increases the intensity and interconnections of human actions and will create new sites and logics of representation. The global network founded by Lindner is an example of this (see Chapter Nine, this volume).

Benhabib (2004, p 221) rejects the right of a sovereign people not to permit naturalisation, arguing that 'no human is illegal', but that this takes place within the 'institutional and normative necessities of a democracy as a form of government based upon public autonomy, namely that those subject to the laws also be their authors' (Benhabib, 2004, p 221). She also argues for 'moral universalism and cosmopolitan federalism', advocating 'porous' not open borders, to include 'first admittance rights', for democracies to regulate the shift from 'first admission to full membership' and for law governing naturalisation to human rights norms (Benhabib, 2004, p 221). While I accept and agree with Benhabib's suggestions, the notion of porous borders and 'first admittance rights' does not go far enough, and I wonder how and in what ways would nations police their porous boundaries and first admittance rights and routes to citizenship. Would the tragic situations faced by many people seeking asylum and refuge in the West today be improved? Furthermore, whilst I agree – no human is illegal – I do not think that Benhabib's porous borders and first admittance rights go far enough in promoting the right to have rights.

Social justice

> If you wish peace, care for justice…. Absence of justice is
> barring the road to peace today. (Bauman, 2007, p 5)

I suggest that an holistic understanding of social justice includes distributive, cultural and associational justice (see O'Neill et al, 2005). Theoretically, an holistic conception of social justice is of crucial importance in understanding and promoting processes of belonging within the complex dynamics of the asylum–migration–community nexus, especially as they impact on the urban environments where asylum seekers and refugees make their homes. But what is an holistic concept of 'social justice'?

The social and critical theory literature throws up approaches to social justice that coalesce around philosophical analysis and empirical enquiry, equalities of opportunity and social justice through pedagogy (Applebaum, 2004), as well as discourses around rights, redistribution and recognition (Fraser, 1997; Bauman, 2001) linked to the very fabric of modernity/post-modernity/liquid modernity[13]. In earlier work, I argued (O'Neill et al, 2005) that a critical theory perspective embraces cultural justice (issues of recognition), distributive justice (equality of opportunity, redistribution) and associational justice. An holistic view of social justice needs to appreciate the importance and interrelation of each of the three aspects in order to provide a sophisticated conceptual framework for understanding and advancing social justice.

Three forms of social justice are neatly summarised by Cribb and Gewirtz (2003), drawing on but extending models developed by Iris Marion Young (1990) and Nancy Fraser (1997):

- distributive justice, which includes concerns about what Fraser calls 'economic justice', defined as the absence of exploitation, economic marginalisation and deprivation;
- cultural justice, defined (by Fraser) as the absence of cultural domination, non-recognition and disrespect;
- associational justice, defined as the absence of 'patterns of association amongst individuals and amongst groups which prevent some people from participating fully in decisions which affect the conditions within which they live and act' (Power and Gewirtz, 2001, p 41, quoted in Cribb and Gewirtz, 2003, p 19; see also O'Neill et al, 2003)

From a community development (and community arts) perspective, social justice encompasses associational, cultural and distributive justice. It is

> about building active and sustainable communities based on social justice and mutual respect. It is about changing power structures to remove the barriers that prevent people from participating in the issues that affect their lives ... [and] enabling people to claim their human rights, meet their needs and have greater control over the decision-making processes which affect their lives. (www.scdc.org.uk)

However, in late, or liquid modernity sociologists and criminologists have highlighted the problem of the disintegration of more solid communities (communities bound by shared territory, shared interests and shared experiences; mining communities are a classic example of strong communities), social disintegration and division that can result from more diverse, multicultural societal forms. Giddens (1994, p 126) describes the danger as one of returning to 'cultural segmentalism' in which local communities 'function through exclusion, a differentiating of insiders and outsiders'. It raises, in new forms, the longstanding sociological issue posed by modernity, that of solidarity.

For Bauman (2001, p 74), the vision of a final, just society, which characterised earlier modernity, gives way to a '"human rights" rule/standard/measure meant instead to guide the never-ending experimentation with satisfactory or at least acceptable, forms of cohabitation'. This later, more 'liquid' version acts, according to Bauman, as a 'catalyst' that perpetuates the production of difference that leads to 'a keen control over entry and exit visas' (Bauman, 2001, p 76).

In the remainder of this book it is suggested that understanding and advancing social justice can be tackled (drawing on the work of Woods, 2003) by first, 'an appeal to or a belief in *affective change*' (2003, p 157), and that this is rooted in relational dynamics. Second, 'awareness that there is a human need for culture to live a life that is meaningful, and that this implies a particular type of integrating culture – not a universal/ assimilationist version but one that enables multiplicity, equality and difference'. This might be described as interculturalism (counter to multiculturalism), expressive of cosmopolitanism that imagines social justice as togetherness in difference through intercultural bridging (Bianchini and Santacatterina, 1997). Or Nancy's account account of community discussed in Chapter Two that incorporates the relational dynamics of togetherness in difference. Third, that distributive, cultural and associational aspects of social justice are each necessary and interconnected.

The associational model can be seen as bringing in recognition of the importance of what Woods (2003, p 157) identifies as 'interlocking democratic rationalities', which also supports the usefulness of participatory methodologies in research with asylum seekers, migrants and refugees. Participatory research includes the following factors: 'decisional (involvement on decision-making), discursive (participation in debate and dialogue), therapeutic (enhanced self esteem through involvement) and ethical (aspiration to truth and meaning integral to authentic participation)' (O'Neill et al, 2005). Hence a vision of social justice as *affective*, imagined and holistic is presented as a model on which to develop further research and analysis with migrants, forced and free, linked to concepts of 'community' as recognitive community and linked to processes of egalization.

In summary, this chapter has drawn on a number of key themes in the available literature to examine the global, social and relational processes underpinning the production of refugees, the movement of people across borders, the development of refugee regimes and the development of transnational/diasporic communities. Smith's (2006) thesis on the triple helix of globalisation, humiliation and modernity, Lindner's (2006) work on humiliation and human dignity and Marfleet (2006) on globalisation and transnationalism have been discussed in relation to Adelman's (1999) work on refugee regimes. The tension between international human rights law and state-centric protection of 'porous' borders and the tension between humiliation and human dignity are important aspects for understanding globalisation and forced migration at the macro, meso and micro levels. A central theme that has an impact on the lived experiences of refugees, asylum seekers and economic migrants is the growth of human rights discourses worldwide, and the concept of social justice linked to the asylum-migration-community nexus. Within the context of the triple helix, and drawing on Lindner (2006), the future directions for research, policy and practice must surely be to focus on the following:

- accept the impact of migration, both forced and free, and the emergence of transnational communities and identities;
- build decent institutions based on justice, equality and global citizenship;
- develop interventions based on holistic concepts of social justice that will address humiliation, mis-recognition and 'othering'.

The next chapter explores more closely the dynamics of the asylum-migration-community nexus.

Notes

[1] Spybey (1995) defines globalisation as encompassing political, economic and cultural institutions; indeed 'today there is virtually no one on the planet who can participate in social life without reference to globalized institutions' (1995, p 9).

[2] The experiences of expatriate migrants are that they are certainly not all living in situations of privilege and financial security, as O'Reilly's ethnographic work shows. See O'Reilly (2000) and Benson and O'Reilly (2009).

[3] Sales (2007) and Koffman et al (2000) use the concept of migration regime to explain migratory flows in specific historical contexts.

[4] Benhabib defines this particular development of an international human rights regime as 'a set of interrelated and overlapping global and regional regimes that encompass human rights treaties as well as customary international law or international "soft law" ... (international agreements that are not treaties and therefore not covered by the Vienna Convention on the Law of Treaties)' (2004, p 7).

[5] In earlier studies of migration that focused on structural and power inequalities, the agency of migrants was a relative absence (Marfleet, 2006).

[6] Lindner writes: 'Humiliation means the enforced lowering of a person or group, a process of subjugation that damages or strips away their pride, honor or dignity. To be humiliated is to be placed, against your will and often in a

deeply hurtful way, in a situation that is greatly inferior to what you feel you should expect. Humiliation entails demeaning treatment that transgresses established expectations. It may involve acts of force, including violent force.... Indeed, one of the defining characteristics of humiliation as a process is that the victim is forced into passivity, acted upon, made helpless' (2004, p 29).

[7] Margalit (1996) draws our attention to the fact that we need to stand up not just against singular acts of humiliation; we also have to build societies with institutions that do not humiliate their citizens.

[8] The dynamics of globalisation include the pursuit of power, prestige and profit, and survival across three phases: European imperialism (1600 to post–Second World War); global imperialism (1945 to 1991 [that is, to the end of the Cold War]); and global multi-polarity. Smith (nd, p 6) defines global multi-polarity as the ending of 'the uni-polar world dominated by the United States', and the beginning of a third phase in the early 21st century, notable for 'the increasing independence of the European Union, the rise of China, the revival of Japan, the resurgence of Russia, the emergence of India and the clear signs of American weariness with, and distaste for, its present role as "global monarch"'. The regulation of modernity involves social competition, provision of care and protection and control of access to sociocultural benefits. Embedded in modernising processes is the tension between the honour code and the human rights code. The honour code that is very much alive in many parts of the world involves a focus on strength and the capacity to maximise your stake in the world and to destroy enemies. The human rights code focuses instead on respect that all human beings should enjoy a decent life. Most societies operate a mix of the two codes.

[9] Fangen (2006, p 71) points out that the concept of 'humiliation' covers a wide range of experiences, from being a victim of genocide to being an object of gossip and ridicule.

[10] Marfleet's response is to advance the argument for open borders.

[11] Lindner argues that people react in different ways when they feel that they are being unduly humiliated. Some people suffering humiliation may experience rage; this may be turned inwards, as in the case of depression and apathy. However, rage may also turn outwards and express itself in violence, even in mass violence, when leaders are available to forge narratives of group humiliation. Hitler is a classic example. Some people hide their anger and carefully plan revenge. The person who plans for 'cold' revenge may become

the leader of a particularly dangerous movement (see an interesting article on extreme mass homicide by Dutton et al, 2005).

[12] The 1951 Convention, the founding of the UNHCR and the ECHR and the Assembly of Europe.

[13] The paradoxical nature of modernisation/modernity is that the enlightenment ideals of reason, progress and liberation have turned into their opposite in repression, manipulation and unfreedom. Critical theorists explore the paradoxes.

TWO

Asylum-migration-community nexus

If there is to be a community in the world of individuals, it can only be (and needs to be) a community woven together from sharing and mutual care: a community of concern and responsibility for the equal right to be human and the equal ability to act on that right. (Bauman, 2001, pp 149-50)

'Imagine a long free fall without knowing what's going to happen to you whether you are going to smash on the ground or land on something smooth and comfortable and suddenly you get news that your case has been accepted, here it is, the documents I have been waiting for. Yes we are proud of our new home, life and the way that we can gather round the table like this, and just you know, to feel as a family again, that is a wonderful thing. For several months now we have been living here but you know, quite happily, and trying to settle down, lovely neighbourhood. I felt like I was reborn you know and even in the eyes of the family you feel decent, you feel that you have finally managed to protect them, and I feel that I will be able to help these children become decent members of this society, where they live, now their home.' (quoted on www.bbc.co.uk/ learningzone/clips/asylum-seeking-asylum/6375.html)

This chapter discusses the asylum–migration–community nexus as it is experienced in the UK within the context of globalisation and discussions of social justice raised in Chapter One. Concepts and understandings of 'community' linked to asylum and migration are discussed in the context of broader social, relational and historical processes. Indeed, as Schoene (2009) argues, globalisation demands an account and understanding of community, 'how we connect one to the other, starting with the most intimate levels of everyday existence (our lives as family members, lovers and friends) via our communal neighbourhoods right up to the abstract heights of the nation and the globe as a whole' (Schoene, 2009, p 180).

This chapter aims to problematise the concept of *community*, and argues that it is important to explore the tensions between asylum, migration and community in the lives of people seeking asylum and refuge as well as in relation to the broader social processes and structures identified in Chapter One. This chapter examines: 'how can we be receptive to the meaning of our multiple, dispersed, mortally fragmented existences, which nonetheless only make sense by existing in common?' (Kester, 2004, p 154).

What do we understand by 'community'?

Community is defined variously throughout the history of the 20th century as relating to first, a geographical area or place. Mining communities are a common example, as are people living in cities, urban spaces or rural spaces. Second, it can refer to a group of people living in a place, for example Irish community, Polish community, Zimbabwean community, Bangladeshi community. Here people are identified with a nation, an origin, an 'essential' aspect of their identity. Moreover, in this second definition of 'community' a sense of belonging, attachment and identity is often linked to essential or imagined origins (nation) and/ or place. In fieldwork for a research project in 2004 I talked to a group of young people about their identifications with the housing estate where they lived. The young people had demarcated their area into two zones – those living in 'Texas' (newer homes, more aspirational) and the 'Wild West', (social housing, high unemployment) where they lived. The symbolic association with *Texas* and the *Wild West* told me a lot about how they perceived and related to the area.

A third and more common definition of community in the 21st century is as togetherness, marked by shared interests, a life lived in common. Like Willmott's (1989) earlier study, Bauman (2001) writes about 'community' as defined through shared territory, shared attachments, shared identities and shared interests that are less and less tied to place, due to an increase in mobility (for some) and the withering away of traditional forms of solidarity that were class- and place-based. These changes have taken place alongside an increase in technology, internet-based forms of communication and social networking such as Facebook and Skype. Beck (1998) argues that the withering away of traditional forms of solidarity does not issue in a void but rather gives rise to new 'niches of activity and identity' that allow for contingent communities and new modes 'of conducting and arranging life' (Beck, 1998, p 33), and through which new individual and collective identities are formed.

Bauman asks us to consider how 'togetherness' is experienced through increasing mobility/mobilities. Research tells us that mobility gives rise to 'diasporization of communities in the contemporary era' (Urry, 2007, p 35) that can destabilise place and interest communities (Bauman, 2001). For Bauman, the paradox of the contemporary world is that there is a fascination with community while at the same time people are increasingly aware of the fragmentary nature of community relationships (Bauman, 2001). What Bauman (2001) calls 'togetherness' has become fragmentary and episodic – and so contemporary communities become more contingent. Forms of 'togetherness' as the various bases of 'community' may be mediated through place, as in a workplace; communities of interest are matrix like, stretching relationships across time and place, involving connectedness and marked by social networks and postulated, or imagined, communities.

As discussed in Chapter One, Castles (2003) calls the complex relationship between migration (the movement of people across borders) and forced migration (forced movement, for example as a consequence of civil war, natural disasters, decolonisation) the 'asylum-migration nexus'. The distinction between forced and economic migration has become blurred and there are complex factors and outcomes operating that link the local with the global and there are multiple reasons for mobility. For example, a young Muslim woman from Bosnia working in the UK as an economic migrant applies for asylum in 1993 as the war in Bosnia and human rights crimes escalate. A young man on a student visa applies for asylum as the situation in Sri Lanka deteriorates for his family (and his future). Young artists from Iraqi Kurdistan seek asylum not only to flee the war and horror they experience in Iraq but also to fulfil their ambitions, to fulfil their potential, to live in peace and safety. The asylum-migration nexus also involves understanding that people move 'in and out of different statuses. Indeed, migration is 'an integral part of North–South relations' (Castles, 2003, p 9) and global inequalities, societal crisis and social transformations in the South have a profound impact on the mobility of people and forced migration.

The concept of 'community' is contested and contingent, and is of central concern to analysis of forced migration, with diaspora being one expression of 'community'. Migrants may leave territorially bound and localised communities; many of these communities are torn asunder through violent conflicts (Bosnia is a contemporary example). They may form de-territorialised diasporic communities in the new situation or in the zones of transition in key cities (Marfleet, 2006) and become transnational communities with connections in more than one country (Vertovec, 2001). Such transnational communities are also supported by emerging virtual communities. For example, Somalis living in Leicester have family and friends who have gained refugee status in other European countries, such as Sweden and the Netherlands. Together they make up a virtual community supported by technology and media communication, such as the Somali Afro European Media Project (SAEMP) based in Leicester (see Chapter Four) that facilitates online communities of Somali diaspora, not only in Europe but also in Somalia and other parts of the globe.[1]

Multiple mobilities and transnational migration are historically embedded in modernity and late modernity and become more complex in the latter part of the 20th and 21st centuries with the increase in forced migration, people fleeing crisis, war and terror. As Marfleet (2006) shows, these journeys are long and complex and forced migrants may have to wait for months in 'transit zones' in major cities before finding agents to support them or the safest mode of transport to take them forward on their journeys. As Urry (2007) points out, once people are forced to migrate, 'they encounter the legal and social systems ... of the countries they transit which sets up many restrictions and limitations upon their migration and upon their capacity to stay' (2007, p 36). Ahmed and Fortier (2003, p 255) suggest that the 'present global context of flows, fluidity and transnational connections disturbs, if not forever dissolves, the temporal, spatial and emotive certainties of "communities", whether national, regional or local'.

Acknowledging the contingency of the concept 'community', Bauman's analysis is instructive: '"community" stands for the kind of world which is not, regrettably, available to us but which we would dearly wish to inhabit and which we hope to repossess' (Bauman, 2001, p 3). Far from developing a nostalgic return to an earlier time mythically associated with a rural idyll or strong communities based around place, common culture and class, such as mining communities, where social bonds *appeared* stronger and harmonious, Bauman urges us to critically examine community in relation to the tension between freedom and security – individualism and collectivity – freedom and belonging. This tension is also marked in the debates on the subject of community between liberals (individualism) and communitarians (collectivity). I return to this tension later in this chapter.

Ahmed and Fortier (2003) also urge readers 'to think about community as an effect of power and to consider the historical specificity of community formations in their modes of organisation and articulation as well as some of the (new) 'grammars' of collective belonging: the trans(national/gender); the post-(national/modern); the multi(cultural);

the queer; the diasporic; the virtual; the cosmopolitan' (2003, p 256). For now it is useful to examine the concept of 'community' in relation to terms that express asylum-migration-community nexus: diaspora, cosmopolitanism and hybridity.

Community diaspora, cosmopolitanism and hybridity

Discourses of forced migration combine with economic migration in the use of *diaspora*. Refugees and economic migrants and people seeking to reunite with their families are captured in diasporic discourses. The field of refugee and migration studies has been slow in connecting with more cultural analysis, with the related concepts of diaspora (Kalra et al, 2005) hybridity and cosmopolitanism. Cohen (1997) describes 'diaspora' as the dispersal and scattering from one's homeland; there is also the experience of collective trauma linked to home, and in the new situation a cultural flowering, as well as a troubled relationship with the majority, and a sense of community that is transnational and transcends the national borders of home and the new situation. Vertovec (1999) and Brah (1996) also offer complex readings based on multiple meanings and experiences of diaspora.

Brah (1996) raises the question as to whether diaspora is a descriptive category or can be used analytically. Brah advocates the use of 'diaspora' as an interpretive frame for analysing the political, economic and cultural modalities of historically specific forms of migrancy to include migrant, immigrant, expatriate, refugee, guest worker and exile. Brah is especially interested in the forms of identity and subjectivity in social relations and in the way that exile and the 'politics of location' form what she calls a 'diasporic space', tinged with discourses of 'return' (p 209).

Vertovec (1999) defines diaspora as: a social form, a type of consciousness and a mode of cultural production that intersects with global and local contexts as well as the homeland:

> 'DIASPORA' is the term often used today to describe practically any population which is considered 'deterritorialised' or 'transnational' – that is, which has originated in a land other than in which it currently resides, and whose social, economic and political networks cross the borders of nation-states or, indeed, span the globe. (1999, p 1)

Diaspora as a social form includes: the process of becoming scattered through voluntary or forced migration; the communities living in various locations and the places where the dispersed live; a collective identity often sustained through an '"ethnic myth" of common origin, historic experience and some kind of tie to a geographic place; a feeling of not being accepted by the host society; networks of communication and exchange that "create new communal organisations in places of settlement" and also transnationally' (Vertovec, 1999, p 4, 2001).

Diaspora as a form of consciousness includes a focus on identity and belonging and can be articulated through what Gilroy (1999) and de Bois (1897) describe as a sense of 'double consciousness' generated by transnationalism and an awareness of multilocality that includes a 'diaspora consciousness' (Vertovec, 1999, p 10). The latter can be expressed through 'ethnic mobilisation, identity or community politics, or the politics of recognition or difference' (Vertovec, 1999, p 10).

Diaspora as a mode of cultural production is identified through 'cultural objects, images and meanings' and 'constructed styles and identities ... evident in the production and reproduction of forms' (Vertovec, 1999, p 19). Hence, in this latter sense we can explore cultural production and configuration such as music, film, art and literature (Kalra et al, 2005). Artist Houston Conwill and Trinh. T. Minh-ha's work (1989, 1991) are two good examples of the way that experiences of diaspora are articulated through cultural forms and products, which also include (through their artworks) cross-cutting themes of diaspora as a social form and as a mode of consciousness. Similarly the arts-based research discussed in Chapter Five is an example of the articulation of experiences of diaspora.

Conwill's art work involves making large-scale maps either on the floor or on the ground of public, civic sites (Rogoff, 2000). Systems of organised knowledge are layered on top of each other with each layer transparent (see Figure 3). 'The result is that we must read each of the organizing systems, whether it be cartographic, historical or spatial, through one another' (Rogoff, 2000, p 106). So, in the 'New cakewalk humanifesto' the south of the US is overwritten with the civil rights marches of the 1950s and 1960s and words of Martin Luther King, Sojourner Truth and Langston Hughes, producing 'layered, geographized histories that not only add to existing knowledge but restructure it' (Rogoff, 2000, p 110). Rogoff (2000) describes Conwill as being engaged in a process that undoes the universalism of the dominant ideology and produces 'a spatialized history charted on to an articulated location which in turn becomes a concrete manifestation of double consciousness' (2000, p 110). The double consciousness that Conwill works through is African-American.

Figure 3: 'New cakewalk humanifesto'

Minh-ha's filmic and theoretical work also deals with the hyphenated experience of migration, belonging and unbelonging (www.trinhminh-ha.com/). *Surname Viet Given Name Nam* was released in 1999 and is based around interviews with Vietnamese immigrants living in the US. The film explores 'identity and culture through the struggle of Vietnamese women' (http://pages.emerson.edu/organizations/fas/latent_image/issues/1993-12/print_version/trinh.htm). Minh-ha's feminist theoretical work also explores these themes particularly in relation to post-colonialism.

For Kalra et al (2005), the concept of 'diaspora' shifts our attention away from viewing migration as a 'one off, one way process', but it is not at all clear if these concepts offer a positive understanding of 'transnational affiliation or a defensive posture by communities in the face of a hostile host saying "you do not belong"' (2005, p 14). Diaspora does allow us to move beyond the 'static fixed notion of immigrant' (p 14), emphasising transnational belongings and multiplicity of identities and subject positions (Anthias, 1998) but, for Kalra et al, it is not linked to possibilities for praxis. Ultimately, the concepts of diaspora 'divorced from organized politics, is largely unable to help us in resisting the globalizing and transnational ravages of local and contemporary capitalism' (Kalra et al, 2005, p 27).

For Brah (1996, p 238), the usefulness of the concept of 'diaspora space' is that it can mark the 'intersectionality of contemporary conditions of transmigrancy of people, capital, commodities and culture'. Moreover, the way that 'diasporic collectivities' mobilise resources, identities and power 'is also crucial to the construction of diaspora space' (p 238). Importantly too, for Brah, the concept of diaspora articulates the construction and experience of 'borders' (social, political, territorial, psychic and cultural) and together 'diaspora', 'border' and 'the politics of location' are 'immanent' (p 238). Brah's analysis draws attention to identities, belonging, otherness and the multiple ways these are contested and constructed, including configurations of power, particularly the 'multi-axiality 'of power at global level (the World Bank and the International Monetary Fund are given as examples of the 'multi-axiality' of power).

The related concept of *cosmopolitanism* is used in a number of senses to express identity and belonging beyond the nation state. Criticised by Bauman (2001) as a term that celebrates an elitist 'irrelevance of place' linked to business and the culture industry, 'it does not matter where we are, what matters is that we are there' (Bauman, 2001, p 56). Bauman goes on to define cosmopolitanism and the cosmopolitan outlook as a community-free zone:

> More than anything else, the 'bubble' in which the new cosmopolitan business and culture-industry global elite spend most of their lives is – let me repeat – a *community-free zone*....The 'secession of the successful' is, first and foremost, escape from community. (2001, p 57)

Thus, for Bauman, cosmopolitanism is marked by individualism, difference and what he calls 'cool secession', the distancing of the powerful and wealthy from collective responsibilities and concepts of redistribution and collectivity. Drawbridges are pulled up, and 'out as well is community understood as a site of equal shares in jointly attained welfare: as a kind of togetherness which presumes the responsibilities of the rich and gives substance to the hopes of the poor that such responsibilities will be taken up' (Bauman, 2001, p 62). In this sense, cosmopolitanism is marked by an 'aesthetic community' generated by identity concerns, the entertainment industry, mobility, consumption and individual desires. This, he defines, by 'no long term commitments', marked by 'peg' communities: 'the "experience" of community without real community, the joy of belonging without the discomfort of being bound' (2001, p 70).

Schoene (2009) takes a more productive approach to the concept of cosmopolitanism.[2] For Schoene a cosmopolitan outlook involves a particular stance to the world that includes a philosophy of world citizenship that transcends the boundaries of nation states open to the idea of global community, not in a homogenising sense, and 'thrives on recurrent reassemblage' (Schoene, 2009, p 21):

> ... to imagine ourselves as belonging to something far less securely defined and neatly limitable than the nation, that is, to conceive of ourselves first and foremost as members of humanity in all its vulnerable, precariously exposed planetarity. (2009, p 180)

For Schoene it is the role of art and literature to provide the cosmopolitan imagination to achieve a fundamental shift in 'the way we conceive ourselves in relation to one another' (2009, p 183), for it is artists that 'take an active role in the mediation of its emergence' (2009, p 183). Moreover, the hope placed in art and especially the novel is for a cosmopolitan imagination not only 'to combat the worst effects of globalization' but also drawing on Nancy's work, to 'recast' the world (2009, p 186).

The call to cosmopolitanism involves an attitude where difference is respected, combining local/national belonging with a sense of interdependence (Hall, 2002, pp 25-6). However, given Bauman's analysis, cosmopolitanism is a horizon we might move towards but ultimately may not fully grasp or realise, for 'some communities and nation states demand a commitment that contradicts a cosmopolitan stance ... and many communities exert material constraints and apply force to ensure conformity to norms and expectations' (O'Neill et al, 2005, pp 77-8).

Hence, as an expression of 'community' diaspora enables us to focus on migrant communities through a critical reflective process of identification, recognition and analysis of forms, consciousness and products that, as Vertovec argues, enables analysis of structure, agency and history 'in the face of life worlds that are constantly in flux' (Vertovec, 1999, p 27). 'Diaspora and hybridity recognise the disruption of that privilege, but do not offer the means to displace it, and the massive military-legalistic force that ensures its continuity' (Kalra et al, 2005, p 137).

The concept of diaspora is useful in expressing the experience of transnational belonging and hybridity, while enabling an understanding and an expression of double consciousness of identities marked by both 'here' and 'there'; in so doing it contributes to a fuller understanding of 'community', especially the need for a 'recognitive' community.

As a term 'diaspora' invites us to examine the contested and contingent experiences of belonging from the perspective of diasporic groups that may also include 'cosmopolitanism', in Schoene's sense. 'Community' also suggests this but it has a broader meaning that includes the complexities of the encounter with others and the togetherness or collectivity of our being in the world. As Yuval-Davis writes, there is a need for the 'acknowledgement of one's own positioning(s) while empathising with the ways others' positionings construct their gaze at the world' (Yuval-Davis, 1999, para 4.3).

Community is also, therefore, a symbolic and relational structure linked to identity, shared interests, shared places, shared meanings and, in Nancy's terms, '"being-together", "being-in-common", and "being-with"' (Nancy, 2003, p 31). Understanding 'community' also involves exploring processes of boundary formation, where the limits of community are, who is included/excluded (Lee and Newby, 1983; Cohen, 1985; Smith, 2001) at the levels of individual, group and nation.

Community: togetherness, the established and the outsiders

While a focus on diaspora entails understanding the forms, consciousness and cultural production of voluntary or forced migrants it is important to understand these processes within the broader context and understandings of 'community' that include not only an understanding of political community (taken up later in this chapter) but also the relational dimensions of attachments, connectedness and communication that exist in the encounters between established residents and new arrivals. This text argues that it is important to explore the concept of *community* in the tension that is the asylum-migration-community nexus from the perspective also of the established as well as the new arrivals/migrants; and within a broader account and analysis of the imagined community of the nation (Anderson, 1983).[3]

Elias and Scotson's (1994) study of one community in an East Midlands city in the late 1950s is helpful to the concerns of this chapter, integrating, as it does psychosocial and sociological analysis, using what Elias calls 'figurational sociology'. Importantly the study illuminates where and how the boundaries of 'communities' are drawn and can help to understand contemporary mechanisms of inclusion and exclusion that are pertinent to the lived experiences of asylum seekers and refugees in the UK and other parts of the world. This small-scale study of Wigston Parva in Leicestershire enables readers to experience the relationships between community members drawing attention to the power differentials of the 'established' and 'outsider' residents; the sociodynamics of stigmatisation and prejudice, the emotional barriers that are set up against contact with the 'outsiders' and the paralysing emotional impact of stigmatisation, exclusion and humiliation on the 'outsiders'.

The study was undertaken in the late 1950s in a suburban development on the outskirts of an industrial town in the East Midlands. The neighbourhood consisted of three areas, one middle class and two working class. The middle-class residents considered themselves better than their working-class counterparts and one of the working-class groups (an old working-class district) considered themselves better than their working-class counterpart (a new working-class district). The latter appeared to accept their inferior status. The study explores the psychosocial dynamics, distinctions and barriers involved. Elias and Scotson were concerned to uncover why the inhabitants of one district

> felt the need and were able to treat those of the other as inferior to themselves and, to some extent, could make them feel inferior.... The only difference between them was that ... one group was formed by old residents established in the neighbourhood for two or three generations and the other was a group of newcomers. (Elias and Scotson, 1994, p xvii)

In the study Elias and Scotson reveal the dynamics whereby a more powerful group look on themselves as better people, endowed with group charisma shared by its members and lacked by the 'others' and maintain their status 'through social control such as praise-gossip ... and blame-gossip' (1994, p xvi). At the centre of the 'established-outsider configuration' is an uneven balance of power. 'One group can effectively stigmatise another only as long as it is well established in positions of power from which the stigmatised group is excluded' (1994, p xx). Moreover the 'social slur cast by a more powerful upon a less powerful group usually enters the self-image of the latter and, thus, weakens and disarms them (1994, p xxi). As Elias and Scotson state, where the power differential is weakened or goes into reverse 'the former outsider groups, on their part, tend to retaliate' (1994, p xxi).[4]

This configuration can be looked at from the micro politics of the working-class communities in Wigston Parva but it can also be related to the operation of power by nation states and powerful elites and in community relations between established community members and new arrival migrants, asylum seekers and refugees. Elias and Scotson do not focus on which group was right or wrong but on the structural characteristics of the developing community that bound them to each other in ways that compelled one of them to treat the 'other' 'collectively with a measure of contempt, as people less well bred and thus of lower human value, by comparison with themselves' (1994, p xxi). Here the two groups were of the same social class, but one group were long-term residents (established) and the other were relative newcomers (outsiders).

Elias and Scotson identify that the stigmatisation of outsiders shows certain common features in the established-outsider configuration: the outsider group are defined as anomic −'untrustworthy, undisciplined and lawless' (1994, p xxv); the power differential serves to reinforce in the established group 'justification of their elevated position and as proof of their own superior worth' (1994, p xxvi) and in the inferior group the internalisation of their outsider status 'and the humiliation and oppression that go with it' (1994, p xxvi) reinforced by constant exposure to humiliation exclusion. The group processes and group relations are defined in terms of 'we-image' and 'we-ideal' (1994, p xiii).

This configuration can be seen both in the current media responses (see Chapter Four) and the lack of welcome asylum seekers and refugees experience from residents in the areas where they are housed in the UK. One of Rutter et al's (2007, p 78) interviewees said, "Sometimes they told us 'why do you come here?' They kicked us. We passed them and we tried to be nice … two or three friends, also from Ethiopia were beaten in that area."

The study by Elias and Scotson can throw some light on the experiences of new arrivals in communities in the UK in this examination of the asylum-migration-community dynamic.

Next I want to use the study to explore three overlapping aspects of the asylum-migration-community nexus: the imagined community of the nation; the imagined community of governmental discourse/governance (Rose, 1999; Pickering, 2005; Rogaly and Taylor, 2009); and community as a symbolic and relational structure linked to identity, experience, shared interests, shared places, shared meanings – "'being-together", "being-in-common", and "being-with"' (Nancy, 2003, p 31; see also Smith, 1998).

Imagined community of the nation

Anderson (1983) argues that the nation itself is an imagined community, imagined as limited, bounded and as a sovereign state, because 'regardless of the actual inequality and exploitation that may prevail in each, the nation is always conceived as a deep and horizontal comradeship' (Anderson, 1983, p 7). And this fraternity has made possible the willingness of people to kill and to die for 'such limited imaginings' (1983, p 8).

Integral to understanding the asylum-migration-community nexus is analysis of the wider socio-political context. As discussed in Chapter One, the sovereignty of the nation state is a key issue in analysis of migration. Bauman's analysis of modernity and globalisation acknowledges that 'throughout the era of modernity, the nation state has claimed the right to preside over the distinction between order and chaos, law and lawlessness, citizen and *homo sacer*, belonging and exclusion, useful (legitimate) product and waste' (2004, p 33).

Concern about forced migration increased at the end of the Cold War as certain globalising processes brought more asylum seekers to western countries (Sales, 2007, p 92). Bauman describes the figure of the asylum seeker as an exemplar of 'that human waste of distant parts of the globe unloaded into "our own backyard"' (2004, p 56), providing governments with 'an ideal deviant "Other", a most welcome target for "carefully selected campaign issues"' (Bauman, 2004, p 56). 'Refugees, the displaced, asylum/seekers, migrants, the *sans papiers*, they are the waste of globalization' (2004, p 58). And for Bauman, migrants serve an important purpose for nation states who, in a globalising capitalist world order have limited power in the international arena but who can still exercise 'the foundational constitutive prerogative of sovereignty: their right of exemption' (2004, p 33).

In Agamben's terms (1995), Bauman defines *homo sacer* as 'the principle category of human waste laid out in the course of modern production of orderly (law abiding, rule governed) sovereign realms' (Bauman, 2004, pp 32-3). Moreover, still referencing Agamben, the identity of a people is linked with state identity and 'the concept of a people makes sense only if redefined within the concept if citizenship' (2004, p 33). There are some similarities with Elias and Scotson's (1994) study – migration is bound up with the power of nation states to exclude/include in relation to power, order, policing the boundaries, national identity and citizenship. As Sales (2007, p 212) states, individual nation states determine policies on immigration and citizenship despite the fact that at supranational level, the globalisation of trade and investment means that regional and international policy making erodes national sovereignty. And, as Anderson (1991) has argued, the nation, as an imagined political community, has 'finite, if elastic boundaries, beyond which lie other nations' (1991, p 7), and the migrant, especially the forced migrant, becomes 'the visible symbol of globalisation and the insecurities that it brings in its wake' (Sales, 2007, p 212).

The imagined community of the nation state and the sovereign right to exclude is operationalised and embedded in the UK in law and order politics and discourses on immigration and 'race' relations policy (Schuster and Solomos, 1999; Pickering, 2005; Schuster, 2005; Sales, 2007). Asylum and immigration are treated as one in the public imagination. Increasingly restrictive policies, a focus on securing stronger and stronger border controls and the 'securitisation' of migration closes down debate and increasingly presents asylum seekers as 'bogus', 'illegal', competing for 'our' jobs and resources (Bauman, 2004; Sales, 2007).

Imagined community of governmental discourse/ governance

As Pickering (2005) highlights (and as I stated in the Introduction to this book), dominant responses by governments are embedded in law and order politics that are maintained via hegemonic relations across three levels of society: civil society (identified in media representation); law enforcement (administration of the law); and domestic and international legal mechanisms ('courts and international human rights regime' [Pickering, 2005, p 1]). But, I suggest, these responses are also embedded in the relational dynamics of governance – governmental communities – and these inevitably intersect with the hegemonic relations at the level of civil society, law and international rights regimes.

The basis of Pickering's argument is that governments in the North have used 'law and order politics in the development and implementation of refugee policy' (2005, p 3). This 'increasingly relies on unmitigated ideological and coercive force', and importantly this 'distances Western nations ... from their complicity in the production of the refugee deviancy as justification for unbridled denunciation and violent rejection' (2005, p 21). A key concept is that of sovereignty, for it is this that 'gives law and order its decisive push into the realm of the politically unchallengeable by looking inwards' (2005, p 20). The role of sovereignty is explored in relation to state crime against those seeking safety and refuge. Using the example of border protection legislation (2001) in Australia, Pickering identifies the

> crossing of the national territorial border in unseaworthy vessels is represented as the challenge to public morality, decency and way of life. It is in that 'unauthorised' border crossing that the very presence of the asylum seeker becomes deviant and triggers various processes of criminalisation. It is in this moment that the asylum seeker is both victim and offender so many times over. (2005, p 20)

Pickering very importantly and clearly identifies the role of law and order regimes in responding to asylum seekers and refugees:

> Law and order rests on neo-liberal ideas about the responsibility of the individual for their situation: the responsibility of the individual to know what is wrong and to refrain from doing it and the responsibility of the state to administer punishment when the law is contravened. (2005, pp 1-2)

As she goes on to say, this, of course, presumes that the 'crime' is a choice and 'punishment must be administered to deter such choices or similar choices by others' (2005, p 2). Thus a law and order approach does not take into account structural, political and social conditions in the country of origin nor human rights approaches and responses. For, in current times, law and order approaches are based on the irrelevance of social conditions to criminality with a focus on the individual and individual responsibility:

> The asylum seeker who arrives by boat is deviant (in that they 'undermine' the offshore protection process and the territorial sovereignty of the nation-state), while on the other hand the nation-state abrogates the shadow of the rule of law at the international level (most particularly in relation to the Refugee Convention) in order to justify such an approach. In short the alleged deviancy of the nation-state on the international human rights stage. (Pickering, 2005, p 4)

Moreover, consensus can be found in the responses of political parties. Pickering comments that during the '2001 Australian federal election campaign the two major parties were all but undistinguishable on refugee policy' (2005, p 5). This is also mirrored in the UK. The Labour government's approach to refugee policy in the mantra 'faster, fairer, firmer' and the name change of the Immigration and Nationality Directorate to the UK Border Agency also reflects both Labour and Conservative's instrumental approach to asylum/refugee 'issues'.

Most importantly, as Pickering points out, 'when major parties refuse to debate, or only engage in debate on peripheral issues to immigration, then the space for questioning and the space for civil society to exert itself are often reduced' (2005, p 5). Negative and problematic responses and attitudes to migrants go unchallenged and the closing down of debate simply reinforces limited and limiting hegemonic attitudes and knowledge in the general population. For example, political responses that simply seek to protect borders and make deviant and criminalise those who seek entry as 'dangerous outsiders' prepare the ground for asylum seekers and refugees to be seen as deviant outsiders by the general population. As an example of humiliation exclusion (as Elias and Scotson found in their study of Wigston Parva), the outsider group become stigmatised, defined as anomic and internalise their outsider status, along with the humiliation and oppression that goes with it.

The imagined community of governmental discourse involving refugee integration is linked to community cohesion agendas and 'race' relations, and, like the New Labour New Deal and Respect agendas, iterates integration, citizenship and belonging in relation to the imagined community of the nation. Notions of community are 'inextricably bound to ideas of governance', 'citizenship' and 'community' is simultaneously 'the object and target for the exercise of political power' (Rogaly and Taylor, 2009, p 126).

The Europeanisation of restrictive asylum policy, geopolitical changes since 9/11 2001 and EU enlargement have heightened security concerns regarding unregulated migration and porous borders (Griffiths et al, 2005). As identified by Schuster and Solomos (1999), the evolution of a 'race' relations framework has provided a central axis for the development of asylum policy in the UK. 'Anti-immigration rhetoric, short-term electoralism and concerns over mounting welfare budgets are the immediate context for the increased saliency of asylum in the domestic policy agenda' (Griffiths et al, 2005, p 3). With regard to managing migration, 'community' is both a space for neoliberal governance and control as well as a challenge to it (Rose, 1999; Rogaly and Taylor, 2009).

Refugee community organisations: incorporation and support

In the UK, the reception and 'incorporation' (Soysal, 1994) of migrants and refugees largely related to RCOs is embedded within a postwar 'race' relations framework (rooted in colonialism) marked on the one hand, by restrictionism (the right to enter) for certain groups, and a multicultural approach to settlement on the other. The latter developed from British immigration policy (Solomos, 1998; Schuster and Solomos, 1999; Schuster, 2003; Griffiths et al, 2005), and until the Asylum and Immigration Appeals Act 1993, seeking asylum in the UK was treated 'as a type of immigration' (Schuster, 2003, p 132). Griffiths et al (2005, p 23) identify how a 'race' relations framework and multiculturalism underpin asylum and refugee policy:

> In the first instance, a restrictive approach to asylum applications has been framed within the language of increasing numbers, welfare strain and urban decay which is typical of the racialisation of immigration in the post war period.... In the second case, as we suggest at great length in this book, RCOs (refugee community organisations) have been absorbed within the multi-cultural framework of minority ethnic community representation and the discipline of funding regimes which structure the black and minority ethnic (BME) sector as a whole.

What this amounts to is that RCOs are often 'imagined' by the state, in relation to a multiculturalist view of community organisations, as cohesive, representative and homogeneous, which facilitate what Soysal (in relation to migrants, not refugees) calls 'incorporation regimes' based on an individualistic, market-based model (Griffiths et al, 2005, p 26). This also serves to shape the way that RCOs are developed, sustained and incorporated. As Griffiths et al note (2005, p 26), a 'clear implication for the organisation of refugee groups in the UK is that they encounter a distinctive national tradition of migrant incorporation and ethnic representation, which provides their immediate "opportunity structure", the terms under which they enter the public sphere of accountability and legitimate representation'. Since the publication of the Home Office (2004) *National refugee integration strategy* (which makes no reference to asylum seekers), 'RCOs now find themselves increasingly embedded within a broader framework of institutional arrangements that aim to "integrate" refugees' (Griffiths et al, 2005, p 26).

Many researchers have criticised this model. Griffiths' (2002) research with Somali communities counters a homogeneous representation of RCOs and draws attention to the way a multicultural discourse provides a platform for the enunciation of certain identities, the obfuscation of internal politics in RCOs as well as their relation to the political conflict in countries of origin. The latter inevitably leads to marginalisation for those excluded from belonging to these imagined communities.

At the same time, the development of RCOs has aided communities in gaining a voice, networking, having their voices and stories heard within the local and regional context and gaining resources to enable the support of their particular communities. Along the lines of ethnic identity such as the Somalis in Leicester, Bosnians in Derby, Nottingham and Birmingham, these groups are well served by strong community organisations that (in Griffiths et al's [2005] terms) have succeeded in generating networks, resources and social capital. Griffiths et al (2005) argue, however, that it is inconclusive to what extent RCOs aid in the integration of their members.

However, Sterland (2009), in a small-scale study of refugee community workers based within RCOs, argues that 'establishing community networks is essential in refugees' efforts to improve their social and economic position and regaining a sense of *normality* and belonging', but there is a 'significant gap in the government's commitment to support RCOs in carrying this role in practice' (Sterland, 2009, p 3). Sterland's study is premised on the fact that 'the increasing restrictions and negative public attitudes, which perpetuate mistrust and limit freedoms and opportunities to utilise and develop individual resources have become the defining features of the UK asylum and immigration situation' (Sterland, 2009, p 3). Moreover, based on extensive experience of working in and with RCOs, she argues that most 'refugee community *organisations* as they are referred to, exist without or with very few institutional organisational structures' (2009, p 4). And, while highly structured institutional frameworks are not necessary for providing support to people, they are often assumed by outside agencies which, from her experience, leads to 'expectations, engagement, or attempts to engage with RCWs [refugee community workers]/RCOs at an inappropriate level' (2009, p 4). Implicated in this 'is the insufficient understanding of the impact that a range of different, multilevel social, political, economic and cultural factors have on shaping RCOs' reality' (2009, p 4).

As Kelly (2003) and Sterland (2009) note, 'restrictive policies, most notably the dispersal policy, have directly undermined the opportunities for newly arriving refugees to benefit from existing contacts and develop further emotional and geographical ties that are conducive to community formation and development' (2009, p 8). Sterland (2009) and Griffiths et al (2005) challenge the view of RCOs as prime movers in integration. Indeed, Sterland (2009, p 14) says the majority of RCOs have 'weak structures, little money, sometimes with no meeting place, limited knowledge of the British system, and dependency on a small number of enthusiastic individuals whose dedication led them to work very hard'. Indeed, she argues that 'RCOs' main strength is in "knowing" their community and acting as a link between the mainstream agencies and refugees, and a mediator between refugee communities and the wider community' (2009, p 16).

Ultimately, the multidimensional aspects of exclusion and the de-humanising asylum system and process have a negative impact on asylum seekers and on refugee community workers.

> [The] challenges of rebuilding their lives in the new environments are exacerbated by the reactive politics of restrictionism and escalation of exclusionary measures and practices that not only hinder dealing with problems that refugees have on arrival in the UK but create multiple new ones. (Sterland, 2009, p 54)

Moreover, based on her empirical research, Sterland suggests that refugee community workers who are usually volunteers should proactively try to utilise their resources in order to positively manage their situation. At one level, their 'unmet needs as arising from the position of displacement and multilevel exclusion inherent within their current contexts, provide incentive, motivation and shape the agenda for community involvement' (2009, p 54).

Korac's (2001) comparative study of refugees in Italy and the Netherlands suggests that ability to participate freely in the social life of the receiving country, as in Italy at that time (unlike the UK), through 'freedom of movement, access to employment and the ability to mix with members of the receiving society – may be more effective in promoting integration than state-directed programmes, or other formal community-based organisational means' (Griffiths et al, 2005, p 202), as in the UK. Rutter et al, in *From refugee to citizen* (2007), conducted 30 life history interviews with refugees who had arrived in the UK between 1956 and 2008. They found that:

> Interviewees defined their integration in terms of their labour market success, their social interactions and their

personal happiness. Many interviewees also felt that the responsibility for social integration was placed on refugees, but the problem lay with the majority community who were unwelcoming. (2007, p 179)

The factors impeding integration included: 'an interrupted prior education in the home country or in transit to the UK; initial housing mobility in the UK; difficulties accessing English language support; inappropriate careers advice' (Rutter et al, 2007, p 192). Factors that aided their integration included: 'rapid asylum decisions; English language fluency; secure housing; tolerance; the long-term support of a professional, such as a lecturer or teacher; opportunities to volunteer' (2007, p 192). Indeed,

> one of the most important conclusions from our research is that refugees experienced what we term a '*discongruity of belonging*'. Britishness was not fostered by local integration in the workplace and immediate neighbourhood, but was experienced nationally, through refugees' appreciation of freedom and peace. (Rutter et al, 2007, p 193)

At the local level a lack of belonging in their neighbourhood or locality was due to 'The unfriendliness of neighbours and hostile social interactions' (2007, p 193). Unemployment, underemployment, discrimination alongside racial harassment and alienation were key defining features of interviewees' lived experience.

> Two thirds of our interviewees had experienced racial harassment in their neighbourhoods. Most of those we interviewed did not know or had never spoken to their neighbours and did not feel any attachment to their locality. (Rutter et al, 2007, p 197)

In the UK, Sales' (2007) analysis of New Labour's managed migration policy provides a key critique around which further research could be developed that intersects with concepts of social justice and human dignity. Sales identifies the conundrum in 'managed migration policy' as on the one hand, imposing increasingly restrictive and selective regimes on control of entry while operating 'a more market-oriented labour market policy' on the other (Sales, 2007, p 183):

> Social inclusion has been more narrowly defined, with the main route out of exclusion seen as incorporation into the paid labour market rather than through broader notions of social justice and equality. Certain groups, particularly asylum seekers and those who enter through clandestine means, are denied routes to inclusion. At the same time, migrants are expected to conform to more prescriptive rules both in relation to the conditions of their stay and, for those seeking citizenship, in the notion of Britishness that they are expected to embrace. (Sales, 2007, p 183)

And most importantly, Sales argues that as the UK government focuses on targets and numbers, 'the human faces behind these numbers sometimes refuse to disappear' (Sales, 2007, p 208), as evidenced in the many campaigns and qualitative, narrative-based research with asylum seekers and refugees. Sales concludes her critique by calling for a review of the basis of immigration policy and a shift away from current policy based on 'the premise that immigration is a problem to be curtailed as far as possible and managed in the name of the "national interest"' (2007, p 237), which has meant specific groups have been targeted for exclusion and in the process, government policy has played a role in creating fear and xenophobia and constructing immigration controls 'has created and sustained divisions and legitimised the racist attitudes that demand ever-further controls' (Sales, 2007, p 237).

Migrants become nameless and faceless, de-humanised, and this 'situation corrupts not just those involved but also the society whose interests it claims to protect' (Sales, 2007, p 237). Unsustainable both practically and morally, Sales asks for an opening up of debate and an examination of the 'real social and human implications of migration controls' in order that we 'can move beyond the agenda that is doing so much damage to individuals and society' (Sales, 2007, p 238).

Governance through community and active citizenship

New Labour governance is symbolised in the competing discourses of (a) strong centralised control and (b) more open systems, network and partnership-based governance (Newman, 2003, pp 17-23; Clarke, 2004; Lewis, 2004). Open systems are made up of partnerships and networks – 'joined-up government' – 'that transcends the vertical, departmental structures of government itself' (Newman, 2003, p 20) to develop or foster a consensual style of governing. Newman (2003, p 15) defines progressive governance as involving a significant shift from governance through hierarchy and competition to governance through networks and partnerships, with an emphasis on inclusion. Progressive governance involves the production of techniques and strategies of responsibilisation of citizens, operationalised through the development of networks, alliances and partnerships, with a strong focus on active citizenship.

It is important to explore the governance of the asylum-migration-community nexus, especially at the level of the imagined community of governmental discourse and decision making. Taking a Foucauldian approach, Rose talks about 'government through community' (1996, p 332) and the ways that community is a new specialisation of government imbricated into knowledge, programmes and policies, but also the ways that community is used to deal with social problems. As Marinetto observes (2003, p 109), this has 'demarcated a new sector for government, one in which the capabilities and resources of communities could be utilized by policy programmes through placing the onus on responsible self-help'. Drawing on Cruikshank's (1994) analysis of community empowerment programmes in the US, Marinetto describes 'a technology of citizenship' that works by encouraging active citizenship in the provision of social services based on the empowerment of members, which ultimately reduces their dependency on the state in circumstances where welfare is rolled back. In this sense 'active citizenship is regarded as a strategy of government that provides an efficient means for regulating the population' (Marinetto, 2003, p 109). Hence 'incorporation regimes' operationalised largely through RCOs, community cohesion agendas as well as the promotion of 'citizenship' are intrinsic to the governance of refugee integration.

Marinetto (2003) argues that 'modern democratic forms of government, have tended to be structured around representative rather than participative forms of democracy', (p 117) partly due to the size and complexity of industrial society. And despite the usefulness of Foucault-inspired analysis of community and active citizenship as strategies to enable the state to govern more effectively, there is evidence that New Labour has sought to make community a central theme and that this has been invaluable in promoting community involvement.[5]

A focus on citizenship and what it means to be a citizen is at the heart of recent responses to migration and integration and recent research, as well as the Nationality, Immigration and Asylum Act 2002 that highlights belonging as tied inextricably to citizenship. New Labour's focus on citizenship draws heavily on communitarian principles. In his report and review of citizenship, *Citizenship: Our common bond*, Lord Goldsmith (2007) writes:

In effect, the history of legislation on citizenship and nationality has led to a complex scheme lacking coherence or any clear and self-contained statement of the rights and responsibilities of citizens. My report discusses measures to address that and makes a range of proposals that touch every stage of an individual's life. My recommendations are intended to promote the meaning and significance of citizenship within modern Britain. (Goldsmith, 2007)

As Rutter et al (2007, p 16) argue:

National citizenship, with its rights and responsibilities, is increasingly mediated by their membership of other collectives: political, social, ethnic, local, regional, supranational, as well as transnational. European societies, however, seem unable or unwilling to acknowledge multiple and multi-layered citizenship, other allegiances and belongings, especially when cultural difference and transnational belongings come under attack from some politicians and media commentators.

Lister's (2007) body of work on citizenship and its intersections with poverty define 'citizenship' 'as a multi-tiered concept and practice' (2007, p 58), marked by the dynamics of inclusion/exclusion. Lister writes that Naila Kabeer's work on citizenship provides 'four values of inclusive citizenship that emerge from empirical work in the Global South and accounts from below'. These four values are: justice, recognition, self-determination and solidarity. Lister writes that Kabeer articulates them as follows: justice involves 'when it is fair for people to be treated the same and when it is fair that they should be treated differently' (Kabeer, 2005, p 3, quoted in Lister, 2007, p 50); recognition involves 'the intrinsic worth of all human beings, but also recognition of and respect for their differences' (Kabeer, 2005, p 4, quoted in Lister, 2007, p 50); self-determination involves 'people's ability to exercise some degree of control over their lives' (Kabeer, 2005, p 5, quoted in Lister, 2007, p 50). And solidarity is 'the capacity to identify with others and to act in unity with them in their claims for justice and recognition' (Kabeer, 2005, p 7, quoted in Lister, 2007, p 51). Lister states that this 'value could be said to reflect a horizontal view of citizenship (developed most strongly in Nordic accounts in the North) which accords as much significance to the relations between citizens as to the vertical relationship between the state and the individual' (Lister, 2007, pp 50-1).

In defining the development and momentum of the concept of citizenship, Lister highlights the work of Mouffe (1992) and Young (1990), specifically the benefit of an 'ethos of pluralisation' that 'makes possible a radical plural, rather than a dual way of thinking about citizenship and identity' (Lister, 2007, p 52). For, in the process of working with group differences, 'rather than suppressing them', a radical plural ethos is possible 'without sacrificing citizenship's universalist emancipatory promise as expressed in the ideals of inclusion, participation and equal moral worth' (Lister, 2007, p 52). Let us have a closer look at this concept of radical pluralism in relation to the asylum-migration-community nexus.

Radical democratic pluralism as a counter to governance of the asylum-migration-community nexus

Smith's (1998) analysis of the work of Laclau and Mouffe is instructive as she argues that their theory of radical democratic pluralism breaks new ground, beyond liberal and communitarian camps. I argue that this approach resonates deeply with Yar's (2003) notion of recognitive community (based on Honneth's 1996 work).

Citizenship in a radical plural tradition involves an understanding of the individual as a socially situated self (not just a bearer of rights). For Laclau and Mouffe, the individual 'self' is the articulation of multiple subject positions inscribed within diverse social relations. 'Insofar as each subject position preserves within itself traces of past articulations even as it is transformed through articulation, it brings with it elements of previously sedimented shared traditions' (Smith, 1998, p 120). Moreover, the political is a site of identity construction, contestation and renegotiation (1998, p 125). And these processes reflect power relations.

Warning against an ideal type of 'community' as *Gemeinshcaft* for this communitarian vision is 'organized around a single set of moral values and a substantive idea of the common good, will never adequately respect pluralist differences between micro communities ... and within each micro-community, nor will it accommodate the complexity of each individuals membership' (Smith, 1998, p 127). For Smith, the 'space for radical indeterminacy, must be preserved' (Smith, 1998, p 127).

Mouffe argues that we should be striving for values of democracy, equality, freedom, rather than the idea of the good (Smith, 1998, p 127). This struggle revolves around citizenship, 'for the radicalisation of citizenship creates conditions necessary for substantial and progressive social change' (Smith, 1998, p 127). This also resonates with Lister's work on citizenship as including civil, social, political and cultural rights (2007).

There is no blueprint for Mouffe, for by its nature the democratic tradition is heterogeneous and indeterminate, and the ground for contestation includes 'how the principle of democratic participation and solidarity can be reconciled with the principle of defending diversity, and how can we move towards a more egalitarian society without sacrificing individual freedom' (Smith, 1998, p 128). Preserving space for contestation is crucial.

> The neutral state model has all too often resulted in the subjection of disempowered minorities to the will of the majority.... Under radical democratic pluralisms diversity principle, the democratic demands of newly included groups must be satisfied as much as possible. (Smith, 1998, p 140)

These 'newly recognised groups should not be treated as the childlike recipients of the established group's generosity'; indeed they should 'be recognised as valuable teachers who can reveal the anti democratic moments within the established group's traditions and provide alternative solutions' (Smith, 1998, p 141). Moreover, cultural minorities should have access to resources to sustain their traditions within a framework of basic human rights, and 'the logic of autonomy must be mobilized against the logic of assimilation to preserve genuinely multicultural pluralism' (1998, p 143). Mouffe maintains that citizenship becomes an articulating principle, but 'it can only become the site of democratic articulations to the extent that it is centred on a firm commitment to equality and human rights' (Smith, 1998, p 146).

Hence citizenship provides an 'articulating principle' through which 'linkages between each individual's diverse membership and between individuals and micro communities are mediated' (Smith, 1998, p 135). Displacing the idea of the social agent is pre-constituted and fixed; instead the social agent is conceived as an articulation and 'ensemble of subject positions' constructed within specific discourses and always precariously and temporally sutured at the intersection of those subject positions. In this sense 'an approach to citizenship becomes thinkable' (Smith, 1998, p 135).

This productive version of citizenship is limited by a focus on the nation state as the 'primary site of political identification', and a 'fixed territorial imaginary' (Smith, 1998, p 137). Certainly global capitalism and transnational political activism challenge the framework of the nation state and its frontiers. For Mouffe, resistance to domination ideally takes grass roots forms and leads to mobilization from below that would 'guard against bureaucratisation and containment from above' (quoted in Smith, 1998, p 140). Thus, power should not accumulate in one group or social sphere and participatory mechanisms facilitate democratic interaction.

Laclau and Mouffe caution against the imposition of a concept of the common good, and in contrast to the communitarian focus on harmonious dialogue and shared discourse they stress the 'Foucauldian principle of the ubiquity of domination and resistance in all discursive situations' (1998, p 119). Pluralism is 'constitutive of modern liberal democracy', and the task is not just to cope with this but to 'create the conditions in which radical democratic forms of plural differences would thrive' (1998, p 119). Creating such conditions necessitates 'the preservation of a legitimate space for genuine dissent' (Smith, 1998, p 120) for without this, the 'unpredictable harms that could be caused by even the most apparently progressive institutions would not be revealed and addressed' (1998, p 120).

Politically 'it is through the discursive interruption of a "constitutive outside" that the democratic revolution is extended and politicised resistance becomes possible. Every social formation is destabilized by its "constitutive outside"' (Smith, 1998, p 123). The Black power movement and feminists are used by way of example. The constitutive outside is made up of marginal resistances that survive in 'the shadows cast by the hegemonic value system' (1998, p 123). Based on a commitment to egalitarianism, overcoming domination, oppression, sexual and social inequalities and the instrumentalism and alienation specific to capitalism, radical democratic pluralism is based on the valuing of multiple individual goods and the right to self-determination.

Laclau and Mouffe's work provides us with an account of community situated within radical democratic pluralism that prioritises the articulation of citizenship, recognising the importance of both autonomy and collectivity, similarity and difference. This recognition is based on democratic principles that value egalization, respect, rights, difference and dignity as well as critical theory's focus on reason/rationalisation as both the grounds for individual liberties and the basis or material of subjugation. Identities are formed in relation to others, there is no reconciliation between subject and object, and, like Adorno, Laclau and Mouffe see the necessity of political struggle, in contrast to communitarian focus on progressive rationalisation where 'citizens deliberate on the common good in a coercion free environment, and progress towards justice is made in each new era as laws and norms become increasingly rational' (Smith, 1998, p 150).

I want to add to this focus on citizenship within an ethos of radical democratic pluralism by drawing on Yar's 'recognitive community' and Nancy's 'inoperative community' to sketch out possibilities for a generative (radical democratic imaginary) relational concept of transnational citizenship and community that transcends the limited and limiting notions of citizenship we find in the UK and many other European governments responses to asylum, migration and community.

Community as being-together, being-in-common and being-with

I end this chapter with an examination of community situated within this account of radical democratic pluralism that challenges exclusionary principles and discourses and prioritises recognitive forms of community. A recognitive theory of community involves relational dimensions of being-together, being-in-common and being-with, in the sense articulated by Nancy (1991, 2003). Recognitive community provides the basis for a productive relationship between asylum, migration and community that counters the forces of humiliation, abjection and othering through processes of recognition, cultural citizenship and social justice. The struggle for recognition is the struggle for community.

Nancy (1991, 2000, 2003) talks of the dangers inspired by the word 'community' and how, mindful of this, he prefers to focus his work on community around 'with' as opposed to 'co'. 'The "with" is dry and neutral: neither communion nor atomisation, just the sharing and sharing out of a space, at most a contact: a being-together without assemblage' (Nancy, 2003, p 32).

Distancing himself from totalitarianism and identity politics contained within understandings of community, he cites the rape of Bosnian women as an examplar of such 'unitary community', an affirmation of the fantasy unity of the perpetrator's community, and the will to realise an essence ('we' as opposed to 'them'). The problem of the latter is seen very starkly in Elias and Scotson's (1994) study, and the ways that governmentality homogenises in the process of social order and social control, erecting and demarcating borders and boundaries. Nancy's 'community' of being together, in common and with, highlights the deeply relational aspects of togetherness, for our identities are always in negotiation, 'formed and reformed through our encounters with others' (Kester, 2004, p 154). 'What we have in common is also what always distinguishes and differentiates us' (Nancy, 2000, p 155). And 'com-passion' is the 'contact of being with one another in this turmoil ... it is the disturbance of violent relatedness' (Nancy, 2000, p xiii). Nancy writes: 'there is no meaning if meaning is not shared, and not because there would be an ultimate or first signification that all beings have in common, but because meaning is itself the sharing of Being' (Nancy, 2001, p 2).

Schoene (2009) describes Nancy's outline of community as 'inoperative being-in-common' the 'unwieldy structure of our shared existence, which at any moment remains prone to affiliation and capable of dispersion' (2009, p 17). It is in fact the very structure of our shared existence, the co-existence of singular pluralities. *Being singular plural* (2000) and *The inoperative community* (1991) articulate Nancy's philosophy.

Yar (2003) mobilises Honneth's work on recognition (1996) to define a 'recognitive' theory of community rooted in the legacy of the Frankfurt School in order to move beyond both liberal and communitarian models of 'community'. Human self-making is defined as intersubjective and is defined (following Hegel) as a struggle for self-realisation. This attempt to self-realise 'is seen as a generative process by means of which shared normative grounds come into being' (Yar, 2003, p 116). Moreover, mutual recognition is necessary for Yar, 'such that each must recognise the value and dignity of others if the recognition that others are to confer upon the self is to be meaningful' (2003, p 116). This ripples outwards in that 'coming into oneself through the other develops into a shared medium, the moral-ethical substance of society' (2003, p 116). This is constitutive of both the self and of 'the common ground which mediates, connects and embeds selves in a shared form of practical life' (2003, p 116).

The subject comes into being through the social process. Both Nancy and Yar's accounts of community transcend the dualism of liberalism (individuality, rights and autonomy) and communitarianism (collectivity, solidarity and responsibility). For once autonomy is 'reconceived in decentred terms, as something which can become real socially only through mediation via another, then communalised ethical orientations and solidaristic commitments cease to be the antithesis of autonomy, but instead are seen as its correlates' (Yar, 2003, p 116).

Relational dynamics are crucial to understanding 'community'. Community in this sense is a process through which shared 'self conceptions and structures emerge' (2003, p 121).

> Community qua relationality is something split between
> the present actually existent and the futurally promised or
> anticipated. The struggle for recognition is always a demand
> or claim for the establishment of mutuality, reciprocity, or
> symmetry which does not yet exist. (Yar, 2003, p 121)

So there is an appeal to an ideal and the gap between the actual and
the ideal 'is what preserves community as an ongoing and open ended
activity' (Yar, 2003, p 121). Honneth (1996) identifies a threefold
typology of recognition-oriented intersubjective relations: the desire
for emotional support; cognitive recognition; and social esteem. Each
of these forms of recognition is related to love, rights and solidarity.
The struggle for recognition can take place on any and all of these
registers. Yar also suggests that this recognitive theoretical approach to
community has the capacity to accommodate social conflict and to
maintain a commitment to critical reflection on, and transformation
of, social structures.

In contrast to the communitarian logic of social conflict as an absence
of community remedied by a commonly held 'core of thick normative
commitments' (Yar, 2003, p 123), the struggle for recognition is also
the struggle for community. Critique and social struggle also emerge
from experiences of a 'lack of community', denied recognition of
selfhood, refused participation in forms of mutual affirmation and
hence prevented from social self-realisation. Honneth describes this
experience as 'disrespect'. '[T]hree forms of disrespect … [are] the
violation of the body, the denial of rights and the denigration of a way
of life; each of course, amounts to the experience of a failure to secure
a positive self-relation via recognition in the forms of "love", "rights"
and "solidarity"' (quoted in Yar, 2003, p 123).

Drawing on Mead, Honneth argues that the self as a social being 'is
always a being that is recognised by, and recognises itself in terms of, a
communal framework of understanding and evaluation' (quoted in Yar,
2003, pp 119-20). Ultimately, Yar argues that a recognitive theory of
community 'can satisfy the demands of establishing solidarity, preserving
singularity (or difference) and keeping open a space for critique' (p 125).

Acknowledging the contingency of the concept 'community',
recognitive community as being-together, being-in-common and
being-with, embedded with radical democratic pluralism, is a concept
and theory that I want to hold on to, and indeed, want to revisit in
the remaining chapters through research that counters exclusionary
discourses and practices, challenges sexual and social inequalities and
develops praxis (purposeful knowledge) not 'on' or 'for' but 'with'

people situated in the asylum–migration nexus who are living in, being with and creating communities.

Chapter Three looks at methods of doing research that foster a radical democratic imaginary regarding the asylum–migration–community nexus. This involves an understanding of the counter-hegemonic role of participatory action research (PAR) and participatory arts (PA) as 'ethno-mimesis' (Cantwell 1993; O'Neill, 2001, 2002, 2003). Ethno-mimesis can lead to the production of knowledge and a radical democratisation of images and texts that can move us, pierce us, challenge identity thinking and bring us in touch with our feeling worlds in a subjective, reflexive relationship with the feeling worlds of the 'other', so important for a recognitive and radical democratic theory of community.

Notes

[1] Somali Afro European Media Project: www.saemp.org.uk/ See also Chapter Four.

[2] Linked to the role of the cosmopolitan novel's transformative possibilities.

[3] That is rooted in an analysis of modernity, globalisation, humiliation and social justice.

[4] As was the case in responses to humiliation in Rwanda (Lindner, 2006).

[5] Marinetto observes that despite this, evaluations of programmes such as Best Value show 'community involvement tends to be conflated with mass focus group-style public consultations'; and despite the adoption of active citizenship by recent governments they are 'yet to encompass the actual redistribution of political power: the emergence of a truly "citizen-centred government", a modern type of *Ekklesia*, is still far from being realized' (Marinetto, 2003, p 118).

THREE

Researching the asylum-migration-community nexus

This chapter argues that the articulation of identity and belonging for those situated in the tension that is the asylum-migration-community nexus[1] can helpfully be understood within the context of: (a) renewed methodologies for social research that are participatory, relational, interpretive and action-oriented; (b) a deep understanding of the economic and political relations of humiliation, inclusion and exclusion that includes the role of the mass media (print and broadcast); and (c) the related issue of governance at national, European and international levels. There is a need to develop alternative forms of representing and analysing the lived experiences of refugees and asylum seekers living in the UK.

At the centre of this work is the importance of renewing methodologies in the process of re-imagining the asylum-migration-community nexus, especially within the context of globalisation, humiliation, increasing mobility, the emergence of transnational communities, the need for radical democracy that includes a recognitive theory of citizenship (beyond the nation) towards an holistic concept of social justice. Also discussed are the importance of renewing methodologies for the work we do within the area of forced migration, humiliation, 'egalization' and human rights (Lindner, 2006); the role of the arts in processes of social inclusion; the importance of the relational and connective aspects of sociality; and the vital importance for creating spaces for dialogue and performative praxis through participatory methodologies.

Forced migration, research and public scholarship

Reflecting on the possibilities for a sociology of forced migration, Castles (2003) reminds readers that the field of migration studies is new, dating back only to the 1980s, and as pointed out by Richard Black (2001), the field has been 'intimately connected to policy developments' (Castles, 2003, p 26). However, a narrow concern with policy measures within the framework of what is possible or what government departments can work with is too narrow a remit. The problem of working within government funding and government agendas is that creative and theoretical thinking is bracketed in the interests of practical and pragmatic results and recommendations. A practical orientation dealing with empirical realities is, of course, a strength, but as Castles remarks:

> Migration policies fail because policymakers refuse to see migration as a dynamic social process linked to broader patterns of social transformation. Ministers and bureaucrats still see migration as something that can be turned on and off like a tap through laws or policies. (Castles, 2003, p 26)

These concerns expressed by Castles are of pressing concern at the current time within the social sciences in debates about public scholarship, public criminology, public sociology and the impact of social science research. These discussions tend to bifurcate around research that is 'critical' and interpretive, or research that serves a legitimating or administrative function (Bauman, 1992). Public sociology is defined by Burawoy and van Antwerpen as 'a sociology that is oriented toward major problems of the day, one that attempts to address them with the tools of social science, and in a manner often informed by historical and comparative perspectives ... designed to promote public reflection on significant social issues' (Burawoy and van Antwerpen, 2001, p 1).[2] What underpins these debates is analysis of the role of the state and governance in the commissioning/production, dissemination of social science research.[3]

With reference to communities, Castles (2003) suggests undertaking 'ethnographic studies of specific groups, studying: community studies on settlement and inter-group relations and identity formation in exile' (p 30). Methodologically such an interdisciplinary undertaking requires the full range of research methods involving primarily ethnographic and qualitative methods, connected also to survey and larger data sets where possible. The basic methodological principles should, for Castles, include historical and comparative studies, with a view to exploring 'transnational social transformation' as well as 'local, national and regional patterns of social and cultural relations' and how they connect to broader social relations, taking account of the agentic dimension of lived experience and the use of participatory methods (Castles, 2003, p 30).

Taking up these issues, a special edition of the *Journal of Refugee Studies*, edited by Voutira and Doná (2007, p 164), aimed to create a forum for ongoing discussion by providing a comprehensive overview of debates in the field, revisiting key terms, conceptualising the particularities of refugee research as an interdisciplinary field of study and identifying emerging trends. Voutira and Doná refer to three key methodological issues intrinsic to the field of 'refugee studies': 'multi- and interdisciplinarity, bottom-up approaches and the relation between advocacy and scholarship'[4] (Voutira and Doná, 2007, p 165), and these themes are taken forward in the remaining chapters of this book.

The relationship between advocacy and scholarship is another aspect of the tension between interpretive and legislative sociology, and central to debates about public scholarship. Voutira and Doná (2007) argue that social transformations in the lives of refugees have had an impact on the way scholars conduct research with refugees, making it more difficult; and this adds to the complexity of interdisciplinary endeavour. These transformations include: 'the "securitization" of migration', with an increased focus on security of the state in contrast to the protection of refugees; a shift from permanent to temporary protection that includes increased use of camps, detention, 'all of which point to a "re-temporalization" of protection' (Voutira and Doná, 2007, p 167), making it harder to access refugees; and the growth of supranational actors, that include the EU and non-governmental organisations (NGOs) as well as transnational communities.

Voutira and Doná's (2007) collection include contributions on the range of methods used in research with refugees and forced migrants that are reflective of multidisciplinarity and bottom-up approaches. It includes papers discussing the role of surveys (Bloch, 2007), comparative research (Chatty, 2007), life history interviews (Eastmond, 2007), gatekeepers, accessibility, physical and bureaucratic barriers to doing research and who speaks on behalf of who (Harrell-Bond and Voutira, 2007), participation in research with refugees (Doná, 2007), the concept of generation and identity in forced migration (Loiozes, 2007) and issues relating to the label 'refugee' (Zetter, 2007).

The bottom line, and one that is strongly resisted by public scholarship, in sociology, criminology or anthropology, and a key issue for research on forced migration, is the relationship between the knowledge requirements of the state[5] and the way that 'research evidence is rapidly becoming subservient to political expediency' (Haggerty, 2004, p 219), rather than 'being the soil from which sound governmental policy emerges' (Haggerty, 2004, p 219).

Bauman (1992) has written eloquently about the role of the sociologist as interpreter rather than legislator and, moreover, that this interpretive role takes up the mutual understanding of diverse communities, valuing plurality of cultural traditions, subcultures and fostering tolerance of diversity as well as making the unfamiliar familiar.

For Bauman, there is little choice to be made between an engaged or neutral way of doing sociology. For a 'noncommittal sociology is an impossibility....The job of sociology is to see to it that the choices are genuinely free and that they remain so, increasingly so, for the duration of humanity' (Bauman, 1992, p 369). With this in mind, I propose that critical and cultural analysis using participatory methods could move us beyond the binaries of legislative research that serves the purposes of the state, and interpretive research that is easily ignored by government. Such research could also help us to access a richer understanding of the complexities of forced migration, develop knowledge and analysis that might foster a more radically democratic imaginary that challenges exclusionary discourses and connects to more relational ways of promoting social justice and egalization.

Critical theory and researching the asylum-migration-community nexus

Within the methodological and epistemological context defined earlier, I now want to explore the possibilities for researching the asylum-migration-community nexus using critical theory that engages with meaning making and the relational and community-based aspects of lived experience for people situated in the asylum-migration-nexus. This approach is necessarily aware of the glocalisation of our being in the world. 'There can be no local studies without an understanding of the global context and no global theorization without a basis in local research' (Castles, 2003, p 22). My research approach entails an understanding of the relationship between the particular and the general, and the need for analysis that takes account of the embeddedness of small-scale phenomena in the broader social totality. For example, Adorno's aphorism, 'the splinter in your eye is the best magnifying glass' (Adorno, 1978, p 50), brings into focus the interrelationship and the mediation between the 'micrology' of lived experience and broader structures and contexts that are not only the outcome but the medium of social action and meaning making.

Adorno's statement encourages us to focus on what is ordinarily overlooked: the small scale, the minutiae of lived experiences. In focusing on the small scale, we can often reach a better understanding of the bigger picture. In Adorno's critical theory it is only by trying to say the unsayable, the 'outside of language', the mimetic, the sensual, the non-conceptual, that we can approach a 'politics' that undercuts identity thinking/identitarian thinking, criss-crosses binary thinking/territories and resists appropriation. For Adorno the social world is marked by identity thinking (the equivalence between an object and a concept such as asylum seekers being represented as 'bogus', or 'illegal') and instrumental reason.[6] The exemplars of instrumental reason and identity thinking are no more obvious than in the psychic and social processes that led to war in Bosnia and Rwanda. They are also present in the British government's response to asylum seekers, as enshrined in the latest raft of asylum and immigration acts.

For example, the 1999 and 2002 Asylum Acts instantiate in law a rational individualist diaspora. They engender a 'culture of disbelief' towards asylum seekers – it is very difficult to prove asylum status. The 1999 Act enabled the British government to prepare removal documents and deportation orders before the decision on an asylum claim was made. The Act extends criminal offences that cover trying to enter or remain in the UK using 'deception' to include asylum seekers and their representatives who 'knowingly' make false statements on their behalf. The Nationality, Immigration and Asylum Act 2002 introduced a further raft of legislation that erodes the basic human rights of people seeking asylum in the UK. The fundamental right to protection and sanctuary has been significantly and seriously reduced, partly the result of the impact of sections 55 and 57, which came into force on 8 January 2003. The measures deny automatic access to food, shelter and clothing to destitute asylum seekers, and they leave already vulnerable people, which may include pregnant women, children and those with special needs, exposed to victimisation, exploitation, bullying and harassment. The Borders, Citizenship and Immigration Act 2009 introduces a new 'path to citizenship' for refugees. Once the initial five-year period of protection is over, there is another period of temporary leave as probationary citizens before refugees get a permanent right to stay and they must also fulfil a period of volunteering activity as part of the government's 'active citizenship' measures. Section 25 of the Act 'changes the definition of the places where detainees can be held short term and allows some to be held there for unspecified periods. The Refugee Council are concerned that this will mean that immigration detainees will be held in facilities where they are with people held on criminal matters' (Refugee Council, 2009).

It would appear that the state wants individual tourists to enter the UK and those with professional expertise under the new points-based system, not families dispersed and separated, not families, communities and 'others'. For those seeking asylum, their post-kinship diaspora – marked by archaic depths of loss of kinship, history and politics – combine with the experience of cultural repression. As discussed in

Chapter Two what constitutes 'citizenship' and 'community' can be explored through patterns of inclusion and exclusion.

I argue in this chapter that renewed methodologies that incorporate the voices and images of 'refugees' and 'asylum seekers' through scholarly/civic research as participatory research not only serve to enlighten and raise our awareness of certain issues, but could also produce critical reflexive texts that may help to mobilise social change. Thus critical, participatory and arts-based research with migrants could produce work that is both, interpretive and may impact on policy, and can be defined within the rubric of public scholarship.

The interrelationship between social research and praxis is, of course, fraught with tensions. The tension between a modernist ethos of resistance and transformation through participation as praxis (working *with* research participants towards social renewal), and a post-modern ethos of hybridity, complexity and intertextuality (anti-identitarian thinking, representing the complexity of lived experience through performative praxis, working across genres and borders) is uneasy, but represents the complex dynamics of this work, and it uncovers important messages about the complexity of everyday life.

I have argued elsewhere (2004, 2009) that representing social research through art forms can create multivocal, dialogical texts and can make visible 'emotional structures and inner experiences' (Kuzmics, 1997, p 9) that may 'move' audiences through what can be described as 'sensuous knowing' or mimesis (Taussig, 1993). As a researcher, interpretive ethnography grounded in the stories of the co-creators of the research (participatory research) rooted in critical theory is my chosen method. This method privileges the voices of participants and triangulates their voices with cultural texts representing and imagining the lived experiences of new arrivals through 'feeling forms' (Witkin, 1974). The point about such methodologies is that they deal *with* the contradictions of oppression *and* the utter complexity of our lived relations in the 21st century, within the context of technologisation and globalisation, and indeed, within the context of what Piccone calls 'the permanent crisis of the totally administered society' (1993, p 3).

Renewed methodologies: ethno-mimesis

In 1994, but rooted in earlier PAR, I began to develop research at the borders of art and ethnography in order to explore ways of transgressing conventional or traditional ways of analysing and representing research data and developing what I called 'ethno-mimesis' as a politics of feeling. Keen to explore the sensuousness of ethnography and our immersion in the life worlds of participants as well as valuing their knowledge, experience and expertise, I looked for ways of exploring and representing the complexity of psychic and social lived relations by combining art and ethnography. Already using PAR as a methodology for working with marginalised groups (women and young people who sell sex), I described the work I was then developing as being situated in the tension or intersection between feminist theory, sociocultural research and experimental alternative forms of representation and interpretation.

I introduced the concept of ethno-mimesis to express the combination of ethnographic, participatory research with participants, and mimetic representations of lived experience using art forms, poetry, film – sensory modes of representation and analysis. I use mimesis following Benjamin (1992) and Adorno (1978, 1984, 1997) to express not the imitative dimension of social life but rather as sensuous knowing, the playful, imaginative and performative relationship we have to each other and to cultural forms and processes – indeed, to culture. Cantwell's (1993) text on ethno-mimesis and folk culture also defines mimesis as more than simply imitation. He uses mimesis in three senses: as imitation or mimicry; as the imaginative interplay between people in the sense used by Plato of 'impersonation', the 'embodiment, in a person, of a total sense of life, which is the cultural infrastructure of personality'; and the 'figuring forth' or 'summoning up of both elite and popular culture' (Cantwell, 1993, pp 5-6). Ethno-mimesis for Cantwell is identified with folk culture and culture more broadly: 'Ethno-mimesis is my word for culture and for my conviction that, although it is embedded in social practices, manifested in art, and reproduced by power, culture is essentially imaginative' (1993, p 6).

Ethno-mimesis in my own work is a theoretical construct, a process and a methodological practice. It is a combination of ethnographic work and artistic representations of the ethnographic work through PAR. It is a process and a practice, but it is ultimately rooted in principles of equality, democracy and freedom, as well as what Jessica Benjamin (1993) describes as a dialectic of mutual recognition. The key concept used here to express the representation of life stories in artistic form is 'mimesis' and the dialectic of mimesis and constructive rationality.

Following Adorno (1984, 1997), 'mimesis' does not simply mean naive imitation, but rather feeling, sensuousness and spirit; the playfulness of our being in the world in critical tension to constructive rationality; reason; and the 'out there' sense of our being in the world. Hilde Heynon writes, 'Mimesis, however, is not simply equivalent to a visual similarity between works of art and what they represent. The affinity

Adorno refers to lies deeper. It can be recognized, for example, in an abstract painting that, in mimetic fashion, depicts something of reality's alienating character' (Heynan, 1999, p 175). Taussig understands 'mimesis as both the faculty of imitation and the deployment of that faculty in sensuous knowing' (Taussig, 1993, p 68).

As performative praxis, ethno-mimesis seeks to speak in empathic ways with people, represented here through photographic and performative texts in ways that counter post-emotionalism, valorising discourses and the reduction of the 'other' to a cipher of the oppressed/marginalised/ exploited (see Mestrovic, 1997). It seeks to develop a radical cultural imaginary, to challenge exclusionary discourses and produce counter-hegemonic knowledge as a resistance to instrumental rationality and identity thinking, especially regarding the governmentality of the British government's response to forced migration, border control, asylum seekers, refugees and undocumented people. Ethno-mimesis is both a practice (a methodology) and a process aimed at illuminating inequalities and injustice through sociocultural research and analysis, but it also seeks to envision and imagine a better future based on a dialectic of mutual recognition, care, respect for human rights, cultural citizenship and democratic processes.

This new approach focuses attention on the importance of renewing methodologies through interdisciplinarity to better interpret social issues such as: (a) migration, both forced and free; (b) the experiences of new arrivals; and (c) to facilitate the production of new knowledge and counter-hegemonic texts to support the shifts taking place, borrowing Roger Bromley's (2001, p 20) words, that counter 'exclusionary processes' and offer 'representational challenges as part of a counter formulation and potentially radical cultural imaginary'. This brings an approach to knowledge production as collaboratively made, not found, that in turn loosens the knowledge/power axis involved in knowledge production and expertness. This counters the instrumental rationality underpinning the government's need for research evidence that supports the management and control of migration, but especially the 'undeserving' 'forced' asylum seekers and refugees (Sales, 2000).

Renewed methodologies such as ethno-mimesis can serve to focus our attentions on history and the unspeakable, the transgressive acts, everyday resistances, the relational dimensions of shared experiences and the democratic processes and possibilities for social justice, citizenship, rights and freedom – within the realm of relative unfreedom marked by the instrumental reason, and what Mestrovic (1997) calls 'postemotionalism'.

Ethnographic approaches to research prioritise exploring the micrology of lived cultures, lived experiences through the frame of reference of asylum seekers, refugees and undocumented people through sensuous knowing, listening, and connecting. It fosters understanding of the meaning and meaning-giving practices people engage in. Listening to the voices of people seeking asylum encourages us to engage with ethics, within a moral order and reasoning based on thinking, feeling and compassion. The importance of empathy, of relational connectedness, of working *with* people experiencing forced migration, not on or for them, cannot be overestimated. Such research may inspire praxis. The worry is that during the 21st century there will be an increase, not a decrease, in war and crimes against human rights, and an increased breakdown of law, justice and protection of people. Research on the asylum-migration-community nexus that uses narrative, biographical and participatory methods can contribute to cultural politics at the level of theory, experience and praxis, and I argue that it can be constitutive of critical theory in praxis in earlier work (O'Neill, 2004, 2007, 2009). I developed a case for theory building based on lived experience using biographical materials, both narrative and visual, as critical theory in practice towards a vision of social justice that challenges the dominant knowledge/power axis embedded in current governance and media policy relating to forced migration.

Emotionality/feeling is embedded in the materiality of social life and, through interpretive ethnography, we can access feeling worlds to provide a fuller understanding of lived cultures and the interrelation of psychic and social processes and structures in all our lives. *Ethno-mimesis* provides a theoretical organising construct that describes a research process, as relational 'feeling form'. The materiality of everyday life and indeed relationships between ideology, knowledge and power, need to be understood within the context of wider structures of signification and legitimation and control (Giddens, 1984). Our lived experience, our emotional lives, are wrapped up in materiality. Coming to understand in a reflexive and purposeful way, through ethno-mimetic processes, the relationship between lived experience, wider social and cultural structures, processes and practices, is constitutive of what I call a 'politics of feeling'.

Immersion, identification in the lived cultures of individuals and groups and subsequent commentary and criticism, may lead to praxis (purposeful knowledge); for example better informed policy and practice, shifts in attitude and perception, a form of consciencisation or critical consciousness.

Ethno-mimetic research seeks to understand, express and re-imagine the complexity of the asylum-migration-community nexus through a combination of participatory, biographical/life history work and representation/re-imagining through artistic forms that one can describe as performative praxis. This is a dialectical/constellational project rather than one that deals in binaries. Millar (1992), like Cantwell (1993), Witkin (1974, 1995, 2002) Cornell (1995) and Schoene (2009), looks to art, literature and aesthetics as one means to re-imagine and renew our social worlds. Research methodologies, such as PAR, that create spaces for the voices and images of the subaltern – refugees and asylum seekers – through narrative methods that are rigorously ethical can serve not only to raise awareness, challenge stereotypes and hegemonic practices, but can produce critical texts that may mobilise and create 'real' change. This approach connects well with Pain (2008) and Askins' and Pain's (2009) research on the transformative possibilities of PAR, conscientisation and the importance of analysis on emotion.

Participatory action research

My introduction to PAR in 1990 (by Richard Harvey Brown who was then Professor in Sociology at the University of Maryland) was through the work of Orlando Fals-Borda (1988) and William Foote Whyte (1989). Rooted in western Marxism and in particular the work of the Frankfurt School, I was committed to producing knowledge as praxis. Fals-Borda's work therefore had huge resonances as a way of seeing and knowing through participatory democratic ways of doing research that included asking questions such as 'knowledge for what? Knowledge for whom?' (Fals-Borda, 1995, p 78).

Through PAR knowledge is gained *with* the participation of marginalised groups with a view to transforming social and sexual inequalities. Praxis is developed via mutual recognition and also via the practical commitment of the PAR researcher with local groups. In contrast to positivism, Fals-Borda focused on hermeneutics and phenomenological methods. Drawing on what Heller (1984) calls 'true knowledge', Fals-Borda describes PAR as a transformative methodology linked to social justice, especially for those who are most marginalised. Methods used include in-depth interviews, biographical methods, diaries, maps and photographs. Fals-Borda describes two core orientations of PAR as, first, *vivencia*[7] or *Erfahrung* (life experience gained through immersion in fieldwork with local communities), identifying with them without giving oneself over or projecting oneself onto the other; and second, *commitment* with change processes and their actors.

He describes the existential concept of experience (*Erlebnis*) following Spanish philosopher Jose Ortega y Gasse:

> Through experiencing something we intuitively apprehend its essence, we feel, enjoy and understand it as a reality, and we thereby place our being in a wider, more fulfilling context. In PAR such an experience, called *vivencia* in Spanish, is complemented by another idea: that of authentic commitment resulting from historical materialism and classical Marxism (Eleventh Thesis on Feuerbach: 'Philosophers should not be content with just explaining the world, but should try to transform it'). (Fals Borda, 1988, pp 87-8)

Whyte (1989) suggests that PAR can advance sociological knowledge in ways that would be unlikely to emerge from more orthodox sociological research. For Whyte, the element of creative surprise (which comes with working with practitioners whose experiences and knowledges are different from our own) is a central aspect to conducting PAR and advancing social-scientific knowledge.

This approach gives rise to a subject–subject approach to generating understanding and knowledge and, as Fals-Borda states, takes us beyond the classical 'participant observer role' (subject–object) in fieldwork. This methodological approach can give rise to the 'critical recovery of history' (Fals-Borda, 1995, p 81), fostering mutual recognition, trust and responsibility; it also enriches the life experiences and skills of the researcher. Moreover, respect for communicating such knowledge is written into the processes and practices of PAR so that meanings are understood by all involved.

Fals-Borda talks of four key aspects or skills that are part of PAR's contribution to social research methodology: an emphasis on collectivities (helpful in ensuring cross-referencing of data and triangulation); critical recovery of history based on use of personal, folk and archival materials, the oral tradition that is supportive of community dignity and facilitates inclusion and involvement; devolving knowledge in understandable and meaningful ways through the production of 'symmetrical communication', indeed 'symmetrical reciprocity', which reinforces the need for dialogue, interpretation and can lead to conscientisation.

Ultimately, drawing on Heller (1984), Fals-Borda suggests that there is no such thing as a final solution to a problem and that social science is a 'treasure trove' that we revisit in a hermeneutical spiral via interpretation–reinterpretation. Thus the fourth key aspect is 'praxis' (based on Gramsci and Marx), purposeful knowledge that involves turning common sense into good sense, drawing on the knowledge and experience of participants. Fals–Borda (1995) draws parallels with his work and that of Agnes Heller. Heller talks about the use of 'imagination with good judgement' and 'truth' consisting of an agreement between researcher and participant member. Moreover, a 'more meaningful paradigm is possible if, to academic knowledge, one adds and takes into account the knowledge and wisdom of the common people in a plural universe' (Fals–Borda, 1995, p 85). Attention to rigour, validity and ethical imperatives are also central to good PAR.

PAR is a methodology that encompasses social research, action or intervention and the production and exchange of knowledge. Typically it enables the participation of the very people who might be the subjects of traditional research methods. It seeks to develop purposeful knowledge leading to social change by valuing the knowledge and experience of community members. Methodologically the focus is on the process as well as the outcomes of research. In practical terms PAR involves *collective research, valuing all voices* and *producing and exchanging knowledge*.

Community members are trained as co-researchers and may be involved in the entire research process, from research design to writing up and disseminating the work. The sum of knowledge from participants in the research, community co-researchers, academic researchers and the steering group facilitate the acquisition of a more accurate and richer picture of the issue or problem we want to understand in order to change or transform it.

PAR is based on democratic principles and processes including the principle of mutual recognition. A key aspect of this is that inequalities of power between different groups and community members need to be handled carefully and sensitively. 'In any community, it is likely that women, children and disabled people will have difficulty getting their point of view heard. The poorest people out of any group will be in the same position' (Laws et al, 2003, p 52).

The element of creative surprise is central to advancing knowledge and this is more likely to emerge in the PAR process where learning is shared, based on mutual recognition and where collectivist approaches are prioritised. PAR is rooted in the principles of inclusion, participation, valuing all local voices, transformation/social change and partnership working that is community-driven and sustainable. It involves a commitment to research that develops partnership responses to facilitate learning and social change and includes all those involved where possible, thus facilitating shared ownership of the development and outcomes of the research (stakeholders). 'Inclusion' involves working with participants as co-researchers (community members, as experts through democratic processes and decision making. This involves mutual recognition (what Paulo Freire calls dialogic techniques); uses innovative ways of consulting and working with local people, for example through arts workshops, forum theatre methods, stakeholder events; and is transformative, rigorous and ethical. PAR is a process and a practice directed towards social change *with* the participants. It is interventionist, action-orientated and interpretive.[8]

What is the impact of participatory action research?

If conducted ethically, with integrity and not as a token gesture, PAR can enable the coming into voice for marginalised people (without reducing them to versions of ourselves); enlighten and inform; raise awareness; make visible people's experiences and ideas for change (for example the visual artistic can say so much more than words alone and can reach a wider audience); and feed into social policy.

Fals-Borda defines PAR as anticipating post-modernism as it drew on a range of conceptual elements to guide fieldwork: 'Marxism, phenomenology, and classical theories of participation, including action' (Fals-Borda, 1999, p 1), and yet went beyond them. Fals-Borda defines PAR as *vivencia* (life experience akin to Husserl's *Erfahrung*), 'necessary for the achievement of progress and democracy and as a complex of attitudes and values to give meaning to our praxis in the field' (Fals-Borda, 1999, p 17).

PAR is a social research methodology, which includes the stereotypical subjects of research as co-creators of the research. It creates a space for the subaltern to become involved actively in change or transformation. It uses innovative ways of consulting and working with people; and it facilitates change with communities and groups. Thus PAR provides safe spaces for dialogue; in Benhabib's terms, an 'ethics of communication' (2004), fostering polyvocality and involvement in producing knowledge as well as action and in so doing can contribute to social justice.

In summary, PAR is reflective (provides opportunities for people to think through issues and make visible their concerns, experiences, hopes); it can produce change at any and every part of the process; it can be transformative *with* the participants, not *on* or *for* them; it can challenge stereotypes and address the multilayered problems of urban decline, especially in relation to multiagency working/partnership working. Working together to develop analysis and collective responses and outcomes enables people to have a stake in their community/ society fostering inclusion. At the very least PAR can help highlight, reinforce and support skills and capacity development. It uses a range of research methods as appropriate – mixed or multiple methods including creative consultation. In a nutshell, PAR can empower, be inclusive, mobilise and can transform.

Temple and Moran (2006, p 6) argue that participatory approaches can help to maximise local participation (which is especially significant for people who speak little English and/or do not access services); lead to a sense of ownership, responsibility and self-esteem; recognise and value people's skills and capacities; and lead to community development processes and capacities. Additionally, because the research methods used involve rigorous checking and cross-checking of interpretations, a deeply embedded reflexivity emerges in the research design, process and outcomes.

However, participatory approaches are by no means a panacea and must be used with caution (Pain and Francis, 2003; Pain, 2004). There are risks in doing participatory research: the power balance can become skewed, especially where tokenism replaces partnerships and genuine collaboration; expectations and outcomes can be disproportionate to what is possible; collaborations may go nowhere and if the 'research' is unduly prioritised over the participatory processes, this can lead to mistrust, resentment and, at worst, participants feeling 'used'. Participatory research at its best is conducted over and through time, with a keen eye on the dynamics of power, relationships and with deep attention to reflexivity. PAR can often lead to the production or carving of democratic spaces where genuine dialogue happens and dissent can be worked with and through and the collaborative work is sustained by relationships of trust and mutual recognition: 'we have learned that a mutual inquiry space requires a very honest conversation about roles, tasks, boundaries, authority, and power in the context of each particular project and as relationships are being built' (Ospina et al, 2004, p 66; quoted in Arieli et al, 2009, p 265).

Participatory action research and participatory arts

Conducting PAR with individuals and groups can promote purposeful knowledge about the asylum-migration-community nexus that may be transformative, and certainly counter paralysis and pessimism. The relationship between thinking, feeling and doing (Arendt, 1970; Tester, 1992), commitment and collective responsibility is central to PAR.

Representing social research in art forms can help audiences access a richer understanding of the complexity of lived experiences, and representing research using photography, poetry or creative writing we reach a wider audience, beyond academic communities, that may encourage people to think differently. Webster (1997) defines PA as a set of techniques and practices that help to make visible people's experiences and ideas for change. They are involved directly in making art, individually or as co-creators, not as the audience or recipients. PA is reflective, transformative and problem solving, with an emphasis on process and production. It is linked to community arts, a strong movement in the UK underpinned by democratic values that seek to challenge inequalities and support participation in art and art making.

Community arts organisations with a strong tradition in working with the various waves of migration to the UK, as well as the more recent work with asylum seekers and refugees, includes Charnwood Arts in Loughborough since 1985, and indeed the East Midlands Participatory Arts Federation and B Arts in Stoke on Trent.[9] The power of community and participatory arts to enable voice, to tell stories, to contribute to social change are evidenced in the range of research and practice-based work ongoing for some decades now in the UK. Ultimately the arts are perceived and experienced as transformative. For Kevin Ryan (Director of Charnwood Arts), relationships, dialogue, creativity and expression are basic aspects of our experience, and when explored within the context of the community arts movement the arts can be transformative in relation to both policy and practice.

Part of a perceived 'turn' to art in the social sciences, PA has come to the fore in a multiplicity of attempts to understand the ways in which people experience, mediate and intervene in the diverse areas of everyday life. The kind of creative, cultural, participatory and arts-based research documented in this text is inherently linked to specific conceptions of social justice and cultural citizenship. The arts and culture in the broadest sense are integral to processes of belonging and important to fostering cultural citizenship and social justice. Cultural citizenship is understood (following Pakulski, 1997) as the right to presence and visibility, not marginalisation; the right to dignity and maintenance of lifestyle, not assimilation to the dominant culture; the right to dignifying representation, not stigmatisation.

Social justice is understood in the sense summarised by Cribb and Gewirtz (2003) that extends the work of Iris Marion Young (1990) and Nancy Fraser (1997, 2000, 2004), and includes distributive justice (economic) involving the absence of exploitation, economic marginalisation and deprivation/destitution; associational justice including networks of support that enable people to fully participate in decision making and governance; and cultural justice that includes the absence of cultural domination, non-recognition or mis-recognition and disrespect. The power of art is also linked to the power of narrative and to history and the past.

Narrative, biographical methods

Scholars with expertise in biographical research have noted a turn to biographical, life history and narrative-based methods since the 1980s (Miller, 1995, 2005; Chamberlayne et al, 2000; Roberts, 2002; Miller et al, 2003; Merrill and West, 2009). Beyond the disciplinary boundaries of biographical sociology and criminology there is a growing interest in narrative theorising. Bruner, referenced in Horrocks et al (2003), defines the self, in part, as a 'library of stories' and what matters is 'that we try to characterise people's lives ... there is an acceptance of the need to look at how people actually live and make sense of their lives' (Horrocks et al, 2003, p xv). For Craib, emotional life is 'complex and contradictory and too disruptive to be grasped in a coherent way, thus we tell ourselves stories to ease our anxieties' (quoted in Horrockes et al, 2003, p xvi). Moreover, as Roberts (2003) has shown, the narratives we construct are subject to 'repetition and revision'. Individuals are constantly engaged in rewriting the self. For Roberts, telling our stories through narrative practices is an 'artistic endeavour' that enables us to 'do' coherence. Some narratives can help us; others, as Craib documents, can keep us passive and 'separate people from the authenticity of their lives' (Craib, 2003, p 1). Ultimately, 'the intent of biographical research in its various guises is to collect and interpret the lives of others as part of human understanding' (Roberts, 2002, p 15).

For Walter Benjamin (1992, pp 89-90), storytelling has a primary role in the household of humanity. Biographical research is involved in the production of meaning and offers resistance to the dominant power/ knowledge axis that we find in the current politics of representation of marginalised groups such as asylum seekers, and some media messages and images. For both Benjamin (1992) and Adorno (1984, 1997), art has a transformative role, and 'mimesis' is a key concept when exploring the relationship of art to society. A feeling form (art) is created in the tension between sensuous knowing, playfulness, the creativity of the artist and historically given techniques and means of production. And the combination of biography/narrative (ethnography) and art (mimesis) becomes a 'potential space' for transformative possibilities.

A key issue in narrative-based research with migrants is articulated well by Eastmond (2007, p 262):

> The challenges and limitations of narrative research notwithstanding, we need to continue seeking ways of listening to and representing refugees' experiences, in their great diversity. This is particularly urgent as solidarity with refugees in their plight appears to be giving way to distrust in many parts of the world. As a result, refugees' stories are either not deemed relevant or credible or, increasingly, not heard at all.

And as Eastmond states, as a field of knowledge production, narrative provides a site to examine the meanings that actors ascribe to experience. Many of the complexities of a narrative approach, notably the tension between empirical and interpretive demands, between reality and its representation, are those that most qualitative approaches have to tackle. However, beyond these, forced migration presents special challenges to narrative research.

Biographical research and PAR methodologies are involved in the production of social justice through knowledge production that is 'authentic' or 'typical', revealing 'social actors' own way of knowing the field' (Fowler, 1996, p 12). Drawing on Bourdieu, we can say that PAR produces a 'socioanalysis', facilitating 'the return of the socially repressed', and thus creates an 'archive which contains a genuine popular culture' (Fowler, 1996, pp 14-15). For Bourdieu,

> 'understanding' involves attempting to situate oneself in the place the interviewee occupies in the social space in order to understand them as *necessarily what they are....* *[T]o take their part* ... is not to effect that 'projection of oneself into the other' of which the phenomenologists speak. It is to give oneself a *general and genetic comprehension* of who the person is, based on the (theoretical or practical) command of the social conditions of existence and the social mechanisms which exert their effects on the whole ensemble of the category to which the person belongs. (1996, pp 22-3)

Key aspects to consider in life history/biography research (as explored by these authors) include: the importance of memory and forgetting; life as a psychosocial project; and recurrence, time and space, and the fact that micrology can throw light on broader structures and processes.

Svensson writes about the power of biography as a way to order 'life and time just as a map orders the world and space....We live in a biographical era.... Both life and time are biographically ordered in modernity ... we shape the present against the background of our earlier life history and with our sights set on the future' (Svensson, 1997, pp 99-100). Moreover, that biography has a therapeutic power, creating forms of subjectivity within particular discourses linked to what Giddens has called 'the project of self' (1991, p 11).

Narrative and memory

Biographical narratives can heal, empower, challenge and transform our relationship to the past and the future. They are also important psychosocially, as we have documented, as narratives of self-making, fostering ethical communication, producing counter-hegemonic discourses and critical texts that may mobilise change. The process of memory making is important to how we produce biography. Winter and Sivan (1999) document the process of recollection in relation to memory traces. Most experiences, we are told, leave 'long term memory traces, recorded in our *episodic memory* system – the system which encodes "what happened"' (p 12). Furthermore, '*autobiographical memory* appears to be the most enduring kind of memory ... combat experience is particularly dense because it is personal and dramatic. Harrowing moments are denser still' (Winter and Sivan, 1999, p 12).

Kuhn (2000), discussing memory work, suggests that it involves an active staging of memory; a questioning attitude to the past and its reconstruction through memory; and questions the transparency of what is remembered. And takes what is remembered as material for interpretation.

> In acknowledging the performative nature of remembering, memory work takes on board productivity and encourages the practitioner to use the pretexts of memory, the traces of the past that remain in the present, as raw material in the production of new stories about the past. These stories may heal the wounds of the past. They may also transform the ways individuals and communities live in and relate to the present and the future ... how we use these relics to make memories, and how we then make use of the stories they generate to give deeper meanings to, and if necessary to change, our lives now. (Kuhn, 2000, pp 186-7)

Biographical research is involved in the production of meaning, and offers resistance to the dominant power/knowledge axis related to asylum and refuge in the current politics of representation we find in some media messages and images. Biographical research can do this in the production of alternative and renewed narratives that generate social knowledge to inform, raise awareness and empower. Ultimately biographical research counters the sanitised, demonised or hidden aspects of the lived cultures of exile and belonging as well as the normative, stereotyped stories we access through some mass media institutions. In so doing, biographical research helps to produce knowledge as a form of social justice. PAR develops social knowledge that is interventionist in partnership with migrants and communities and, because it seeks to promote social change, is action oriented. It also provides the possibilities for participation in local governance. The knowledge produced can shed light on broader structures, practices and processes and might lead to better governance of migration.

Methodologically, PAR and PA seek to foster social justice and can provide resistance and challenges to the fixed identity of the 'asylum seeker' or 'refugee' as abject 'other'. PAR is a social research methodology, which includes the stereotypical subjects of research as co-creators of the research. It creates a space for the voices of the marginalised to become involved actively in change or transformation. PAR seeks to understand the world from the perspective of the participants. Outcomes of participatory research can inform, educate, remind, challenge, empower and lead to action/interventions.[10]

PAR can provide important counter voices that document subjecthood amidst narratives of deeply painful experiences and migration journeys, and the resilience and courage of the people involved. Immersion in the life worlds of migrants through participatory research enables the foregrounding of feelings, meanings, emotions and experiences from their multiple standpoints that facilitates the development of 'thick' descriptions of lived cultures, provides more accurate accounts of their lives and resists identity thinking.

Ethno-mimesis and community/participatory arts

Thus the ethno-mimetic process can help to create a space for the marginalised to speak for themselves, without an intermediary speaking on or for them as subjects and objects of their own narratives. The process is reflexive and phenomenological and looks to praxis, given the participatory process, both in terms of the research and arts-based practice. Life history narratives are re-told via arts and in the process and practice of the workshops a reflective, safe space for dialogue, listening and understanding emerges. This deeply relational process is crucial to 'understanding' transnational identities, home and belonging, involving 'subjective–reflexive feeling'. Indeed, the space or hyphen between ethnography and arts-based practice within the research process can create a potential space, a holding space (or third space) that is creative, relational and potentially transformative for those involved (see O'Neill, 2008).[11]

Thus, I argue that through narrative, biography, art works, performing arts, live arts, film, painting poetry, literature, photography and architecture we are able to get in touch with our 'realities', social worlds and the lived experiences of others in ways that demand critical reflection and can help us transform these worlds. For Shierry Nicholsen (1997, 1999, 2002), the critical potential of art is that it can 'pierce us' and 'help us to grasp reality in its otherness within the context of the image society that attempts to tame and inhibit critical reflection' (1993, p 14).[12]

Recognitive community: two examples

In the next section I reflect on the ethno-mimetic process in relation to two examples. 'Global refugees: exile, displacement and belonging', an ethno-mimetic research project conducted in 1999 with artist Bea Tobolewska and a Bosnian community living in the East Midlands (fleeing war and ethnic cleansing) using PAR, PA and biographical methods. The second is Tom Scheff's account of his participation in a memorial to soldiers killed in Iraq. I want to suggest that both are illustrative of a recognitive theory of community and, I suggest, look towards a radical democratic imaginary, egalization and social justice.

1. Global refugees

'Global refugees: exile, displacement and belonging' combined PAR and PA using ethnographic approaches including biographical interviews and arts-based workshops facilitated by myself and four artists and Exiled Writers Ink,[13] in order to represent people's experiences of exile, displacement and belonging. Two communities took part in the research: a newly arrived Bosnian community living in the East Midlands who were 'programme' refugees arriving from the same UN camp in Croatia and an Afghan community living in London, made up of three waves of Afghan migration. The people involved were keen to represent themselves, raise awareness about their community with their neighbours and wider communities and develop connections with other community groups to facilitate belonging.

'We wanted to show how quickly things can change and how much we hope this will never happen to you. Everything changed so quickly. One morning my best friend said that her parents had told her she could not play with me anymore because I was Muslim. Soon afterwards my Father arranged safe passage across the border and we ended up in a refugee camp in Croatia. We were then given a choice Britain or America. My Mother chose Britain because it is closer to home.1 (V, quoted in O'Neill and Tobolewska, 2002a, p 124)

The partnership included Nottingham City Arts, a community arts organisation, managed by Bea Tobolewska, and Exiled Writers Ink, a London-based support group for exiled artists, performers, film-makers and writers. Myself and community co-researchers conducted biographical interviews and the participants then represented their life stories in artistic form with the support of artists and writers in creative arts/research workshops. Bea commissioned artists with experience of working on sensitive issues and facilitated the participants representing their stories in artistic forms. The London-based group worked with Exiled Writers Ink to produce creative writing, poetry and short stories.

Figure 4 was created first as an installation, then digitally photographed and developed in Photoshop. The narrative in English and Bosnian tells that the woman's neighbours held a meeting and decided to protect the three non-orthodox families in the block. She needed her neighbour's key for three years and would hide in her neighbour's flat when soldiers were looking for Muslims. She baked bread for her neighbour (having had supplies from the Red Cross) and took the bread to her neighbour – a soldier was in her neighbour's flat asking for the Muslims – she kept silent. The soldier asked "who are you" and she replied "you know who am I, I would not be here if I were Muslim". The image and text tells of the possibility and actuality of a greater humanity than experienced by many during the war, of protection, care and thanks offered through gifts to her neighbour – the good things denied during war and sanctions – bread, chocolate, lights, fruit – it is a hopeful image. A crucial point here is that in her experience of being 'protected' by her neighbours, Fahira's Muslim identity was acknowledged, and she was able to hold on to this. The art work represents this experience, as well as the emotions involved, in the intersection of the image and the text (see also O'Neill, 2009).

Figure 4: 'Good neighbour'

This project was exhibited in galleries and community centres and reported on in the local press; it helped to challenge attitudes, myths and stereotypes about 'asylum seekers' and 'refugees'. At one exhibition in a community centre a woman, clearly moved by her experience of seeing the work, said to Bea and myself this could be us, my family, my grandchild (see O'Neill, 2009).

Our collaborative work also led to awareness that refugees and asylum seekers should be included in arts and cultural infrastructures in the region. A subsequent research exchange project (between Maggie and Bea), 'Towards a cultural strategy for working with refugees and persons seeking asylum in the East Midlands', led to the development of a cultural strategy. Supported by the Arts Council, funding was later provided for a conference, 'The long journey home', which led to the development of an artists in exile regional support organisation and funded post. The research also fed into other policy and practice discussions in the region, and dissemination of the exhibition and text-based outcomes and presentations by the team meant that the importance of arts and culture in integration processes were considered in addition to the pressing issues of housing and health policies for new arrivals. These first two PAR projects led to a 10-year trajectory of research in the East Midlands with groups and emerging communities, artists and individual asylum seekers, refugees and migrants, including undocumented people (see O'Neill, 2008, 2009).

Subsequent research focused on examining new arrivals' access to education (O'Neill et al, 2003), and new arrivals' access to employment, training and social enterprise (O'Neill et al, 2004), the arts–based outcomes illustrated in Figure 5 provide very powerful messages.

Figure 5: New arrivals' access to employment (billboard)

2. Silence and mobilisation

In an article called 'Silence and mobilization: emotional/relational dynamics', Scheff (2006) writes about the experiences of visitors to an Iraq War memorial that he was supporting at the invitation of a friend:

> The monument itself, dubbed Arlington West after the US military cemetery in Washington is only temporary, as per city ordinance. Early Sunday morning the crosses, flags, and other materials are brought to the site and installed by members of the local chapter of the Veterans for Peace. A

nametag is then attached to each cross. In the evening, we remove everything, leaving nothing behind. (2006, p 1)

The monument is organised and removed every day, and so every day brings a renewed immediacy. 'Immediacy' is an important concept for Benjamin (1992) and Adorno (1984) – meanings are not encoded in images, instead meanings emerge in 'now time' like a flash, dialectically in the form of a constellation ... and uncovering layers of meaning in past experience. A combination of the sensory, sensuous experience of narrativity 'that preserves and concentrates its strength and is capable of releasing it even after a long time' (Benjamin, 1992, pp 89-90), and dialectical images may together generate 'understanding' (in the sense given by Bourdieu) and be transformative. There are resonances here with Scheff's description of the 'strollers' and visitors to the monument. Scheff argues that emotions and social bonds might play an important if disguised role in political mobilisation and also in silence. Using Stern's concept of 'attunement', he refers to the cognitive connectivity between people as experienced by some, of helpers, visitors and 'strollers' to the monument:

> Stern was referring to the momentary states of unity that occur between a mother and her infant. In my usage, the word attuned or attunement alone, unqualified, will refer to a balancing of the viewpoints of self and other, neither engulfed (too close) nor isolated (too far). (Scheff, 2006, p 2)

Scheff writes that he resisted going to the monument at first, for what could a monument tell him that he did not know:

> My own response on first visit was intense. When I arrived, Bob had me install some of the nametags he had just made. Crawling in the sand between the crosses, I read the names and ages of the fallen. It was their ages, mostly 18-26, that I couldn't shake off. I became quite upset, like something was stuck in my craw. After finishing the stack of nametags, I returned to where Bob was working. He asked if I would do more. I said 'Let me take a breather; I didn't realize how young....' I couldn't finish the sentence, silenced by convulsive sobs. Tears streamed down my face. The deep feeling of loss revealed by my fit of crying was probably the reason I had resisted visiting. I hadn't wanted to feel

it. Resistance to feeling turned out to be a theme for our visitors also. (Scheff, 2006, p 2)

Some of the visitors commented:

> 'Very emotional and touching.' 'Thank you for showing us what a tragedy the war is. These crosses really bring it home....' 'Seeing this brings a face to war, not just headlines.' 'Thank you from my heart. We must remain conscious of our losses.' 'Thank you for being our conscience, for waking us up....' 'Thank you for keeping us in touch....' and 'Thank you for jarring me into reality – it's so easy to forget....' 'This makes it real....' 'Thank you for being a voice for conscience. [We need] reminders that the numbers are real people....'

In a letter to a local paper, a visitor commented:

> Walking out into the memorial for the first time, I found myself overwhelmed with grief. One thousand casualties is just a number. One thousand crosses, with names and dates, will drive you to your knees like a sledgehammer.... (Scheff, 2006, p 9)

Scheff comments that seeing and talking to people who stop at the monument gives a more detailed picture of their responses and feelings. Scheff argues that the element of surprise combined with the relational element of attunement compel a connection to deeply hidden feelings/ emotions that may lead to a change in attitude or response. And in this moment of attunement, one is able to 'feel' some of the grief that has been 'covered over'. 'Until this moment, one knew about the loss of lives only intellectually, without feeling it' (2006, p 10).

> ... for most people, deeply hidden feelings can be accessed only when they feel attuned to at least one other person. Being attuned, rather than isolated, provides the security needed to access emotions that are anticipated as extremely painful, if not unbearable. Note that in my own first day at the memorial, described above, my own response was delayed until I spoke to Bob, my colleague. (Scheff, 2006, p 10)

And particularly in conflict situations, 'paying particular attention to emotional/relational issues' and feeling 'deeply heard' for both parties may begin the process of facilitating negotiation. Scheff argues that the emotional/relational world is important 'since it constitutes the moment-by-moment texture of our lives', and 'it is intimately linked to the larger world; it both causes and is caused by that world' (2006, p 2). Weaving a path between mobilisation into action through moral shock and collective denial, Scheff argues that what is needed is rituals such as those enacted through the monument to help uncover and deal with grief, but also other emotions such as shame, humiliation and fear.

To summarise, art and participatory methodologies can challenge exclusionary discourses and processes. They can also offer representational challenges that can be change causing, challenging identity thinking, helping the connectivity defined in 'attunement'. The work art engages us in is relational. It involves, quoting Witkin's, 'subjective–reflexive' feeling. The methodological contribution of combining biography/narrative with art forms (ethno-mimesis) in creating a 'potential space', a reflective/safe space for dialogue and narratives to emerge, is also a space where connectivity/attunement can become – at many levels, internally, between participants, between participants and researchers and also in the gallery or space or place between audience/participant and art works/performance.

Adorno (1984, 1997), Benjamin (1985) and Wolff (1981) discuss the way that art represents the sedimented 'stuff' of society, in that 'society' emerges/unfolds in works of art. De la Fuente expressed this as follows:

> Art entails objects (or situations) that have the capacity to draw upon 'social-psychological associations' which are heavily compressed and give that object (or situation) an air of 'transcendence'. Art transcends mundane and routine perception, by compressing experience in the following manner: the magic of art is in the way complex social and psychological stimuli are made to conjoin, a kind of *lash up* of sensualities. (Molotoch, quoted in de la Fuente, 2007, p 419)

The counter-hegemonic role of PAR and PA, through ethno-mimesis, can lead to a radical democratisation of images and texts that can move us, pierce us, challenge identity thinking and bring us in touch with the micro-relational worlds, helping us to connect with our feeling worlds in a subjective–reflexive relationship with the feeling worlds of the 'other', destabilising the relation between us and them, self and the 'other' into a subject–subject relationship. A politics of feeling that emerges through the potential space and the attunement that occurs in and through PAR projects can counter identity thinking and mis-recognition, destabilise regressive discourses and help us move towards egalization (Lindner, 2001, 2002, 2006, 2007), a recognitive theory of community and social justice. This kind of research runs counter to the kind of messages and images we find in the mainstream media and ultimately feeds into the public imagination.

Notes
[1] This is the complex relationship between migration (the movement of people across borders), forced migration (forced movement, for example as a consequence of civil war, natural disasters, decolonisation) and community (at macro, meso and micro levels). The distinction between forced and economic migration has become blurred and there are complex factors and outcomes operating that link the local with the global.

[2] Burawoy and van Antwerpen (2001) see sociology as organised around four types, that can overlap and even be conducted by the same individual. These are: professional ('claiming an archimedean point outside of the world it studies'), policy ('marked by instrumental serving the needs of various clients'), critical ('marked by reflexivity and critical analysis of professional sociology that denies the very possibility of detachment and insulation, and denounces the pretence of professional sociology as an act of interested self-deception') and public ('designed to promote public reflection on significant social issues') Burowoy and van Antwerpen (2001, pp 2-3).

[3] Haggerty (2004) discusses the impact of the rise of neoliberal forms of governance on the increasingly superfluous and interventionary potential of criminological research. Alongside the growth of administrative criminology, the neoliberal focus on individuals as being responsible for their own fate, welfare and security has impacted on a shift away from criminology rooted in sociological analysis to a focus on the 'monitoring and control of risky individuals and dangerous places' (Haggerty, 2004, p 218) through increasingly technocratic and administrative criminology. For Haggerty, the bottom line is that 'the state is interested in a fairly narrow set of questions: 'They want help in running the state. They want research based on the problems as defined by the state' (Haggerty, 2004, p 219).

[4] Indeed, the editors stress that refugee studies is 'multidisciplinary as a field and interdisciplinary in its approach' (Voutira and Doná, 2007, p 165).

[5] To help rationally and efficiently manage the growth of experts proffering policy-relevant knowledge within the context of the rise of neoliberal governance, not only of the asylum issue but broader issues of welfare, crime, protection and justice (O'Malley, 1995; Haggerty, 2004).

[6] I have argued elsewhere (see O'Neill, 1999) that the usefulness of Adorno's oeuvre is that his work gives voice to the critical, moral and creative potential of non-identity thinking, *Kulturkritik*, and the social role of art in dialectical tension with the role of subjective experience, within the context of a social world marked by identity thinking and instrumental reason.

[7] PAR is therefore a combination of experience and commitment. Certainly a combination of experience and commitment allows us to see and shape the relationship between knowledge and social change. For Fals-Borda, the sum of knowledge from both the participants and academics/researchers allows us to acquire a much more accurate picture of the reality we want to transform. For him, academic knowledge, combined with popular knowledge and wisdom, may give us a new paradigm. Certainly, renewed methodologies that aim to get at the reflexive nature of human thought and action, the meanings given, both conscious and semi-conscious, could enable us to better understand people's everyday experiences and at the same time enable us to better understand broader social institutions and work towards social change.

[8] An excellent text just published by The Policy Press provides detailed accounts and discussions of some of these themes; see Ledwith and Springett (2010).

[9] There are many other examples, such as ICAR Focus. Connecting Futures Through Film used PAR to produce films with local young people and new arrival young people in Coventry and Peterborough to help foster cohesion/ better community relations (see www.icar.org.uk/10006/introduction/ introduction.html). The 'Towards a sense of belonging' project led by Creative Exchange worked with 73 projects across the UK to look at the role of culture and arts in the resettlement process (http://cultureartsrefugees. creativexchange.org/car/asenseof/). Exiled Writers Ink (www.exiledwriters. co.uk/), and many community arts organisations are working in participatory ways with new arrivals through film, arts, crafts, photography and dance.

[10] Yet PAR is little used in the UK. Rarely will it get a mention in research methods texts, other than in the literature on development, and it is most prevalent in countries of the South, North and South America and India. In contrast to this situation see the work of Rachel Pain, Kye Askins and colleagues at Durham University (www.dur.ac.uk/beacon/socialjustice/).

[11] In summary, the methodological contribution of combining ethnography and art/mimesis relates to a 'potential space', a 'dialogic space', a reflective space for dialogue, narratives and images to emerge around the themes of transnational identities, exile, home and belonging. This in turn feeds into cultural politics and praxis (a radical democratic and cultural imaginary) that may help processes of social justice via a politics of recognition, as a counter to mis-recognition (O'Neill, 2008).

[12] Shierry Nicholsen (1997, 1999) looks to photography and psychoanalytic psychotherapy to help us develop a broader, more compassionate and accurate consciousness.

[13] Bea Tobolewska, Maggy Milner, Simon Cunningham, Karen Fraser, Jennifer Langer, Director of Exiled Writers Ink.

FOUR

Representing refugees and asylum seekers in the mainstream and alternative media: discourses of inclusion and exclusion

If you wish for peace, care for justice....Absence of justice is barring the road to peace today. (Bauman, 2007, p 5)

Everyone has the right to freedom of opinion and expression; this right includes freedom to hold opinions without interference and to seek, receive and impart information and ideas through any media and regardless of frontiers. (Article 19 of the 1948 UDHR)

In previous work (O'Neill and Harindranath, 2006) I suggested that people come to understand the lived experience of 'asylum' and migration through the mediated images and narratives of mass media institutions as well as advocacy groups, networks and academic research. The media politics of asylum can be seen as constituted through the weaving together of legal, governance and media narratives/messages for general consumption. Moreover, while the mainstream media contribute to debates on the notion of asylum, they are thus crucially implicated in the politics of representation of refugees and asylum seekers.

Research on the media representation of asylum seekers and refugees illustrates 'the relentless repetition and overemphasis of precisely those images that reinforce particular stereotypes and a failure to source more diverse images to illustrate the many other aspects of the asylum issue' (O'Neill and Harindranath, 2006, p 40). Bailey and Harindranath (2005, p 274) argue that in media representations there often takes place a 'discussion of policy issues in an outwardly reasonable language, but one using words and phrases that are calculated to carry a different message to the target audience'. The asylum seeker is represented as an undesirable alien, occasionally represented as a possible threat to national sovereignty and security. This is humiliating at the level of lived experience, representation and embedded in the institutional processes of media production.

Much of the knowledge generated by advocacy groups, organisations, self-organised groups and services supporting asylum seekers and refugees provides much needed alternative voices, dispelling myths and promoting better understanding and knowledge. However, the knowledge generated is also subject to media representation and this tends not to be constituted by the voices of refugees and asylum seekers. Thus asylum seekers and refugees are represented by others, such as NGOs, advocacy and support groups. Organisations such as Refugee Action, the Refugee Council and the European Council on Refugees and Exiles are examples. The nearly complete absence – apart from a few exemplary reports and television documentaries – of an alternative voice in the mainstream media from the perspective of the refugee or asylum seeker raises important ethico-political issues relating to the politics of representation, democracy and immigration.

My central argument in Chapter Three was that PAR/ethno-mimesis as a methodology and artistic practice offers the opportunity for such groups to represent themselves, without a cultural or political intermediary talking 'on their behalf'. PAR/ethno-mimesis transgresses the power relations inherent in traditional ethnography and social research as well as the binaries of subject/object inherent in the research process – the participants involved in PAR are both objects and subjects (authors) of their own narratives and cultures. In Chapter Three I also suggested that PAR/ethno-mimesis can facilitate and envision a more holistic model of social justice.

Crucially, PAR/ethno-mimesis is reflexive and phenomenological, but also looks to praxis. Thus, it is vitally important to develop innovative methodologies in order to: (a) interpret the issues of migration, both forced and free; (b) share the experiences of new arrivals; and (c) facilitate the production of new knowledge and counter-hegemonic texts to address the way in which, to borrow Roger Bromley's words, 'the circulation in politics and the media of a set of negative images and vocabularies relating to refugees and asylum seekers has become part of a new exclusionary process' (2000, p 20).[1]

In this chapter I focus not only on the representation of asylum seekers and refugees in the mainstream media and the research that has taken place documenting this, but also on the creative ways in which refugee communities in the UK have not only survived but also managed to construct lives for themselves very effectively in the ~t countries, despite problems and barriers (including humiliation, ɔn and domination). I focus on two examples: the work of

SAEMP, set up by a Somali organisation (http://saemp.org.uk/home. htm), an online community television station based in Leicester; and a workshop organised as part of the Making the Connections: Arts, Migration and Diaspora Regional Network funded by AHRC and the Arts Council East Midlands on media representations of destitution.

Representations of 'asylum' in the mainstream media

As described earlier, the British public learn of the lived experiences of asylum seekers and refugees through the media, and much less frequently through advocacy groups, research or face-to-face experience. Media institutions are therefore crucially implicated in the politics of representation, with asylum seekers/refugees usually represented by others through forms of representation that emphasise questions of difference and (the abject) 'other' through such terms as 'illegal' and 'bogus' (O'Neill and Harindranath, 2006; Bailey and Harindranath, 2005; Bailey et al, 2007). While the public do not assimilate dominant discourses in an unreflexive manner, and may question some representations, the role of the media in setting agendas is thought to be one of its strongest impacts (ICAR, 2007). In this respect, it is notable that national press coverage around asylum issues has bolstered the 'us' and 'them' divide, with the 'otherness' of asylum seekers reproduced through discourses that identify them as a burden and as potentially disruptive (Buchanan et al, 2003). Moreover, the figure of the asylum seeker as abject 'other' helps to reconfirm a sense of national identity, with Tyler (2006, p 186) arguing 'the figure of the asylum-seeker increasingly secures the imaginary borders of Britain today'. Moreover, she argues:

> The identification of a person as an asylum-seeker has become an 'instrument for the refusal of recognition' (Butler, 2002, p 11), which in turn shores up a normative fantasy of what it means to be British. Indeed, as it shall be argued, the identification of the figure of the asylum-seeker is increasingly constitutive of public articulations of national and ethnic belonging. (Tyler, 2006, p 189)

In 2001 in a report commissioned by Oxfam called *Asylum: The truth behind the headlines*, Mollard writes:

> There can be little doubt that negative press coverage has helped to create a climate in Britain where it is acceptable

to detain asylum seekers, to give them support payments
worth only 70 per cent of Income Support levels, to
make that payment in vouchers, to provide sub-standard
accommodation, and to disperse people across the country
without recourse to individual need. In some cases the
outcome of this coverage has been worse: asylum seekers
in poor communities have been harassed and intimidated
by people who believe that their presence has affected the
quality of services, access to housing, and even access to jobs
(although asylum seekers are not allowed to work for at least
the first six months after their arrival). (Mollard, 2001, p 4)

The research on which the report was based took place over a two-
month period in 2000, in Scotland, just before asylum seekers were
to arrive under the dispersal programme into Glasgow. Between
March and April 2000 'all weekday news coverage of asylum issues
was collected from six Scottish newspapers. The papers were the *Daily
Record, Herald, Scotsman, Scottish Daily Express, Scottish Daily Mail*, and
the *Scottish Sun*' (Mollard, 2001, p 6).

Mollard found that 'most of the press coverage during the period
monitored was negative to the point of being hostile' and 'In order to
sustain this level of hostility, the reporting had to be partial, based on
false assumptions (myths) and on the exaggeration of specific incidents'
(p 6). Moreover, that the 'media sought to justify this position through
the publication of letters from the public which reflected back the
papers' own negative reporting on the issue' (Mollard, 2001). The
report concluded that the

consequences of this sustained negative coverage have been
disturbing: public opinion is now less well informed than
it was, as demonstrated by key findings in opinion polls
(*Mori Poll for Readers Digest*, November 2000). Government
policy is no longer subject to independent scrutiny: the
press reflects the government's line that making conditions
less welcoming and more hostile for asylum seekers will
deter them from travelling to Britain.... The lack of desire
to use information and comment from NGOs and other
organisations who support asylum seekers, and of course
the lack of interest in quoting asylum seekers themselves, is
a problem which needs to be addressed by the newspapers.
(Mollard, 2001, p 6)

Ultimately 'the impact of all this hostility is to increase the threat under which the asylum-seeking community lives and to enable the government to send potentially legitimate claimants back to situations where they will face personal danger. The net result is an overall increase in human suffering in local and refugee communities' (Mollard, 2001, p 25).

Three years later, Buchanan et al (2003), together with Article 19 (the global campaign for free expression) and Cardiff University School of Journalism published research that explored the ways in which the issue of asylum, and asylum seekers and refugees, is represented in the media, the extent to which asylum seekers and refugees feel able to participate in the public debate on asylum and immigration, and the impact media coverage has on their everyday lives. The research was developed in consultation with organisations concerned with supporting the rights and welfare of asylum seekers and refugees. The direct involvement of asylum seekers and refugees as researchers was a central feature of the project. 'Our research took us to four regions of the UK, where forty-five individual refugees and asylum seekers were interviewed by a team of researchers who were

Figure 6: *What's the Story* (Article 19)

Figure 7: *What's the Story* (Article 19)

themselves asylum seekers, refugees or exiled journalists' (Buchanan et al, 2003, p 9). The main findings from the report were as follows:

- Media reporting of the asylum issue is characterised by the inaccurate and provocative use of language to describe those entering the country to seek asylum.
- Media reporting, particularly in the tabloid press, consistently fails to correctly distinguish between economic migrants and asylum seekers or refugees. The numbers that are presented in print and broadcast reports are frequently unsourced, exaggerated or inadequately explained.
- Images are dominated by the stereotype of the 'threatening young male'.

- News and feature articles on asylum rely heavily on politicians, official figures and the police as sources of information and explanation. Asylum seekers and refugees feel alienated, ashamed and sometimes threatened as a result of the overwhelmingly negative media coverage of asylum. Asylum seekers and refugees are not hostile to the media, in spite of the negative coverage, and many describe their sense of duty to speak out and highlight human rights abuses in their own countries and to counter the myths about refugees in the UK.
- The media fails to adequately reflect the experience of refugee women in Britain. Asylum seekers and refugees are reluctant to complain about inaccurate or prejudicial reporting. Interviewees expressed a mixture of doubt that their views would be accurately represented and concern about the consequences of being seen to complain.

Figure 8: *What's the Story* (Article 19)

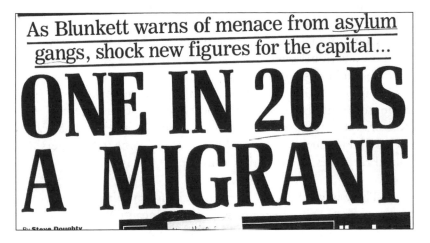

Buchanan et al write about their concerns, such as the links between government discourses, media discourses and the impact on asylum seekers and refugees:

> Press releases from the Home Office speak principally in negative terms of 'extending and securing Britain's borders', 'searching vehicles to root out would-be clandestine' and 'clamping down on benefit shopping'. Policy is presented as a series of combative measures

designed to weed out those who 'abuse the asylum system' and to prevent 'illegal immigrants' from entering the country in the first place in order to free up resources and help 'genuine refugees'. But are these definitions so clear-cut? Are we being informed by the media or merely having our prejudices confirmed? Are government policies really being questioned? How does media coverage reflect the views of the subjects of this debate – asylum seekers and refugees living in Britain – and how does it impact on their daily lives? (Buchanan et al, 2003, pp 12-13)

Finney (2003a, 2003b) found that local press portrayals tend to follow national coverage, with a focus on 'numbers of asylum seekers, the use of negative and sensationalist language. Flood metaphors are frequently used. Headlines are often misleading and can be inaccurate' (2003b, pp 13-14). Finney did find some variations in local press reporting, with the most sensitive and balanced reporting where there was a dedicated asylum reporter and where there were good links between the local press and local refugee sector. Crucially, following other research, the role of the press in setting agendas for debate on asylum issues was a key issue in the links between local attitudes and press portrayals.

Greenslade (2005) provides an illuminating history of press responses to migration from the postwar reception of Jews fleeing Nazism to the 1950s 'race' riots and present-day reception of 'asylum seekers' contextualised within the lack of welcome to 'strangers' and mixed responses by the mainstream press:

> There was little newspaper sympathy for the plight of Jews trying to come to terms with the holocaust. When Jews complained about anti-Semitism some of the comment was hostile and unpleasant, with particularly bad examples in the provincial press: one referred to 'aggressive and cock-a-hoop post-war Jewry' while another urged Jews to acquire 'thicker skins'. (Greenslade, 2005, p 16)

Using a case study from the 1950s riots, Greenslade illustrates 'how newspapers, either by exaggerating race disputes or covering them in such a way as to suggest that migrants were the cause of trouble, helped to set the political agenda which led to immigration legislation' (2005, p 17). And in the wake of the Race Relations Act 1968, Greenslade documents Enoch Powell's speech to his Wolverhampton constituents and the mixed responses by both the left and right wing press:

> He referred to 'wide-eyed, grinning piccaninnies' and, in a classical allusion to the River Tiber, spoke of it 'foaming with much blood'.... We must be mad, literally mad as a nation, to be permitting the annual inflow of some 50,000 dependants, for the most part the material of the future growth of the immigrant-descended population....
> (Greenslade, 2005, p 19)

The Sunday Mirror compared Powell to Alf Garnett, a racist character in a popular TV show 'Till death us do part'. *The Sunday Times* described it as crude and inflammatory and predicted a race war. *The News of the World* stated: "'... most people in this country will agree with him", and concluded, in capital letters: "WE CAN TAKE NO MORE COLOURED PEOPLE. TO DO SO, AS MR POWELL SAYS, IS MADNESS" ... and *The Sunday Telegraph* columnist, and associate editor, Peregrine Worsthorne argued that voluntary repatriation was "the only honest course"' (Greenslade, 2005, p 19).

Both Edward Heath (former Conservative leader) and *The Express* stated that whatever the deficiencies of the statistics and exaggeration of language, he was only expressing the anxieties and feelings of a large number of the population (Greenslade, 2005, p 20). Yet Bob Edwards, editor of *The People*, called for Powell's resignation. Greenslade documents that Edwards received 127 letters opposing his view and only three in support. Edwards 'published a picture which showed 50 hospital workers of varying hues and of 47 different nationalities under the headline: "Dear Enoch Powell, if you ever have to go into hospital, you'll be glad of people like these..."' (2005, p 20).

Greenslade found that between 2001 and 2005

> there has been an identifiable competition between certain papers to see which can attract the greatest number of readers by publishing the most hostile stories, features and opinions about asylum-seekers and refugees. This distasteful contest has been most obvious at the *Daily Mail*, *Daily Express* and *The Sun*. (Greenslade, 2005, p 21)

Key themes include fears about the 'influx' of Roma. The terminology used by newspapers such as 'tidal waves' and 'asylum crisis' made links between asylum seekers and crime, drugs and devastation of neighbourhoods. Inflated figures were given describing the resources wasted on asylum seekers, and strong links between Islamic fundamentalism asylum seekers and terrorism. Moreover, *The News of the World* reported on

> Britain's £1bn asylum bill alleged that the housing of asylum-seekers will cost the British taxpayer more than £1 billion in a year. That's £33 for every one of the nation's 30 million taxpayers ... enough to build up to TEN 450-bed new hospitals or pay off the combined £200 million debt of the NHS five times over. It could also pay for 50,000 new teachers, 40,000 beat police officers or 80 secondary schools. (Greenslade, 2005, p 22)

Greenslade's conclusion is that 'newspapers appeal to deep-seated racist and/or xenophobic views among their readerships' and so, 'however well-intentioned and committed we might be to doing something positive towards asylum-seekers and refugees, we have to recognise the immensity of the task' (Greenslade, 2005, p 29). Moreover, 'negative, inaccurate, distorted reporting on a large and frequent scale is bound to awaken feelings among readers that may otherwise have lain dormant' (2005, p 29). And the 'drip-drip-drip of negative stories and alarmist headlines in papers that command the attention of a huge swathe of the adult British population cannot but have a negative impact on public opinion' (2005, p 29).

Of course we do not read or listen to the news in a vacuum. And while current media stories link migration to security, Islamic fundamentalism and terrorism, and there is much evidence of local resistance to the location of detention centres (Hubbard, 2005), there are also more sympathetic approaches, as Finney (2003a, 2003b) discusses. Such sympathetic approaches occur most often where there are positive links between refugee communities and organisations, with local reporters stressing more positive impacts of diversity in local communities in addition to sympathetic journalists challenging the hegemonic view. Greenslade (2005) suggests that we should all act against this by writing to the Press Complaints Commission, and that 'groups representing asylum-seekers and refugees must consolidate their efforts to develop a media strategy' (Greenslade, 2005, p 31). This would include making links with journalists; we should be putting pressure on editors and journalists through letters and blogs to constantly remind the press about their responsibilities and shortcomings and keep up constant pressure to do so.

The situation as described by the research evidence documented earlier, marked by the near absence of alternative voices of refugees and asylum seekers in the mainstream media, raises important ethico-political issues relating to the politics of representation and democracy given that the right to speak, to be heard and recognised, is a central aspect of social justice.

Much of the knowledge generated by advocacy groups suggests there is a need for alternatives to dominant media messages that construct refugees as a problem or threat and engage in a particular form of policy agenda setting. This alternative voice can dispel myths and promote a more empathic understanding. Bromley (2000, 2007) states that the overwhelmingly negative representation of asylum seekers/refugees perpetuates exclusionary processes and that it is vitally important to explore the issues by empowering and mediating alternative voices and experiences. This is not just a matter of increasing public understanding; it is also essential for developing a fuller academic appreciation of the failures of the asylum system. Social justice is, after all, developed and sustained through participatory democracy.

Making the Connections between arts, migration and diaspora:[2] the role of the alternative media?

As part of the Making the Connections: Arts, Migration and Diaspora Regional Network, a workshop organised by Roger Bromley (University of Nottingham) and Olga Bailey (Nottingham Trent University) focused on the role of alternative media as a response to the issues defined earlier. It was agreed at the launch event and all of the workshops that it is very important that refugee groups have space to represent themselves; this would feed into a politics of presence and representation as well as discourses of rights and recognition (Fraser, 1997; Bauman, 2001). In her report on the workshop, Bailey wrote:

> The premise of this workshop is two fold: firstly, migration is one of the most pressing issues of our times, in particular the dispossession of internationally displaced people.... Secondly, in the UK, as in other parts of the world, there is a paradox between the fact that refugees and asylum seekers have become one of the top political and media topics of the day, and the silent and tragic narrative of the predicament

of these people. These are stories that do not often reach, or even come close, to the top of the political/public agenda. On the contrary, misperceptions and misinformation lie at the heart of how asylum seekers and refugees are received and perceived, with the mainstream media playing a key role in filling what is often a vacuum of accurate information on the dynamics of social change at the local level. Regrettably, the media tend to fill in this gap with misrepresentations and the demonisation of asylum seekers and refugees. These misperceptions and misrepresentations are largely forged along the fault lines of race, ethnicity and religion, whereby displaced people become victims of intolerance. (Bailey, 2007, p 1)

Given the fact of media agenda setting and that 'we live in a world of mediated experiences, the media in part shapes our "common sense" and views about asylum seekers, refugees and migrants' and

because the centrality and power of mainstream media is so pervasive, the role of alternative spaces of mediated communication are acquiring increasing importance as means of representation of public and private ideas and action, and as their stimuli. Alternative media thus, have an important role in mediating the asylum seekers' life stories and in contesting their systematic exclusion from the public sphere and their relegation into 'zones of silence'. (Bailey, 2007, pp 1-2)

At the workshop alternative media were discussed as a space for supporting and reinforcing cultural identities and diversity and for facilitating spaces for self-presentation and the rights of communication. Additionally there was a real need to counter the way that the mainstream media could desensitise people to important messages about asylum and migration such as the homogeneous representation of 'asylum' 'refugees'. Responses to this might include personalising stories to reflect the media representation of asylum seekers and highlighting differences such as cultural, gender and age-based differences. One of the workshop discussants argued that

there is a need to engage and educate the media about the issues affecting asylum seekers in order to get the right message across to the public. Specifically, in her experience, personalising their situation by using examples of individual asylum seekers' life-stories has facilitated a positive response from the locals. It is also important to make contacts with the local media – mainstream and alternative – to discuss issues of migrants' representation. She also suggested that it is important to be 'smarter' at engaging with the media by for example creating events that receive media attention. (Bailey, 2007, p 3)

Saeed (2007, p 182) confirms that a substantial amount of research documents hostile public opinion towards asylum seekers, yet when people encounter asylum seekers on a personal level there is greater tolerance and understanding. However, as Tyler (2006) shows, while we need to address and counter the 'xenophobic discourses that depict the asylum-seeker as a dehumanized, undifferentiated foreign mass, hoard, influx, etc' (Tyler, p 196), we must also be careful that in using humanitarian discourses to 'ask the public to recognize "the human face" of specific asylum-seekers, assuring us that "close up" they are "just like us"', we do not in fact simply use our agency to '"speak" on behalf of asylum seekers' (p 196). In doing so, we need to be careful that we do not project ourselves into the place of the 'other' and represent the 'other' as a 'victim', thereby 'eliding substantive differences', other ways of representing and speaking, so that differences are concealed in the singularity of such accounts that 'fetishize the refugee by universalising the condition of displacement' (Bailey, 2007, pp 197-8). Similarly, Salverson (2001, p 123) writes that there is a danger in perpetuating injustice in representations of the suffering of asylum seekers, and she calls this 'aesthetics of injury'. Adorno refers to this as the de-substantialisation of art – when suffering is consumed something of its horror is removed (1984, 1997).

Alternative media and diasporic voices: strategies for representation, participation and belonging

Leicester SAEMP is a web-based media project and television station that was launched by the Leicester Somali Education and Community Centre using support from the Community Cohesion Fund from Leicester City Council. SAEMP is now made up of a media project and a newspaper, and defines itself as a global community multimedia network and a universal virtual community comprehensive education institute. SAEMP serves a community of around 15,000 Somali people across the city and is a good example of the transnational reach of the alternative ethnic media, with listeners and participants across the globe.

The mission statement defines SAEMP as: connecting to Somali communities locally, nationally and internationally; supporting the integration of Somali people into mainstream Leicester and UK life; fostering inclusion and positive representations of Somali communities; reaching out to other communities to build positive relationships; and promoting mutual understanding, access and effective information sharing. They broadcast in as many languages as there are within Leicester. As such, SAEMP will minimise language and information barriers that currently exist for Somali and other communities in Leicester, creating an effective communications network.

SAEMP steering committee is made up of academics from regional universities, local policy makers and SAEMP board members. There are five key strands to SAEMP's activity including: a key focus on the education of young people and the wider Somali community; business and enterprise to foster new businesses and to reduce the unemployment of Somali people; community news/community cohesion that includes information sharing about a range of intra- and inter-community activities with a focus on community cohesion initiatives; sport and culture; and community empowerment. 'Information on health, housing and other social issues that affect families will be broadcast for the Somali community but will be equally accessible to and will benefit other communities' (Yar-Yari, personal communication with the CEO).

> The great flexibility of SAEMP NEWS is the fact that as a multimedia organization, information will be accessible, on Radio, Television, and Satellite and on line and in the near future on mobile phones as well. The possibilities are infinite, as SAEMP will seek to take advantage of IP technologies as they develop. This technological flexibility empowers people in communities with the greatest of opportunities to communicate effectively with public authorities and with each other. (www.saemp.org.uk)

Local communities are encouraged to get involved in local democratic processes, as illustrated in Figure 9.

Figure 9: SAEMP newsletter, July 2006

The Somali community in Leicester are a 'transnational' community with multiple affiliations in other European countries as well as Somalia. Marfleet (2006) urges us to think about transnational communities in relation to 'circuits of migration' and diasporas (scatterings) as 'networked communities'. Within the context of migration research he argues that three developments have been crucial to the growth of transnational communities. First, changes in new technologies of mass transport (international tourism, mass air transport); second, changes in the means of communication (virtual communication, satellite, internet and cyber environment); and finally, 'the generalisation worldwide of ideas about human entitlement' or human rights that 'require new frameworks of understanding' (Marfleet, 2006, p 216). 'New networks themselves play a role in shaping global movements, drawing in and re-circulating migrants as part of a process of flux and flow' (Marfleet, 2006, p 218).

Key themes emerging from SAEMP's focus on integration, community cohesion and empowerment via cultural associational and distributive aspects of social justice are:

- the role of global media in contributing to discourses of rights and social justice;
- the impact of local media organisations that have a global reach in contributing to public sphere discourses on social justice, citizenship and discourses of exclusion and inclusion;
- the possibility of such local/transnational organisation contributing to visions of social justice in a world marked by globalisation, humiliation and the regulation of modernity (Smith's 2006 concept of the triple helix).

This chapter has so far drawn attention to the lack of media self-representations of refugees/asylum seekers and the importance of challenging this by highlighting the lack of a platform for subaltern voices and attempts to overcome this. Methodologically it is important to challenge the approach currently taken in the West, especially in relation to asylum policies, that result in the instrumental rejection of people who are vulnerable, for this is tantamount to abandoning responsibilities for humanitarian protection by closing/tightening/restricting border controls. Elaborate legal frameworks have been developed and dominant media messages are involved not only in agenda setting but also in representing new arrivals as a menace, as aliens, as 'others' violating the borders of the nation.

I also reinforce messages from earlier chapters, that there is a need to accept the impact of migration forced and free and the emergence of transnational communities; that we need to build decent institutions, based on social justice, equality, global citizenship as well as developing interventions that address the multiple impacts of 'othering'. The role of media institutions is vital in this regard, in representing a counter public sphere, and in contributing to recognitive and communicative ethics.

Hence the focus of scholars, researchers, journalists and media specialists must address both the current lack of refugee voices in mainstream media as well as develop specific strategies that take into account the complex realities of refugee experiences (Harindranath, 2007). Broadcast media are generally held to be the main contributors to the functioning of a public sphere in democratic societies, even if such an argument is used primarily to point out the inadequacies of television and radio in terms of their social roles. However, there has been sufficient research that suggests the centrality of diasporic media to the maintenance of cultural cohesion among immigrant communities. The role of broadcasting and the public sphere are therefore crucial in the development of strategies for representing refugee experiences and exploring/providing a platform for the development of transnational cultural formations and belonging.

The main issue in terms of representation and refugee experience is the provision of perspectival diversity that redresses the prevailing lack of representation from such communities in mainstream media (Harindranath, 2007). For example, in relation to the 'big' and 'small' media, the former, in the shape of satellite and cable television, cinema and radio, require more policy interventions to address the problem. The latter, in relatively low-cost, low maintenance forms such as pamphlets, podcasts and internet sites, provide the opportunity for refugee communities to display their own narratives that highlight their experiences and concerns. Moreover, the internet and Skype is the main connection linking transnational communities and people dispersed across the globe, serving to link such communities to their homeland in complex and productive ways.

Broadcasting and the role of the public sphere

> Broadcasting now has a major role – perhaps the crucial role – to play in 're-imagining the nation'; not by seeking to re-impose a unity and homogeneity which has long since departed, but by becoming the 'theatre' in which [Britain's] cultural diversity is produced, displayed, represented, and the forum in which the terms of its associative life together are negotiated. This ... remains broadcasting's key public cultural role – and one which cannot be sustained unless there is a public service idea and a system shaped in part by public service objectives to sustain it. (Hall, 1993, quoted in Born, 2004, p 507)

Georgina Born suggests that the challenge, in an age of diversity, is to contribute to the formation of a more adequate communicative democracy than we have yet seen, by providing a 'unifying space in which plurality can be performed, one in which the display and interplay of diverse perspectives can animate and reshape the imagined community of the nation' (Born, 2004, p 517), offering on the one hand (drawing on John Dewey), 'the universal orientation, the moral and often consensual address of generalist public service channels and of "impartial" news functions', and on the other (drawing on Stuart Hall), 'a rich array of communicative channels for the self representation, participation and expressive narrativisation of minority and marginalised groups, addressed both to and among those groups and to the majority' (Born, 2004, p 517).

Although her thesis focuses on the role of public broadcasting and the BBC in particular, she asks 'what is the role of public broadcasting in a word of conflictual pluralism, concretised in the "war on terror"?' (2004, p 507). She answers that 'the face of international conflicts and domestic tensions, if it offers ... [an] independent arena for staging a "politics of complex cultural, dialogue" that is required in order to cultivate commonality, reciprocity and toleration' (Born, 2004, p 508).

Of course, the role of public service broadcasting mediating such processes as nationhood and identification, 'the realities of multi-ethnic, multi-cultural and multi-faith societies' (2004, p 512), is complex and problematic, but for Born, public service broadcasting takes a leading role in maintaining and reshaping the boundaries that define the national community – engaging in 'a dialectic with goverment, delegated by it to secure the conditions for democracy's expanded well-being' (Born, 2004, p 515).

In looking to the future, and acknowledging competing media outlets 'such as international news, entertainment channels, alternative online news sites, transnational satellite networks and minority media with their often pronounced ethnic, territorial and ideological allegiances' (2004, p 513), Born argues for the existence of 'channels for counter-public to speak to counter-public as well as the integration into an (always imperfect) unitary pubic sphere' (Born, 2004, p 515).[3] Born asks 'how can the BBC orchestrate a pluralist communicative ethics?' She responds by arguing that from the variety of current strategies it is possible to draw out five structural forms of mediated exchange that together 'flesh out the complex cultural dialogue demanded by present circumstances' (Born, 2004, p 515).

First, the established form in which divergent and minority perspectives are hosted by the majority. Second, inter-cultural communication – when minority speaks to majority and other minorities. Born gives as examples cross-platform events such as the BBC's asylum day, video diary format on both television and the web, Asian sitcoms, drama or current affairs. The third form is intra-cultural communication, such as when minority speaks to minority or to itself via radio, video, cable, satellite TV or the net. Examples given are Asian and black digital radio stations and the Australian national network SBS, where a 'continuous flow of niche broadcasts serving each minority community by turn, offers another model' (Born, 2004, p 516). SAEMP is a clear example of this format. Fourth, territorially based local and regional community networks, served by all media such as the BBC's Hull interactive project, as well as experiments in online democracy. The BBC Capture Wales project using digital story techniques is a good example. The fifth form 'is when issue based, non territorial communities of interest are linked by point-to-point networks ... primarily associated with the net' (Born, 2004, p 516). SAEMP are a useful illustration of this, as is the Making the Connections: Arts, Migration and Diaspora regional network. Taken together, these forms, for Born, affirm the BBC's inventiveness 'in orchestrating a plural public media space' (Born, 2004, p 516).

Bailey et al (2007) draw attention to the fact that diasporic media are not necessarily more inclusive and democratic than mainstream and national media. Indeed, many aim to maximise profits as well as audiences, and others, like SAEMP, are committed to playing a role in community development. What is particular to diasporic media institutions and organisations is 'their growing cultural presence in cosmopolitan societies' and the fact that

> diasporic media's presence within western mediascapes destabilises the dominant hierarchies of control over cultural resources. The symbolic presence and real availability of different media open up new possibilities for expression and representation and thus of imagining the self and belonging within and across space. (Bailey et al, 2007, p 2)

The work of FOMACS (Forum on Migration and Communication), based in the Centre for Transcultural Research and Media Practice at the Dublin Institite of Technology, is an excellent example of a collaborate public media project that seeks to influence social change and public policy with migrants (see www.fomacs.org).

These examples may take us one step forward towards social justice and cultural citizenship as a counter to forces and processes of humiliation, and offer possibilities for fostering a politics of recognition (Taylor, 1994; Fraser, 1997; Harindranath, 2007) and recognitive community. As Lister (2007) writes, the values of inclusive citizenship emerging from 'accounts from below' include: justice; recognition; self-determination; solidarity; and, I would add, human dignity. Stevenson (2003), quoted in Lister (2007, p 51) defines cultural citizenship as being concerned with questions of imagination, identity and belonging, and that struggles for inclusive citizenship are about the demand for cultural respect. Hence, the 'very essence of cultural citizenship lies in a genuinely cosmopolitan dialogue underpinned by the shift from identity politics to a politics of difference' (Lister, 2007, p 52). To what extent the alternative and minority ethnic media and some quarters of the mainstream media can support these processes towards a recognitive theory of community and collective belonging is the subject of further research.

Notes

[1] His paper goes on to explore alternative discourses for a potentially radical imaginary through analysis of four films.

[2] A regional network convened by Maggie O'Neill and Phil Hubbard and funded by the AHRC; see www.lboro.ac.uk/departments/ss/global_refugees/

[3] The alternative is the extreme segmentation of the commercial media in the US.

FIVE

Diasporic communities: citizenship, social justice and belonging

This chapter picks up on the methodological issues raised in Chapters Three and Four and documents a research trajectory conducted over a 10-year period using ethno-mimetic research, PAR and PA methods with new arrival groups and communities situated in the asylum–migration–community nexus.

Chapter Three stressed the benefits of working in participatory ways using arts-based research with refugees and asylum seekers to: represent lived experiences; claim a voice; raise awareness of relations of humiliation, exclusion as well as inclusion; and challenge exclusionary processes and practices. I suggested that such methodologies can support the articulation of identity and belonging for those situated in the asylum–migration nexus and that this is vitally important to the development of dialogue, a recognitive theory of community, cultural citizenship and social justice.

The research discussed in this chapter includes a series of Arts and Humanities Research Board (AHRB)-funded research projects: 'Global refugees: exile, displacement and belonging' (1999-2001); and a linked AHRB-funded research exchange (1999-2001) 'Towards a cultural strategy for working with refugees and persons seeking asylum in the East Midlands'; Making the Connections: Arts, Migration and Diaspora Regional Network (2006-08); and a knowledge transfer fellowship 'Transnational communities: towards a sense of belonging' (2008-09). All were conducted in partnership with migrant groups and four community arts organisation in the East Midlands region.[1] All of these projects are underpinned by the principles of PAR and PA that include a focus on inclusion, participation, valuing all local voices, as well as being interventionist, action-oriented and interpretive. All illustrate that in the collaborative process between migrant, artist and social researcher, a 'thick' (Geertz, 1973) 'understanding' (Bourdieu, 1996) of the lived experiences of processes of migration, belonging and transnational communities emerge that challenge identity thinking.[2] This brings an approach to knowledge production as collaboratively made, not found, which also loosens the knowledge/power axis involved in knowledge production and 'expertness', and sidesteps the thorny issues raised by Tyler (2006) and Salverson (2001) in representing the 'other' (see Chapter Four).

Committed to fostering an interpretive role that includes creating spaces for the marginalised/subaltern to speak for themselves, the combination of art and ethnography, as ethno-mimesis, enabled the production of a more sensuous understanding of social relations and lived experience through the inclusion of visual, poetic, performance texts in the research process. By representing ethnographic data in artistic form we can access a richer understanding of the complexities of lived experience that may also throw light on broader structures and processes. The outcomes of this work can reach a wider population, beyond academic communities, and facilitate understanding, interpretation and action as praxis in relation to the issues of asylum and migration.

I argue that this work supports processes of cultural citizenship[3] and social justice and connects with principles of a recognitive theory of community as part of a radical democratic process and imaginary. All four projects are examples of performative praxis in that they seek to challenge exclusionary discourses that include negative images and stereotypes and offer representational challenges that are transformative, which challenge identity thinking and represent the multiple subject positions and multitiered nature of transnational belonging.

Wider social context to the research

The wider social context in which forced migration takes place (as discussed in Chapters One and Two) involves identity thinking, mis-recognition, the impact of globalisation and processes of humiliation. At national level the governance of migration and forced migration involves conflict and ambiguity; discourses and legislation on human rights exist alongside a focus on protecting borders, speeding up returns and holding people (including children and families) in detention centres. Discourses of fairness and rights exist alongside regressive discourses; for some this means 'Welcome to Britain' and for others 'Go Home'. As we found in Chapter Four, the alterity of the asylum seeker involves mis-recognition, 'otherness', fostering suspicion of the 'stranger'. These exclusionary processes promulgate hegemonic ideologies and discourses around rights to belonging and citizenship, perceived access to resources (redistribution) and mis-recognition.

In the four projects documented later, biographical research involved the production of narrative and meanings that offer resistance to the dominant power/knowledge axis related to the current politics of representation found in the previous chapters. The combination of biography and art (ethno–mimesis) becomes a potential space for transformative possibilities that may facilitate dialogue, discussion and attunement and may support processes of social justice via a politics of recognition. The art/performance process is creative and relational (Jones, 2006). This kind of work, underpinned by principles of participatory research, can support and create spaces for the marginalised to speak for themselves as subjects and objects of their own narratives involving concepts of mutual recognition, cultural citizenship (Pakulski, 1997), publicness and egalization (Lindner, 2006).

Global refugees: exile, displacement and belonging

First, as documented in Chapter Three, 'Global refugees: exile, displacement and belonging' explored the transformative role of art and the methodological approach of working with artists to conduct ethnographic research with refugees and asylum seekers as critical theory in practice. The research was conducted in 1999 with Bosnian communities in the East Midlands and Afghan communities in London in collaboration with City Arts Nottingham and Exiled Writers Ink, London. The aim was to develop alternative forms of representing and raising awareness of the lived experiences of refugees and asylum seekers using life history interviews represented in visual and poetic forms. Community arts organisations and participants including community co-researchers were the co-creators of the research.

This research uncovered the need for a cultural strategy to support the inclusion of asylum seekers and refugees in the arts and cultural infrastructures of the region and the second project 'Towards a cultural strategy for working with refugees and persons seeking asylum in the East Midlands' was conducted with City Arts and Refugee Action. The Arts Council East Midlands supported the research recommendations of the cultural strategy and funding was allocated to a conference and subsequently a regional arts NGO for supporting exiled artists. Refugees and asylum seekers were also included in arts and cultural infrastructures in the region.

At this time some colleagues and myself were commissioned to undertake research on new arrivals' access to education (O'Neill et al, 2003), and then new arrivals' access to employment, training and social enterprise (O'Neill with Galli and Aldridge, 2004). During this phase of research I was struck by the gap or lack of fit between the horizontal and vertical processes of social inclusion, that is, what was going on at grass-roots levels (much excellent work using art, culture and community development) and the gaps in connection with strategic or vertical levels of policy making (the responsible authorities who make decisions about policy and practice). Successful funding was gained from the AHRC in 2006 for a regional network, called Making the Connections: Arts, Migration and Diaspora,[4] to explore and address this issue.

Making the Connections: Arts, Migration and Diaspora regional network

The Making the Connections: Arts, Migration and Diaspora regional network aimed to collaborate with refugee/asylum and micro-communities, arts organisations, support organisations, the Arts Council, policy makers and academics in order to examine the transformative role of arts and culture in fostering integration and belonging for new arrivals in the East Midlands and to build on the strong regional work on going in the region with diasporic communities to create synergies/collaborations across disciplinary boundaries, multiple layers of governance and lived experience. The Network addressed questions of artistic access and cultural inclusion, bridging academic, voluntary and service sector providers in the search for new strategies of participation that might (a) enhance the lives of recent arrivals in the English East Midlands; (b) stimulate high-quality interdisciplinary research drawing on the resources and expertise in the region; (c) facilitate connection, communication and feed into public policy; and (d) contribute to public awareness of issues facing new arrivals.

The Network was launched at a day-long conference on 26 April 2006 where participants[5] identified themes and areas in the East Midlands to act as focus for 10 workshops; explored where the potential lay for collaboration between migrants, artists and those working with newly arrived migrants; and outlined a timetable for subsequent workshops taking place during the next 24 months. Communities of interest formed at this launch event and continued to develop around certain issues, many of these groups taking responsibility for organising and running the subsequent nine workshops/seminars. People volunteered to lead the events, from community groups, NGOs, universities and policy makers, including the Arts Council (see the full report on www.makingtheconnections.info).

Nine workshops or seminars were organised between September 2006 and June 2008, with over 400 people taking part in the programme. An end of programme conference was held at Loughborough University on 3–4 July 2008 to share the work we had achieved together and to celebrate the process and outcomes of the Network with a wider audience made up of migrants, academics, the voluntary, statutory, arts and community sector and policy makers. A website was created to disseminate the work. Conferences, publications and reports were produced. The nine workshops/seminars (agreed at the launch event) were as follows:

- 'What is art? Eurocentric and diasporic processes of art practice', organised by Arts Council East Midlands and the Peepul Centre, Leicester.
- 'Therapeutic features of working with the arts', organised by the University of Derby.
- 'Learning in the real world: using local diversity to promote inter-cultural understanding', organised by Soft Touch Arts cooperative and the Long Journey Home, a regional organisation for artists in exile.
- 'Refugee lifelines', organised by NIACE and Artists in Exile.
- 'Destitution and the role of ethnic minority media', organised by Nottingham Trent University and University of Nottingham.
- 'Distant voices: migrant workers, representation and the arts', organised by Culture East Midlands.
- 'Telling tales: migration, identity and the postcolonial', organised by University of Northampton in collaboration with local voluntary sector organisations.
- 'Making connections: helping asylum seekers through arts inclusion' Conference, organised by Dreamers, an unaccompanied young asylum seekers youth project, Leicestershire Youth Service and Charnwood Arts, a community arts organisation.
- 'Women and migration: art, politics and policy', organised by Loughborough University, Department of Social Sciences and Business School, in collaboration with Artists in Exile, Refugee Action and NIACE.[6]

An image makers subgroup formed after the launch event[7] consisting of a group of artists working with visual media who came together to explore ways of promoting integration, understanding, and participation through visual arts projects that creatively address issues of diaspora and migration in collaboration with migrants' groups and to bid for practice-based funding. This included the development of relationships and connections that supported and mentored exiled artists and fed directly into the subsequent research project that explored transnational communities: 'Towards a sense of belonging'.

Figure 10: Making the Connections: Arts, Migration and Diaspora regional network launch event

Figure 11: 'Making connections' organised by Dreamers support project

Figure 12: 'Women and migration: art, politics and policy' seminar

The aim of the Making the Connections: Arts, Migration and Diaspora regional network was to examine (using PAR) the transformative role of arts and culture in fostering integration and belonging for new arrivals in the East Midlands at the levels of history, experience, theory and policy and to build on the strong regional work of the Arts Council East Midlands, academics in regional universities, practitioners and policy makers in the arts, public and voluntary sector, artists and diasporic communities to create synergies/collaborations across disciplinary boundaries, multiple layers of governance and lived experience. The Network also generated recommendations for regional and national policy in relation to issues of migration, diaspora, identity and belonging. More significantly, perhaps, the Network addressed questions of artistic access and cultural inclusion in ways that sought to enhance the lives and well-being of recent arrivals in the English East Midlands.

At the final conference, 22 national and international speakers and artists participated from the arts, academic, voluntary and statutory sector organisations. The 80+ attendees were migrants, academics, researchers, research students, practitioners from statutory and voluntary sector organisations and policy makers.[8] Papers written and presentations delivered for the end of programme conference document the range and depth of involvement and also the impact on the development of people's work/research as a consequence of involvement in the Network and seminars/workshops. In sum, the project enabled dialogue and meaningful and perhaps unquantifiable connections between newly arrived groups, arts organisations, practitioners, policy makers and those within academic communities and regional universities, producing new understandings of arrival and underlining that a participatory approach opens up debate and dialogue, produces new knowledge, connections and understandings rather than reaffirming academics' pre-established views of the world.

The network has made significant contributions to understanding the lives and experiences of recent arrivals to the East Midlands, publicising and disseminating this through arts-based practice and workshop events in which those outside academia have been fully involved (transport and other financial support was made available for unwaged and low-wage delegates). This has included groups with whom the researchers already had contacts, including women's asylum groups and Artists in Exile, but the implications of the project are much wider given the range of recently arrived groups represented in the workshop programme including both 'forced' and 'voluntary' migrants.[9]

The project advanced participatory methods as well as partnerships and collaborations across the horizontal and vertical processes of social inclusion in the East Midlands region. One outcome was a bid for further monies from the AHRC to leave a sustainable legacy for the region as an outcome of this and earlier work. A successful knowledge transfer fellowship project was launched in January 2008 as a direct outcome of relationships built through the Network. The partners in the fellowship included four community arts organisations and the Departments of Social Sciences and Geography at Loughborough University.[10]

Transnational communities: towards a sense of belonging

'Transnational communities: towards a sense of belonging' was a knowledge transfer fellowship that emerged from the Making the Connections: Arts, Migration and Diaspora regional network, funded by the AHRC and led by a partnership between Loughborough University and four community arts organisations and communities of new arrivals, including Artists in Exile.

The knowledge transfer fellowship project aimed to deliver social and cultural benefits to refugee/asylum seekers/migrants in the East Midlands region as well as wider communities by developing three strands of participatory research and arts activity that contributed to public awareness, examined the role of arts and cultural activity in social policy agendas and facilitated knowledge, communication and understanding *with* new arrivals. The three strands of activity were as follows.

First, a diversity pool event (an event bringing together artists and programmers/schools and community organisations that employ artists for various projects, led by City Arts Nottingham in collaboration with the partners) where artists showcased their work, met other artists as well as programmers, schools, arts development officers and local authority representatives, thus aiding not only connection and communication but the employment of artists. A directory/database resource of refugee/asylum/migrant artists and artists with expertise in working with diasporic groups/communities also emerged from this event. This strand of knowledge transfer developed out of the needs/wants of artists in exile and statutory and voluntary sector organisations wanting artists to work in their projects/programmes.[11] The event also enabled exhibiting artists to connect with one another and celebrated their diversity. The event sought to build capacity and aid the professional development of artists as well as connect people through dialogue and the sharing of art forms.

Second, an electronic web resource was developed as an outcome of the PAR activities of the AHRC-funded Regional Network and partner organisations and to house the database of artists, led by Charnwood Arts (www.beyondbordersuk.org).[12] The aim of the website resource is to build and maintain a database of artists who have arrived in this country from around the world alongside regional artists, in order: to promote their work, explore the issues they face and to support work with new and established 'arrival' communities.

Third, a participatory arts/research project, 'Towards a sense of belonging', that took place simultaneously in four geographical areas of the region (Derby, Nottingham, Loughborough and Leicester). Launched by a series of guided walks,[13] following the arts practice of Misha Myers (artist, educator and consultant to the walks), the project explored relationships between cartography (mapping), home, emplacement and belonging in the lives of new arrivals. PA/ participatory research workshops explored and documented visually and poetically the various senses of belonging and the themes and issues raised during the walks and launch event. Narrative and visual outcomes were exhibited at the Bonington Gallery, Nottingham, in January 2009[14] and subsequently at three regional and local conferences. They are also documented on the Making the Connections gallery pages (www.makingtheconnections.info) and online at the *Guardian Society* pages.

The arts/research workshops were designed to put art at the heart of social research and explored the issues raised on the walks. The arts/research workshops took place in each city/town between June and December 2008, led by City Arts, Charnwood Arts, Long Journey Home, Charnwood Arts and Soft Touch Arts community arts organisations, in collaboration with myself and Phil Hubbard (Loughborough University).

The arts practice communicates what *belonging* means to those participating in the research, exploring their experiences and feelings about home, dislocation, place making, belonging and friendship. The arts practice shows what it is like to live in Nottingham, Derby, Leicester and Loughborough for new arrivals as well as highlighting the perilous journeys people had made to seek freedom and safety from nations including Zimbabwe, the Democratic Republic of Congo, DRC, Iraq, Iran, Eritrea, Albania, Turkey and Afghanistan. The emotional and physical impact of these journeys, and the experiences of 'double consciousness' and being 'home away from home' are represented, alongside the rich cultural contributions and skills migrants bring to the region's cities, towns, cultures and communities.

Walking as ethnography and arts practice

The guided walks involved a participatory, performative process of reflection, conversation and embodied movement/mapping following maps created by the new arrivals. We make places through an embodied process of finding our way (O'Neill and Hubbard, 2010). The walks were led and directed by 'new arrivals' (important given that the voices of new arrivals are often mediated by others), so they held situational authority. Following Misha's guidance, people drew a map from a place they called home to a special place and they then walked the map in Derby, Nottingham, Leicester and Loughborough with a co-walker. Co-walkers were policy makers, practitioners, residents and Network members. What emerged through the process of walking and talking and subsequent reflection at a post-walk lunch event was that a relational, sensuous, kinaesthetic, democratic and participatory process of collaborative co-production leading to 'connection', 'attunement' and 'understanding' took place in the space of the walks and afterwards when we met together as a group.[15]

What Misha calls 'making place through process' emerged – a performing of emplacement, not as a linear process but a dialectical, complex process eliciting multiple modalities of experience – 'between here and there and nowhere', 'home away from home', not only for the new arrivals but also for the co-walkers. In my walk with an exiled artist I saw Derby through new eyes; listening to him talk I experienced the significance of the church that reminded him of a time as a small child out walking with his father, the layers of meaning (and time and space) involved in his multiple journeys before arriving in the UK and also

Figure 13: Walking a map in the Congo in Derby

Figure 14: Sharing a walk in Kurdistan in Derby

in the UK as a result of the Home Office process of dispersal, and the devastating losses that mark the life of a refugee from war-torn areas.

Certain things reminded the walkers of home and connected them with 'home' and here: rivers, birds, trees, sky, monuments, places of worship, as well as objects or people that made them feel at home. It reinforced the fact that people make places, but the processes involved in belonging are deeply relational, and friends, networks and support are crucial. The physical, embodied process of walking, remembering/ feeling/sensing/being, is inherently performative. It is also relational/ collaborative and opens up a discursive space. For one walker what made him feel at home was

> 'the freedom, the opportunities I have, the friends around me, the rights, you know, the basic rights, yes, these things made me fall in love with the land and makes me to feel I am belong to this place and this place is needing me you know.'

The process of walking and talking in a subject–subject relationship (and so avoiding or minimising the power relationship that can be present in orthodox in-depth interviews) facilitates a process that involves layers of meaning and interpretation. The walks were followed up with arts/research workshops (ethno-mimesis) evolving praxis as purposeful knowledge, which tell us something about what it is to feel 'at home' and 'a sense of belonging' in a relational and phenomenological sense, which had an impact on visitors to the exhibition and challenged identity thinking, stereotyping and labelling (O'Neill and Hubbard, 2010).[16]

The process of mapping, walking and making art to express belonging is also about claiming a space and presenting complex stories and experiences in artistic, visual and poetic form, thus claiming a creative space, voice, a personal and political space. The workshops evoke a 'potential space' (Winnicott, 1982), a third space between ethnography and arts practice. I have suggested in earlier work (O'Neill, 2008) that in exploring the in-betweenness, the hyphenated, hybrid space between ethnography and art, we may occupy a third space, a potential space/dialogic space where transformative possibilities and visual and textual products can emerge through 'subjective–reflexive feeling' (Witkin, 1974) that may feed in to cultural politics and praxis. It may help processes of social justice via a politics of recognition, thereby countering the mis-recognition of the asylum seeker, refugee, migrant – the 'other'. This 'potential' space also provides a nurturing space, which can be therapeutic for all involved.

This knowledge transfer activity sought to realise the potential of our separate and combined research by enhancing relationships between the partners, cementing collaboration between the partner organisations and by exploring the role of art in social research, in engaging in interpretation and interventions. Working with ethnographic methods, PAR and PA, the partners took forward the key aims of the Regional Network.[17]

A sense of belonging

In one city we worked with a women's group who were supported by Refugee Action. This group was made up of asylum seekers and refugees, all of whom had children. A crèche was provided for the children. Two artists delivered a range of arts workshops including textiles, sound, word and narrative, that enabled women to learn new skills, explore their creativity and what home and belonging mean to them. The processes involved introduced new skills, reinforced skills they already had and they were able to pass on their own knowledge and expertise to others. The artists documented the process through sound and imagery in an attempt to represent the atmosphere and essence of the sessions themselves. A key focus in this group was expressing a sense of 'home'. Using objects, textiles, food, sound and colour women developed work on what home and belonging mean to them and what it means to feel at home, bringing in transitional objects that had meaning for them such as fabric from 'home', a coffee pot, bowls and recipes. Sensuous knowing was created through the ethno-mimetic process linked to the sensory production of narratives, images around belonging, home and home making. The quotations that follow are fragments of narrative from the sound files which were part of the exhibition.

Figure 15: 'Home-made' (one of a series of postcards capturing images and text produced by women asylum seekers and refugees)

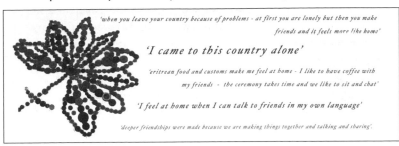

Artist Heather Connelly interviewed women and the supporters of the group and made a sound file for playing at the exhibition as part of the work the women created in the group:

> 'I have been working women's groups for three-and-a-half years and as a member of Amnesty and studying refugee law I became aware that refugee rights … there is a great injustice and some of the most vulnerable people in the world are coming here for sanctuary and they are being treated appallingly by the authorities.
>
> 'Women are isolated at home with their children, they are not allowed to work, most of women in this group have been through extremely traumatic situations before they came to this country so they are trying to deal with that while living in a hostile country.'

Figure 16: Postcard: 'Family'

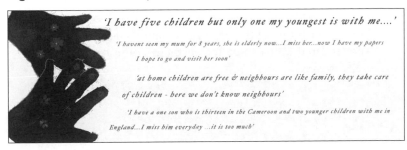

'My name is…. I am 25 I come from Albania. I have one daughter, my family live in Albania.'

'My name is…. my family are in Eritrea.'

'My name is…. I am from Cameroon and 31 years old. Living in UK is better than Africa, we have little bit freedom than Africa here you have free speech, only the government have free speech in my country…. I have three children, two boys and one girl, my first born is 13 and 2nd two and a daughter six months. My first born is in Africa living with mother in law. And two others they are with me here in England. It is hard. It is hard at the moment I do not have status. I did the appeal and so I have to wait.'

Figure 17: Postcard: 'Family'

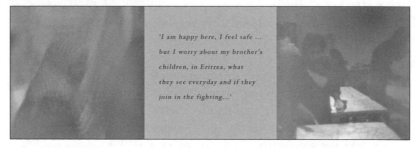

'I am happy here, I feel safe …
but I worry about my brother's
children, in Eritrea, what
they see everyday and if they
join in the fighting…'

'A lot of people in this country do not have a clue and you get the wrong perspective it does bring it home to you being here.'

'All refugees feel isolated but women particularly so and especially those with young children, people are not naturally friendly to them as general rule and Home Office treats people in such a way that their spirit will be broken. The crèche is one of the most important things as children were isolated … it is nice to see them come out of their shells as well.'

Figure 18: Postcard: 'Home'

'I go to college for hairdressers and then go to work. I am happy this year I have got my papers after eight years in this country. I miss my mum very much. Maybe next if they give me my nationality I will go....'

'I would like to be free in this country.... I want to be a nurse....'

'If I go back to my country I want to study police for in my country there is so much corrupt I would like to change that and be nice to the people. I have been learning English for two years, when I came here I could not say hello so I am so happy for my English is so much better.'

Figure 19: Postcard: 'Home'

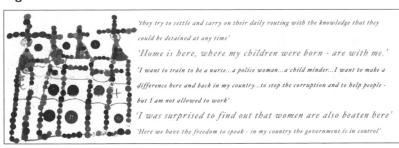

'I went with one lady to Birmingham to get something a registration card from the Home Office and because she was nervous on her own I said I will come with you so we went on the train ... it was the first time I have been to a Home Office immigration office, it was SO demeaning, we were searched and queued up. I can understand the reasons for doing it but it was not done with a smile it was so awful, and never having been in that situation it was awful ... you can understand them being upset ... if we could treat people with a bit of compassion a crumb of smile.... Outside this Home Office place there were two people like me retired and they were from churches standing outside the immigration place and they offered refreshments nearby in a church hall to people coming out and clothes for those who needed. They took us for a cup of tea. People don't come out of choice they come because they are desperate. You can treat people with respect can't you?'

'There are women who have lost family members in conflict or who have been politically active in their country and they are in trouble with the authorities as political dissent is not tolerated. One of the women was almost deported in January because the Home Office did not believe her account of the problems she had in the Cameroon even though there is a warrant out for her arrest in the Cameroon. This woman has been in prison in the Cameroon and her husband disappeared in prison.... I have got to know a lot of their previous life experience, it is very humbling to see how brave and courageous they are and to see how they are coping with life despite.... You cannot even begin to put yourself in their position, you cannot image what it is like.'

'I leave behind my family and friends my house everything, I miss the ground and the stone I miss everything, the ground where I grew up, everything.'

For the women who participated in the workshops a significant outcome was the relational dimension, the chance to talk, share, learn, engage in communication and build relationships and friendships as a consequence of involvement in the creative process. They enjoyed the opportunity to talk in English outside of the ESOL classes, while making art that included felting, silk screening, embroidery and painting. The women attended the private view, bringing children and friends, and were pleased to experience and see others experience their work in the gallery space.

'Home-made' was created for the exhibition to express their senses of belonging and what home meant to them.[18] The group wanted to evoke in a sensory way what home feels like – a table was covered with a cloth decorated in buttons; under the table were packages of

Figure 20: Postcard: 'Friendship'

'We are sewing and we are talking together about our problems. We have known each other two years now, but here we sew and talk we do not need to look and learn.'

cards with images and fragments of their narratives during the sessions and interviews, beautifully decorated with Heather's photographs and images of their art making; silk screen cloth decorated the gazebo and cushions were decorated with felting and embroidery. The sound files were played on a loop and could be heard while people sat in the tent.

In Loughborough, Charnwood Arts and Dreamers Youth Group led two guided walks with young people from Dreamers working in collaboration with youth workers (Dreamers are a youth group for unaccompanied young asylum seekers and they are supported by Loughborough Youth Affairs). These walks were organised differently, with young people taking us to places that were important to them – both good and not so good. Dreamers are currently supporting 150 young people. The initial walks, based on a model developed by Misha Myers, were followed with 'walking voices' sessions, providing the

Figure 21: 'Home-made' (installation)

Figure 22: Artists setting up 'Home-made'

young people with the opportunity to meet with friends and explore their experiences of Loughborough by going on walks in both town and rural locations. The initial walks and post-walk discussions with young people helped to decide what activities to develop in the workshops.

Charnwood Arts ran an extensive programme of activities with the Dreamers youth group in Loughborough: two drama workshops per week with theatre practitioners and a weekly creative session with visual artists. Young people were also taken to see a dance/theatre performance event and two of the young men also attended the Artists Diversity Pool (see page 150). The young people worked with artists Paul Gent and Amy Edwards, and theatre practitioners Gerry Flanagan and Sara Bailey. The group produced a scripted play performed at the private view of the exhibition in the Bonington Gallery. Artist Paul Gent produced 'I had a dream...' (a mixed media collage on a panel 415x135cm, 2008), based on his observations, narratives and the conversations held with the young people.

> '... the impact on the lads is fantastic, the group confidence levels of the lads, the conversations some engaged in at the private view with audience and the press. There is such a positive sense of the whole project.' (Andrew Lake, Dreamers)

Figure 23: 'I had a dream'

Figure 24: 'I had a dream'

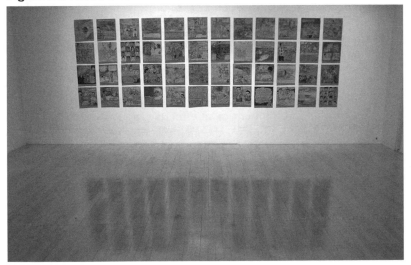

The value of the work was described by Kevin Ryan, CE of Charnwood Arts, as being in the process "the sharing that has occurred between people, the stories, and the walks have all added extra layers of meaning". Thus for Kevin Ryan "the project and process has developed understanding and knowledge between people – about arrival and the process as well as the sense of belonging, especially through the post-walk discussions". A key outcome was relationship building and enhanced cooperation at the local level with the Dreamers group and the Youth Service, but also most importantly with the partner arts organisations. Kevin also stated that overall his response to the exhibition was "so moving and it continues to reveal things to me as things sink in".

Soft Touch Arts ran a programme of activities with young people at a community college in Leicester that incorporated contributions from Chris, one of the artist-walkers. The sessions were led by artists Tove Dalenius and Helen Jewkes, and combined group discussion, games, music making, painting and drawing, photography, poetry and drama to develop dialogue around what makes a special place and how the young people have or have not developed a sense of belonging since arriving in Leicester. The work Soft Touch Arts developed for the exhibition was also interactive. People were invited to think about their special place and write about this and draw a self-portrait while looking in the dressing table mirror. These contributions were then placed in albums for other viewers to look through and contribute to.

Soft Touch Arts described their involvement in the overall research as leading to the development of an effective model for working with young new arrivals through local colleges and would incorporate this into other projects with young people. The project also facilitated the arts organisations' work with local colleges and stronger partnerships with other arts organisations in the region as well as links with refugee journalists:

> 'I think this is great for us as an art organisation to see the young people's work, an art gallery you know it raises the profile both of the work and for the young people, to see their work, to bring them in.' (Tove Dalenius, artist, Soft Touch Arts)

For the Long Journey Home regional Artists in Exile group the research and arts work promoted the contribution that they, as new arrival artists, can make with respect to their artistic contributions, mentoring contributions, as well as involvement and participation in community arts and arts development activities:

'I think we sent a good message to people about why we are crossing borders and seeking asylum despite all the dangers; we gave people some idea about our countries and the hidden realities of different regimes. We engaged people and talked about many issues, for example stoning. As a result I have been asked by two people to exhibit my paintings.' (Jeffer M.-Garib, artist, Long Journey Home)

Figure 25: 'A special place'

Figure 26: 'A special place' (detail)

Figure 27: 'A special place' (detail)

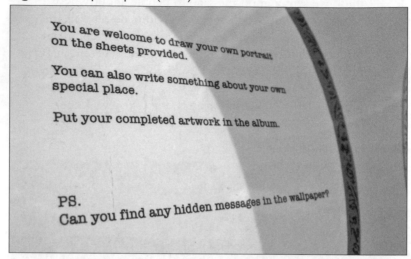

Figure 28: 'A special place' (detail)

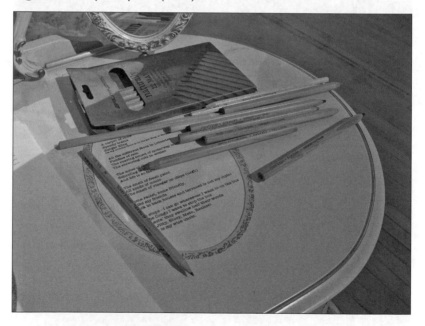

Six artists produced work based on the themes of the project, their experiences and those emerging from the guided walks (see Figures 29–32).

Figure 29: 'The journey of pain'

Figure 30: 'A sense of belonging' exhibition

Long Journey Home artists in Derby worked with an international women's group to produce art that represented the experiences of those seeking safety. The themes and focus for the arts project emerged from the guided walks and post-walk discussion.[19] In the post-walk discussion two people talked about their journeys by lorry. One woman had been separated from her husband, waited two months at Calais before an agent approached her with a possible route to safety: "Some of the agents they care for us, they understand." She travelled alone with her young daughter and son in the back of a lorry, packed in between the boxes, and she described this as a journey she had to make to keep them alive. Her journey to Calais was unbelievably tough and dangerous and at some points she feared for her children's lives and her own:

> 'The English people, they don't realise how much we suffer to get here. We had everything once. The English people, they judge us. They don't ask us why you come here, how was life there, and they don't know anything but they judge us, which is not nice. And today it was very good opportunity to just talk to someone.'

Figure 31: 'Untitled'

Figure 32: 'Neither here nor there'

This work illustrated in Figure 33 was accompanied by an explanatory text that told the reader that the textile pieces that covered the box-like structure were literally created from the stories of the participants. Pieces of thread, cloth and in some cases, photographs had been woven into the squares, and climbing into the enclosed space depicted the refugees' experience of escaping their countries in containers and lorries. Inside senses were engaged through the sounds of ports, stations and engines mixed with the stories of those who had taken the journey, amidst empty chocolate wrappers, an empty bottle and a child's jumper.

Figure 33: 'Home away from home'

To summarise, some of the people involved in working with artists and the researchers spoke about the value of recognition involved in the process, that they had made "a space for themselves and having an exhibition in a gallery like the Bonington especially for people from different backgrounds as they are not familiar with the system". Telling their untold stories was important – "throughout the project and its activities, it enabled refugee artists and refugee groups to engage in the process of showcasing their experiences and the untold stories of people who are forced to flee and seek protection in other countries"

(Jasim Ghafur, artist, Long Journey Home, Nottingham). Participants felt that the process created an "atmosphere for positive discussion and experience sharing between partners and a space for communication between refugee and host community artists". An important aspect of the work was felt to be the invitation to host communities to come and listen to the stories and to see the work, and this enabled "refugee artistic abilities to be seen". And the mutual recognition and sharing across groups was also felt to be positive: "the project provided us with a new experiment in working within a collaborative framework between different art forms and community groups" (Jasim Ghafur, artist, Long Journey Home).

A key concern of some of the participants was the label 'refugee' and 'asylum seeker'; experiences of identity and belonging are bound up with categories such as 'refugee' that may serve to fix the identity of an artist in ways that are experienced as counter-productive and should be transgressed. Participants in the evaluation focus group that took place after the exhibition was over were in agreement that there was a need to acknowledge and be aware of our multiple identities and multiple subject positions – asylum seekers/refugees are more than the label suggests. Indeed, the label/category of 'asylum seeker' and 'refugee' is laden with associations that need to be resisted and transformed.

Alex Rotas (2004) identifies this issue in a paper exploring the identity of professional artists who are also refugees. She writes of how the categories or labels identifying artists and participants as 'asylum seeker' or 'refugee' have many negative connotations within the public imagination. And, rather like the designating of artists with the monolithic term 'black', they may become contained, differentiated and controlled until the people themselves took hold of the term and made it 'Black', a site of resistance and a source of pride. Transnational belonging involves mobility, multiple affiliations as well as loss and dislocation. Lives and roles are transformed in the process, people become a 'refugee' or 'asylum seeker', experience downward mobility and are often located at the margins of the margins.

Participants felt that the media coverage of the exhibition raised awareness and delivered key messages that enabled refugees' and asylum seekers' stories to be promoted in contrast to the dominant and often negative messages in the mainstream media, with the exhibition being documented on the *Guardian Society*'s online gallery pages. The Bonington gallery and staff in the School of Art and Design at Nottingham Trent University commented that a large number of people visited the university as a consequence of the exhibition, thus raising the profile of Nottingham Trent University among populations and groups of people who would not otherwise visit the school/university.

The exhibition elicited dialogue and social awareness and communicated shared experiences with the viewers about the journeys migrants make to seek safety, the pain of exile and dislocation and of the importance of feeling a sense of belonging in the new situation, in time and space, through relationships as well as objects. "Art can be used as kind of like a mediator as a way of creating relationships" (Amy Edwards, artist, Charnwood Arts). The exhibition also raised questions about how migrants' journeys impact on a developing sense of being 'home away from home', on identity as well as belonging:

> '… you never really fully arrive somewhere, you're just on a different part of the journey every day … people are hungry to talk about the changes and these journeys and what those journeys mean and reflect you know the kind of parallels that they might draw in their own lives and maybe you know that kind of place of safety maybe the walk we've done here has created a bit of that, that place of safety so the journey involves people moving towards people who are able to join together for a bit of the journey, you know maybe it's like a point where our paths will come out at different places but for a moment we kind of walk together a bit and then we go off again.' (Gaylan Nazhad, artist, Long Journey Home and City Arts)

> 'I would like to thank everyone who helped with the exhibition and I would like to repeat the Chinese proverb, "the journey of a thousand miles starts with a single step". I think we made some nice first steps and I hope we will continue on our journey with more projects like this and more messages to people about a sense of belonging and use our art to contribute to society.' (Jeffer M.-Garib, artist, Long Journey Home)

Those involved in the walks stated that the walking practice and the performative follow-up discussions (facilitated by Misha Myers) led to genuine communication, listening and understanding leading to embodied and relational shifts that involved affect, feeling as well as enhanced knowledge and levels of experience/understanding. Having a voice, a personal and political space to tell and share our stories, can be facilitated in the process of participatory research. In turn, art based on participatory research is not just a mimetic reflection on someone's origins but brings something new into the world. The 'Towards a sense of belonging' projects demonstrated that this may generate a dialogical process of reflection.

Participants also reflected on the role of art in social change and opened up discussion about the value and role of research linked to arts practice and artist identities. For some of the Long Journey Home artists, social change was tied up with their arts practice – they wanted their art to make people think differently, to inform as well as challenge stereotypes and myths about the issue of asylum and migration. For others it was not a key factor in their work, their art and identity as an artist was not related to politics or social change. For the community arts organisations, stimulating and supporting personal development, enabling a voice for their collaborators and arguments and activities for social change underpinned their work. Indeed, for Kevin Ryan, director of Charnwood Arts, his practice as a community artist "involves 'ethics', 'dialogue', 'relationships' and 'benefit', with an unending desire to understand context, wedded to the capacity to both respond creatively and stimulate creativity in others, these are the factors which underpin my practice as a community artist".

Having a voice, a personal and political space to tell and share our stories, can be facilitated in the process of participatory research. In turn, art based on participatory research is not just a mimetic reflection on someone's origins but brings something new into the world. The 'Towards a sense of belonging' projects demonstrated that this may generate a dialogical process of reflection. Engaging and connecting with the feelings, intellect and politics that mediate the tensions between emotion and materiality can help us to understand better the 'micrology' of migrants' lives and, in turn, can help us conceive more fully our own lives within the context of wider sociopolitical structures and processes, such as the governance of the asylum-migration nexus. The counter-hegemonic role of PAR and PA, through ethno-mimesis, can lead to a radical democratisation of images and texts that can move us, pierce us, challenge identity thinking and bring us in touch with our feeling worlds in a subjective, reflexive relationship with the feeling worlds of the 'other' (O'Neill, 2009).

During my time as invigilator at the exhibition and also at the launch and private view I talked to visitors and listened to what they had to say about the work. The comments in the visitor book also evidenced the impact of the work:

'Well as we know, art is magic, the way we know about each other's emotions. I loved the works and it was something which inspires me so much, the long journey to home.'

'I think these need to happen more – I really gained a sense of what it is like for those forced out of their country and this understanding will have impact upon how I interact with those who are in these situations. Think the art is powerful and well presented, fantastic job everyone.'

'I hope it has built up true bonds of a sense of community! Many thanks!'

'Moving and thought provoking and some of it very beautiful.'

'Really good exhibition, emotional reminding me of home, fabrics, and textile work is fantastic. Came with a group of refugees and asylum seekers they could relate to the artwork, excellent!'

'Congratulations to the artists for their beautiful way of telling their story, their feelings.'

'The peacefulness is all the more powerful because of the trauma and pain represented. Thank you! Lots of powerful images to take away and reflect on.'

'Sobering and thought provoking and brilliant.'

'Very moving works of art. Gives a real insight into people's lives and what they have been through and continue to live with. Thanks.'

'Excellent installations. It makes you feel a little bit, what torments refugees have been through.'

I end this chapter by suggesting that the work between the partners (migrants, some of them undocumented, some seeking asylum and some with refugee status, artists and community arts organisations) reinforced the value of working in interdisciplinary and participatory ways in the space or hyphen between arts practice and social research using PAR and PA. We felt that we had fulfilled our aims and that processes of recognition were fostered involving the recognition of the need for and development of cultural citizenship.

The work produced sensuous knowledge (through narratives and art forms) about the lived experiences, feeling and relational worlds of participants by combining ethnography and arts practice. This involved "a deeper understanding and appreciation of the reasons that lie behind people's migration to the UK" and "an invaluable insight into how refugees and asylum seekers cope with being a stranger in a strange land" (Stuart Brown, coordinator of Long Journey Home).

I have argued in previous work (O'Neill, 2010) and in Chapter Three that the emotional mediation and connections between participants and art works and audience are important aspects to consider. Sarah Ahmed, in 'Collective feelings or, the impressions left by others' (2003), gets to the heart of the matter when she states that 'emotions are not simply "within" or "without", but that they define the contours of the multiple worlds that are inhabited by different subjects' (Ahmed, 2003, p 25). Ahmed argues that 'emotions do things, and work to align individuals with collectives – or bodily space with social space – through the very intensity of their attachments' (2004, p 26). Ahmed defines emotions as what 'move' us but 'emotions are also about attachments and what 'connects us', and she argues that emotions work to create the very distinction between the inside and the outside, and that this separation takes place through the very movement engendered by responding to others and objects. Rather than locating emotion in the individual or the social, we can see that emotionality – as a responsiveness to and openness towards the worlds of others – involves an interweaving of the personal with the social, and the affective with the mediated' (2004, p 28). Similarly Maruska Svašek's (2007) work on art and agency also explores the relationship between art and affect. Svašek writes about an artefact's ability to stir emotions through the embodiment of complex intentionalities and the mediation of social agency. Svašek's point is that 'artefacts "do" things: they reproduce the agency of their commissioners, makers and users; they evoke emotional reactions with and amongst individuals, and urge people to take certain actions and positions' (2007, pp 85-6).

In our work together on the 'Towards a sense of belonging' project there was also recognition that PAR underpins PA, and as Kevin Ryan describes the process, involves "an ethical approach to dialogue, building relationships, exploring meaning and benefits, evaluating outcomes within the context of creatively supported explorations of aspirations, perceptions, stories and possibilities". Our collaborative work also recognised and reinforced the value of participatory and community arts and the tensions that exist between 'professional art', 'public art' and 'community and participatory art'. Related to this is the tension between art as a tool of the state (control/integration/regeneration) and art as a space claimed for voice, representation, marking complexity, disrupting binaries and challenging simplistic policy making. Of course sometimes community art is both – it serves as a tool for inclusion and consultation and it also brings into voice, disrupts and shows complexity.

In this sense community arts may act as a two-way valve between community representation, issues and concerns and the apparatus of state – mediating conflict and advancing arguments for social change or providing the interface for more detailed and informed dialogue in a multifaceted way.

Our collaborations had real and tangible benefits for the participants (refugees, asylum seekers, artists, researchers, arts organisations) across the three strands of activity that included producing new knowledge, making connections, enabling 'attunement', raising awareness and challenging myths and stereotypes. Arguably cultural citizenship and social justice emerge as key aspects of the connections made, the process and the impact of the entire trajectory of research in the first decade of the 21st century. With the strongest impact occurring since 2005 (and in the last two projects) through the process and practices of 'recognitive community' and the collaborative communication and practice (praxis) that has fostered both cultural citizenship and social justice, in the interrelated spheres of redistributive justice (the Making the Connections collaborations and the three strands of knowledge transfer activity), associational justice (networks, collaboration) and recognitive justice (working with, in partnership and collaboration).

Notes

[1] Charnwood Arts, Loughborough (www.charnwoodarts.com/); Soft Touch Arts, Leicester (www.soft-touch.org.uk/site/pages/home_1.php); City Arts, Nottingham (www.city-arts.org.uk/); and the Long Journey Home, a regional arts organisation supporting artists in exile (www.longjourneyhome.org.uk/).

[2] Such as the dominant knowledge/power axis embedded in current governance and media policy relating to forced migration and the sexual, racial and social inequalities experienced by new arrivals.

[3] Following Pakulski (1997), Lister (2007) and Stevenson (2003), cultural citizenship as the right to presence and visibility, not marginalisation; the right to dignity and maintenance of lifestyle, not assimilation to the dominant culture; the right to dignifying representation, not stigmatisation.

[4] The network was co-convened Phil Hubbard and myself.

[5] Migrants, artists, community arts organisations, academics, organisations supporting refugees and asylum seekers, NGOs, community development organisations and representatives from housing, health, Jobcentre Plus, the National Institute of Adult Continuing Education (NIACE) and policy makers.

[6] For reports on each event, see www.makingtheconnections.info

[7] Convened by photographer Dr John Perivolaris, who was also one of the artists working with the 'Towards a sense of belonging' project and who curated the end of programme exhibition.

[8] On average the attendance at each event was around 35-40 participants. Seventy-five people attended the launch event and 80+ attended the end of award conference. There was a good balance of participants from academic and non-academic backgrounds. New arrivals groups and individuals attended from the following ethnic groups: Kurdish (Turkish and Iraqi), Zimbabwean, Somali, Albanian, Polish, African, Congolese, Eritrean, Afghan, Bosnian, Pakistani.

[9] For example, I facilitated a support group for the Nottingham African Women's Empowerment Forum (NAWEF) to help the group develop, put in bids for funding and a link to other regional and local organisations. NAWEF attended the seminar on destitution and following this event, attended all of the remaining seminars. Initially the support group consisted of City Arts Nottingham, the Nottingham Women's Counselling Service, Nottingham Trent University and Loughborough University. I chaired a half-day event that enabled NAWEF to present themselves to local agencies and policy makers in Nottingham. Subsequently, Dr Bailey from Nottingham Trent University facilitated a one-day national conference led by NAWEF to present their work on 'Destitution: still human, still here'. This was also supported by local councillors and Refugee Action.

[10] The arts, migration and diapsora themes are now embedded in the work of the Arts Council regionally as well as the work of EMPAF (East Midlands Participatory Arts Forum).

[11] This strand of knowledge transfer was led by City Arts Nottingham and Artists in Exile.

[12] This strand of activity is looked after by Charnwood Arts.

[13] For example, see John Perivolaris' walk with Thaer at www.flickr.com/photos/dr_john2005/sets/72157605115882016

[14] Over 300 people attended the private view and 1,005 people visited the exhibition between 9 and 29 January, averaging 60 visitors per day (not including the numbers attending the private view).

[15] Photographer John Perivolaris was a co-walker with Thaer Ali in Nottingham and he has documented the walk at www.lboro.ac.uk/departments/ss/global_refugees/image_makers.html

[16] A paper about this process (O'Neill and Hubbard, 2010) has been published in the journal *Visual Studies* in a special edition on walking, art and ethnography. Misha Myers (2010) has also published a paper on her walking arts practice in the same issue.

[17] Namely, enhancing the lives of recent arrivals in the East Midlands; stimulating both high-quality interdisciplinary research and the production of art works; facilitating connection, communication and engagement with public policy; and contributing to public awareness of the issues facing asylum seekers and refugees in the East Midlands.

[18] Supported by artists Rosie Hobbs, Heather Connelly and Alma Cunliffe. The sound files produced by Heather Connelly were played as an integral part of the exhibition.

[19] Karina Martin (Long Journey Home, Derby) and Senkal Yaami (textile artist) ran the arts workshops. Jamie Bird (senior lecturer at the University of Derby in Therapeutic Arts) and one of his students supported and contributed to the work in Derby.

SIX

Children, young people and unaccompanied young people

A range of research conducted with refugee families and unaccompanied children and young people document the failings of the asylum system and deep anxieties experienced by asylum seekers, refugees and support agencies about the asylum process in the UK.[1] Although research has recognised and documented the needs of children and young people, policy responses are inadequate and contradictory. Children situated in the asylum–migration–community nexus often find themselves alone, with little support, facing harassment and bullying, housed in inappropriate accommodation for their years, some are housed in detention centres (pseudo prisons), some are facing age dispute cases, dispersal or return when they turn 18, and ultimately, a hostile asylum process. Acting on the recommendations from key research (Dennis, 2002; Refugee Council, 2002; Rutter, 2006; Lake, 2008; Lorek et al, 2009) would improve the system and enable refugee children and young people opportunities to fulfil their potential. Sadly, the UK is far from operationalising the recommendations from a rich range of research, some of which is documented later.

This chapter starts with the national context and documents the key findings from research; it then moves on to examine in more detail the experiences of children, young people and unaccompanied young people using their own voices through participatory and arts-based research, which raises themes of poverty, humiliation, relational needs and community-based support. The final section draws on the experiences of young people to make some comment on the broader social structures and processes involved, particularly in relation to the impact of globalisation, the role of western nations in the production of the world's refugees and the need for social justice linked to a recognitive theory of community for young people arriving either with families or alone.

National context

Key findings from research conducted since the 1990s show t
refugee children and young people receive inadequate support fr

mainstream services. They have problems accessing health and education services and they experience alienation and racism. They have serious concerns about being dispersed when they turn 18, and they are subject to age disputes, bullying as well as detention. Some experience sexual maltreatment and abuse (Lay and Papadopolous, 2009). They are often treated as asylum seekers and refugees first and children second. Unaccompanied young children are often housed in inappropriate accommodation with inadequate support. 'Reaching 18 can signal a crisis point for many unaccompanied asylum-seeking children who face destitution and homelessness and the risk of removal from the UK' (Mayor of London, 2004, p ii). Additionally, refugee children experience high levels of poverty and social services departments are sometimes unclear as to where refugee children fit into their services. Refugee children's mental health needs are not addressed – teachers do not have the training to recognise this and mental health support does not have the resources to deal with the needs of refugee children.

In seeking to understand the high levels of sexual maltreatment of unaccompanied asylum seekers, Lay and Papadopoulos (2009) undertook research with African unaccompanied asylum seekers:

> Of the 53 (N= 53) former UASM [unaccompanied asylum-seeking minors] who participated in the study only 2 were males.

> Most arrived in the UK aged 15-17. A range of sexual maltreatment, from sexual harassment to rape was reported. Three quarters experienced more than 1 incident. Most initial incidents happened in the first 12 months of their arrival in the UK. Two perpetrators were female carers. Many participants reported being groomed and sexually maltreated by people from their own country. Many described being seriously sexually maltreated, particularly by groups of young males living in the same accommodation or nearby, some reportedly also asylum seekers. Participants that had been warned of the dangers of sexual maltreatment were more likely to both disclose and to seek professional help. (Lay and Papadopoulus, 2009, p 728)

The researchers concluded that 'professionals should assume that UASM will suffer sexual maltreatment in their host country if not protected adequately, which they are unlikely to disclose. They are likely to need more protection from outside sources and help to develop their personal resources than many have received in the past' (Lay and Papadopoulus, 2009, p 728). Practitioners could develop

> preventative measures to include provision of safer environments, ideally single sex housing; more monitoring and supervision; more opportunities to develop trustworthy relationships and have emotional needs met; greater opportunities to develop language skills/access to interpretation; early information regarding the social system, culture, and sexual maltreatment; and improved professional awareness and competence in dealing with minors from other cultures. (Lay and Papadopoulus, 2009, p 728)

Jill Rutter's[2] (2006) *Refugee children in the UK* explores the labelling of refugee children and what this means in relation to educational policy and practice; the impact of the domination in the theoretical and research literature of a focus on discourses of 'trauma' in relation to refugee children; an examination of how the UK context and responses to refugee children emerge and impact on policy; and how young people view the ensuing debates on asylum seekers and refugees. Analyses of educational policy, legislation and school initiatives are complemented by case studies that focus on the three communities of Congolese, Sudanese and Somali children, and the book closes with a chapter devoted to presenting new visions for policy and practice.

Rutter's work provides a complex and thorough analysis of the sociopolitical and educational contexts to researching refugee children in secondary schools (the subject of Rutter's PhD and subsequent case study research), and the complex dynamics operating at meso and macro levels. Rutter develops a Foucauldian analysis of power and discourse in relation to the role of the media, 'race' and anti-racist policy through to the current focus on 'race' and discourses of social cohesion and integration. Rutter's research highlights the under-achievement of Congolese, Somali, Turkish and Kurdish children. She argues that migration involves children and young people losing much of their cultural capital and that this can lead to differential educational achievement. Other factors impacting on educational achievement include racism, deprivation and linguistic problems and their pre-migration experiences. Yet policy measures tend to view refugee children as homogeneous and interventions comprise limited ESOL tuition.

The policy context of the experiences of refugee children includes: *Every Child Matters* (DfES, 2003); the 1989 UN Convention on the

Rights of the Child (UNCRC); the Children Act 2004; *Youth matters: Next steps* (DfES, 2006); *Aiming high: Guidance on supporting the education of asylum seeking and refugee children* (DfES, 2004); the impact of NAM; the Asylum, Immigration and Nationality Act 2006 (from August 2007 asylum seekers aged 18 and over are no longer be eligible for ESOL); and the Borders, Citizenship and Immigration Act 2009.

Resistant discourses of humanitarianism, 'economic asset' and 'cultural enrichment' as they are linked to asylum seekers, refugees and educational policy and practice in the UK are also discussed by Rutter (2006). Rutter demands holistic government interventions to tackle the inequalities associated with class, migration and ethnicity. She asks that we, in the 21st century, accept the arrival of new immigrants in UK schools and faced with this reality we look for new educational visions based on justice, equality and a notion of global citizenship. Notions of justice, equity and global citizenship are far removed from the experiences of children and families locked in detention centres.

According to government figures from November 2009, around 1,300 children were held at immigration removal centres during an 18-month period (http://news.bbc.co.uk/1/hi/uk/8335602.stm). This figure includes: 884 children held at Yarl's Wood immigration removal centre in Bedfordshire between July 2008 and July 2009; 328 children held at Tinsley House near Gatwick Airport between 1 September 2008 and 31 August 2009; 103 children held at the Dungavel centre in South Lanarkshire between October 2008 and 18 September 2009. Pete Wishart, a Scottish National MP, received a letter from Home Office Minister Phil Woolas containing the information. Wishart's response was that detaining children was simply wrong and unacceptable:

> That 103 children have been held in Scotland, where the Scottish government is firmly against child detention, is deeply disturbing. It's time for the UK government to end this practice.... These figures show nearly 200 children a year are being held for more than four weeks. (http://news.bbc.co.uk/1/hi/uk/8335602.stm)

Research by Lorek et al (2009), published in the *Child Abuse and Neglect* journal, found that

> detained children were found to be experiencing mental and physical health difficulties of recent onset, which appeared to be related to the detention experience. These findings support previous Australian studies demonstrating

that detention is not in the best interest of the child. It suggests that current UK policies regarding the detention of children for purposes of immigration control should be re-examined. Further research in the area is required. (Lorek et al, 2009, p 573)

The research team document the practical implications as follows:

Although high levels of mental and physical health problems, as well as child protection concerns were detected, detained families had very limited access to appropriate assessment, support or treatment. The traumatic experience of detention itself also has implications for the sizeable proportion of psychologically distressed children who are eventually released from detention and expected to successfully reintegrate into British society; while those children who are deported are returned with increased vulnerability to future stressors. (Lorek et al, 2009, p 573)

Recently children's authors, including Jacqueline Wilson, Michael Rosen and Quentin Blake, signed a letter to the Prime Minister urging immediate action on the detention of children, supporting previous calls by the Royal Colleges of Pediatricians, General Practitioners and Psychiatrists for the 'immediate cessation of detention for children'. They highlighted the pain and suffering and trauma experienced by children in the prison-like setting of Yarl's Wood detention centre. Writer Beverley Naidoo visited children in Yarl's Wood: 'We spent a morning with delightful, thoughtful young people, which brings home the fact that our government should not be asking Serco to lock up innocent children' (Goddard, 2009). The children's commissioner, Sir Al Aynsley-Green, himself a former doctor, agrees. Labour MP Chris Mullin brought a parliamentary motion signed by nearly 100 MPs, calling for the cessation of detention for children. The briefing paper by the Royal College of General Practitioners, Royal College of Paediatrics and Child Health, Royal College of Psychiatrists and the UK Faculty of Public Health describes the significant harms to the physical and mental health of children and young people in the UK who are subjected to administrative immigration detention. It argues that 'Other countries have developed viable alternatives and the UK should now follow suit' and a 'set of specific recommendations is outlined to minimise the damage caused by the detention of children' (RCGP et al, 2009, p 1):

> On 30 June 2009, 10 of the 35 children in detention had
> been held for over a month. Less than half of the children
> leaving detention are removed from the country. There are
> no data on how many children undergo more than one
> episode of detention, though repeated arrest and detention is
> likely to be particularly traumatising. (RCGP et al, 2009, p 2)

The Home Office response was that detention was the last resort
for families waiting for deportation who might abscond. And that all
inmates were treated humanely. A leading article in *The Independent*
on 14 December 2009 stated:

> While politicians and officials continue to stonewall such
> constructive suggestions and maintain that all is well for
> children in removal centers, suspicions will grow that the
> families of failed asylum-seekers are locked up in such
> numbers because they represent soft targets for deportation;
> and that this is a Government determined to show how
> 'tough' it is on illegal immigration regardless of the
> damage its policy imposes on some of the most vulnerable
> individuals in our society. (www.independent.co.uk/
> opinion/leading-articles/leading-article-the-cruelty-of-
> locking-up-child-asylumseekers-1839893.html)

In Australia and Sweden, detaining children has almost ceased, and in
Scotland refused and detained families are housed in flats before they
are returned.

This enormous gulf left by mainstream lack of support and care is
filled in part by support from voluntary sector organisations. These
are made up of faith groups, youth agencies, arts organisations, some
schools, research and action commissioned by local authorities, NGOs
and charitable trusts such as The Baring Foundation, Paul Hamlyn
Foundation, Save the Children, the Children's Legal Centre, Refugee
Action and the Joseph Rowntree Foundation.

Two case studies from research conducted by leading charities provide
a brief but clear example:

> Peter was 14 when he arrived as an unaccompanied child
> from Sierra Leone. He was already fluent in English. After
> waiting seven months for a place in school, Peter had to take
> the only place he was offered, which was in a project for
> children whose behaviour had led to them being educated

outside of the usual classroom setting. Peter receives one and a half days' education in key skills and has no prospect of getting qualifications. (Dennis, 2002, p 9)

Ahmed was 15 when he arrived in the UK. He was placed in a young person's assessment centre and subsequently placed with a foster family. When Ahmed's uncle appeared, social services said they could live together, even though Ahmed's uncle did not have permission from his landlord. Ahmed had to sleep on the floor in his uncle's room. A year later, Ahmed has indefinite leave to remain (ILR) and his uncle has left the country. The landlord told Ahmed he couldn't stay in his uncle's house so he returned to social services for help. Social services would not help, even though Ahmed requested assistance several times. One of the voluntary organisations involved in this project discovered Ahmed after he had been sleeping in a car. (Dennis, 2002, p 12)

The author of the report, Dennis, is policy adviser for unaccompanied children at the Refugee Council, and she said the following in a press release at the time her report was published:

Policy makers need to take on board the consequences of their policies on young refugees' lives, recognising the unique nature of this vulnerable group. One major issue that this report revealed is that systems designed for adults are being applied to children and young people with devastating effect. Though we recognise the acute pressure and financial constraints on service providers, we hope that the recommendations of this report will help them improve the situation for all young refugees. (Dennis, 2002) www.refugeecouncil.org.uk/news/news/2002/june/20020614newr.htm

Following sustained campaigns from leading charities about the inequities of the asylum system regarding children and young people, the Borders, Citizenship and Immigration Act 2009 introduced under section 55 a requirement that all UKBA staff safeguard and promote the welfare of children seeking asylum. For the Refugee Council, this was a step in the right direction, but insufficient overall:

We welcome this acknowledgement from the UK Border Agency that they should take the safety and welfare of children seriously. We have been calling for this duty to be introduced since the Children Act 2004 was debated in parliament, so we are optimistic that the introduction of Section 55 signals a change of attitude in how children are treated in the asylum system.

This new duty, however, is only a start. There are still many gaps and policies in place that contradict the principles of Section 55 – one being the policy of detaining children for immigration purposes which seriously damages the mental and physical wellbeing of children. Child detention must end without delay, and the Government must now commit to ensuring its policies reflect the duty we owe to children seeking asylum in this country. (Donna Covey, Chief Executive of the Refugee Council, www.refugeecouncil. org.uk/news/archive/press/2009/october/02112009)

In research published a year earlier by Save the Children it was found that young separated refugees experience considerable anxiety over the asylum process, brought about by the difficulty of contacting legal representatives in distant cities, problems with the Home Office and a general lack of information and support (Stanley, 2001).

The report highlighted serious gaps in service provision in relation to access to education, housing and social services support, and made recommendations towards meeting the needs of young separated refugees. Many young people were found to be housed in inappropriate accommodation. There is confusion over what will happen to them once they are eighteen. 'A number of professionals pointed to the potentially disastrous effects of the transition to adult services at 18, especially dispersal, which would entail the loss of friends and support' (Stanley, 2001, p 5). Many experienced emotional and mental health problems, bullying and harassment. Child protection concerns were also raised by the researchers.

Some social services departments enter into contracts with private companies, often located a considerable distance from their area, to provide care and accommodation. This arrangement is leaving these young people without adequate support, recourse to a social worker or independent complaints procedure. (Stanley, 2001, p 5)

Research conducted with refugee families on meeting the needs of refugee families by the Joseph Rowntree Foundation in 1995 (as part of a research and development project by the Daycare Trust) document a range of needs that have remained constant over time for new arrival families.

Families were documented as experiencing a deep sense of isolation, insecurity, poverty and fear. Parents placed great importance on the education and care of their children but recent arrivals had little knowledge of services and were also reluctant to approach official organisations for help. Parents found that professionals in health, social services and education had little understanding of the difference between refugees and migrants, and did not recognise the particular physical and mental problems resulting from their experience as refugees. Long-term support with English language was required to enable families to settle successfully, but access and provision was variable. Language and interpretation needs were a key issue and parents found it difficult to make full use of education and health services because interpretation services were patchy. Parents wanted written and oral material in their mother tongue provided by agencies they trusted. Additionally parents wanted children to have access to additional support, mother tongue teaching and knowledge of their own culture (www.jrf.org.uk/sites/files/jrf/sp86.pdf).

The impact of dispersal has also been well documented by national research and throws up a number of key themes in relation to the management of the dispersal process, including the impact of destitution, housing, health, mental health, employment and education needs (Wilson, 2001; O'Neill et al, 2003, 2004; Refugee Action, 2006). The literature provides evidence of fragmented services, serious language and communication issues, a need for orientation and information about the dispersal area for new arrivals, experiences of racism and unwelcome and emerging tensions between established and new arrival communities. The latter appears to be fuelled by perceived differential access to limited resources. These factors are important to take into consideration in developing strategies for looking after children and young people.

Under an 'agenda for action', the Mayor of London's report (2004) by the Greater London Authority (GLA) recommended that 'The government should be urged to remove its reservation allowing the operation of immigration controls without regard for the UN Convention on the Rights of the Child' (2004, p iii); consider how the duties contained in the Children Act can be built into services for unaccompanied refugee and asylum-seeking children; 'that no unaccompanied asylum-seeking child should be subject to a Section 55 Decision (withdrawal of support to in-country applicants) or dispersed at 18' (2004, p iv).[3] The government were also asked to include in its pledge that no homeless family with children should be placed in bed and breakfast-type accommodation unless it was a short-term emergency, alongside recommendations on better meeting the education, health and mental health needs of asylum-seeking and refugee children, whether unaccompanied or with their families.

The Refugee Council's *A case for change: How refugee children in England are missing out* (2002) documents findings from the monitoring project of the Refugee Children's Consortium. The main recommendations include:

- plans for children should be made at the earliest opportunity;
- no young person should be placed in one area and subject to dispersal at a later date – social services and the National Asylum Support Service (NASS)[4] should work together to minimise the disruption to a young person's life on turning 18;
- children who are not 'looked after' should receive practical assistance for independent living and be enabled to stay in existing accommodation where possible.

The report reinforces earlier work by Save the Children, *Cold comfort: Young separated refugees in England* (2001).

Unaccompanied children are supported by social services until they reach the age of 18. On turning 18 different rules apply depending on the date and location of the application for asylum. Some will be entitled to benefits, some to continued support from the UKBA. Children looked after by section 20 of the Children Act 1989 are entitled to leave care services. Until March 2007 and from October 2001 the agency responsible for managing asylum was NASS and the policy was to disperse young people (as newly arrived asylum seekers) on reaching 18 *unless* they were accommodated under section 20 of the Children Act 1989and qualified as 'former relevant children' (that is, 'looked after'). Many children who arrive are 16 and 17 (the majority), do not fall into this category.

Hence key issues for children and young people are an inhumane asylum process, detention, lack of welcome and a plethora of issues around housing, health needs, support and being looked after, poverty, education and living in limbo with potential deportation or dispersal at 18. The aspirations of asylum-seeking children are dashed in the realities of a system that does not care for them until they are given refugee status, and even then the inequalities of language, poverty and housing can impact on their future lives.

The government published a report in 2008, *Better outcomes: The way forward*, with a foreword by the then Minister of State for Borders and Immigration, Liam Byrne MP, a proponent of communitarianism (Home Office, 2008). The report set out five key improvements for the care of unaccompanied asylum-seeking children that were deeply lacking in any spirit of collectivism and communitarianism; indeed, the report also lacked understanding of the key issues affecting unaccompanied children identified by young people themselves. The report was written from the lens of the UKBA and the 'government' and it contains a superficial understanding of the research outlined earlier. Reading the report one does not feel that young people are at the heart of policy. That being said, the reforms are of course welcome; so far the first reform is instantiated in law in the Borders, Citizenship and Immigration Act 2009. It remains to be seen through evidenced-based research how and if the UKBA manage to achieve this.

Key reforms documented in the report are:

1) Ensuring that the Border and Immigration Agency, in exercising its functions, keeps children safe from harm while they are in the UK.
2) Putting in place better procedures for identifying and supporting unaccompanied asylum-seeking children who are the victims of trafficking.
3) Locating unaccompanied asylum-seeking children with specialist local authorities to ensure they receive the services they need.
4) Putting in place better procedures to assess age in order to ensure children and adults are not accommodated together.
5) Resolving immigration status more quickly and, in turn, enabling care planning to focus on integration or early return to the country of origin.

Until 2008 the government had a reservation in place on the UNCRC. This excluded refugee children from its protection, which meant that such children were not given the same rights as other children in the UK. And under the Borders, Citizenship and Immigration Act 2009 there is now a statutory duty on the Home Office and UKBA to safeguard and promote the welfare of children. Until 2010 the Home Office was exempt from the responsibilities of safeguarding these children, as described in the 1989 and 2004 Children Acts (RCGP et al, 2009, p 3).

In the second part of this chapter I focus on the lived experiences of unaccompanied young people in their own voices through micrology, participatory and arts-based research. I suggest that listening to their voices may help us to understand what it is like living in the asylum-migration-community nexus connected to the broader themes of this book – mobility, migration, globalisation, humiliation, recognitive community and social justice.

Hidden voices: migration and belonging

Michael Winterbottom's powerful film *In this world* (2002) opens with the flight of two Afghan young men, cousins Enayat and Jamal, from a refugee camp in Peshawar, Pakistan. The film is about their journey and the movement of people across borders in search of safety and the opportunity to fulfil dreams and hopes. It presents a moving example of the yo-yoing, circuitous routes that migrants make (Marfleet, 2006); their journey broken up in nodal cities and waystations on the 'silk road' across Pakistan, Iran, Turkey, Italy and France. Filmed in a grainy documentary style it is a fictive tale embedded in real footage of camps and situations experienced by asylum seekers:

> As the film proceeds, they stop being merely 'cases' and become 'characters'. But we never lose sight of the fact that these are not actors but real people participating in a staged journey that follows the route taken by many seeking to travel to western Europe.... *In this world* shows migration and displacement, and the way it works on two human beings ... their seeping through the cracks in checkpoints, breaching porous borders, stowing away in the hold of global circumnavigation. It is this force that propels those forwards on the back of pick-up trucks, in the belly of sea-borne containers and, in one powerfully emblematic sequence, as two tiny figures wedged beneath the wheels of an HGV heading for the UK. (Darke, 2003)

Darke argues, and I agree, that cinema does what mass media cannot:

> ... broadening, deepening, humanising an 'issue' by putting the 'migrants' back into 'migration', watching the toll the journey takes and putting us, the viewers, squarely in their place. By emphasising the experience that lies behind the phenomenon of people-smuggling, by giving it its own

texture of image and sound – rather than having to palliate it with lurid melodrama or sensational sub-plotting. *In this world* powerfully and illuminatingly reveals 'the world inside the world'. (Darke, 2003)

Roger Bromley (2000), in 'Between a world in need and a world in excess: globalized people, migration and cinematic narrative', uses the film to articulate the way globalisation has had an impact on migration to the EU through cinematic narrative. He states:

> Both Jamal and Enayat experience pain and suffering throughout the journey and are forced to improvise, bribe, and 'fake' their way through the harsh, physical and human, landscapes. In some instances, details of their travel are shown in close up and at some length, at other times captions summarise the passage of hours or days. The camera is rarely at a distance from them, they are almost always subjects with primacy given to their point of view. It is never a film about 'victims' in any detached, liberal sense. The worst journey of all is the most subtly conveyed. We see Jamal, Enyat and a Turkish father, mother and child being secured in a freight container (a space designed to store the non-human), aware of them only through whispers, the cries of the child and the occasional flicker of a lighter. We also see the outcome of this stage of the journey – the death of Enyat and of the child – but the lack of food, airlessness and light deprivation, and the enforced silence is not narrated explicitly or melodramatically, but in a simple caption: '40 hours later'. Thus we are not shown, and only barely told about, this unendurable experience. It is in this way that the viewer is forced to imagine, empathise with and complete the 'missing' narrative – what illegal means in human terms, not only in this specific case but in the larger narrative of migration. (Bromley, 2000, p 20)

I mention this film because of its power in telling the story of the experiences of young people migrating within an era of globalisation and human rights, and also because I was involved in screening it as part of a film festival in collaboration with B Arts, Stoke on Trent (emerging from a PAR project with local people seeking asylum and who had refugee status). We screened a series of films chosen for the most part by local people who were seeking asylum or had refugee status. For this film (as for most) refugee families came along, some with babies in pushchairs. I watched as young people thronged to get into the film theatre from local refugee communities – the film theatre was packed. This was largely due to the collaboration with B Arts who had an excellent relationship with local new arrivals communities due to the work they did and continue to do based on principles of community arts and PA. But it was also due to the fact we were showing a film that was highly regarded, telling stories about the lives of the people who came to see, watch and listen.

The experience for me was deeply humanising – the power of the images, visuals and storytelling, and the transnational audience, some of whom were from Afghanistan, had travelled the route. In the space of the cinema mediated by the film we were connected by the narrative, the story and by the journey to the larger processes of globalisation, migration and hopes for a better life, beyond the camps, beyond war, beyond poverty. Here was a good example of the asylum-migration-community nexus.

Dreamers: land of dreams

A few months later I was commissioned by the Government Office for East Midlands to undertake research using participatory methods to examine the experiences and needs of new arrivals' access to training, employment and social enterprise. This followed research I had undertaken on new arrivals' access to education (with Phil Woods and Mark Webster) that had included young people making a film about what it was like to be new arrivals,[5] the issues, problems and barriers they faced regarding education as well as their many positive experiences of the education process (O'Neill et al, 2005). Alongside traditional research methods, interviews, questionnaires and focus groups contextualised within a participatory model (working with community co-researchers in Leicester and Loughborough who were asylum seekers, refugees and also 'community facilitators'), we commissioned two community arts organisations to work with us using creative consultation and arts-based research methods – Soft Touch Arts in Leicester and Charnwood Arts in Loughborough. In Loughborough the research focused on unaccompanied asylum seekers and refugees, working with Charnwood Arts and Dreamers. Paul Gent, an artist working with Charnwood Arts, conducted creative consultation (O'Neill et al, 2005) with the young people and in the process of working with the young men's stories and drawings, he developed a cartoon based on the young men's lives.

Figure 34:
'Land of dreams'

Figure 35:
'Land of dreams'

Dreamers are a Leicestershire County Council youth work project, set up in 2002 when Andrew Lake (area youth work coordinator) met a young asylum seeker on a staircase at Loughborough College. The young man, Selim, told Andrew about his situation and that of other young people, many of whom, like him, were unaccompanied, who felt excluded, marginalised, 'living on the outside of the community, often feeling unwanted and not valued' (Lake, quoted in Ryan et al, 2004, p 4). The young people collectively called the project 'Dreamers'; they said "We are all dreamers. When we travelled and when things got tough it was our dreams that kept us going. We dreamed of freedom and safely. 'Dreamers' it will be" (quoted in Lake, 2008, p 13). The group also adopted a logo of a sleeping boy, because it symbolised safety and security, of having somewhere safe to sleep (www.thejitty.com/clubs/dreamers.html).

Figure 36: Dreamers logo

Dreamers youth group emerged from the conversation between Selim and Andrew they were effectively a self-organised group who were supported and mentored by Andrew Lake. Dreamers are funded through the County Council Youth Service. Since 2002 Andrew and his team (three youth workers) have supported 160 + unaccompanied asylum seekers. Dreamers take a youth work and lifelong learning approach to the group and provide a drop-in place, emotional and practical support, a sense of belonging, a programme of activities that facilitate culturation and citizenship education (again, based on a youth work approach, which is highly successful and valued by the young people), and a warm welcome to Charnwood and the UK. The group run a programme of weekly activities, including sports activities, trips, residential trips, an annual trip to the House of Commons to meet the local MP; basic needs advice and skills learning; citizenship; and sharing of food and cultures. The young people have made a CD of music from their countries/cultures. The support is outreach and centre-based. Shadowing takes place where appropriate and necessary for the well-being of young people.

Land of dreams: New arrivals in Charnwood (Welcome to Britain ... Go home)

The aim of the research was to map the links between strategic and neighbourhood planning, service delivery and projects, with specific reference to new arrivals and opportunities for economic progression, examining distributive justice. The research also mapped the networks, associations and partnerships that addressed the horizontal and vertical processes of inclusion, documenting associational justice, and undertook interviews and creative consultation using arts-based methods with young people in Loughborough and older people in Leicester to explore their lived experiences and lived cultures at the intersections with ethnicity, gender, 'race', age, and class, exploring recognitive justice. Together these strands were also useful in identifying processes of cultural citizenship (as defined by Pakulski, 1997; Stevenson, 2003; Lister, 2007). We also looked at the impact of the Race Relations Amendment Act 2000 and equalities legislation on services to new arrivals.

Responses from questionnaires (created in collaboration with community co-researchers), focus groups, interviews and conversations with young people and the arts worker showed that the key issues facing participants who were aged 11-18 included isolation from mainstream services, racism across the entire trajectory, verbal abuse, violence and assault:

> '... we made it across minefields and countries and across France with nothing to eat ... but we could not get social services to support us together.' (quoted in O'Neill et al, 2003, p 118)

Two young men, cousins, then aged 16 and 13, were separated on arrival to the UK. The youngest was placed in foster care in Lincoln, the older placed in Loughborough. They pressed to be reunited and are now living together in Loughborough. The guardian (now 19) and 15-year-old cousin stated that they have had no social services visit or support in two years. When the guardian became employed (he works permanent night shifts of 12-hour duration) free school meals were taken away and he is not in receipt of child benefit. They said: "Got out of the truck at Leicester and we were seen by social services then moved to London and then to Lincoln ... then I was moved to Loughborough ... we were separated and wanted to be reunited" (young man now aged 19, guardian for his cousin); "I missed speaking my language and speaking to my cousin" (cousin, aged 15).

The young people we worked with are multilingual, speaking between three and five languages, they are incredibly hard working, have high aspirations generally but will accept any work (when they are able) that pays an income.

Employment issues included young men working long shifts for low wages, which affects their ability to go to college, to enjoy leisure pursuits and to go to English language classes. Training, including use of machinery, was experienced by some as inadequate. Young men talked about feeling exploited by employers and employment agencies. They are so desperate to earn that they take what is offered.

Leaving and arriving ... and leaving...

A young person talked about his reasons for leaving Iraq. He was 14 years old when he fled, supported by a family member who paid an agent to help him leave Iraq. His parents fled to North Iraq and were killed. "Saddam dispersed the Kurds and so people migrated to the North." On his 18th birthday he was dispersed to Wolverhampton. A letter arrived with a train travel ticket. He had three days to say his goodbyes and leave his social network – made up of college, home, Dreamers and friends. His college agreed to help find and guarantee accommodation so he could stay in Loughborough. Andrew Lake liaised with NASS to try and ensure the young man could stay in Loughborough. NASS, however, would not agree to this. The young man had a choice, which was to go to Wolverhampton or stay without support and so survive without accommodation. The young man felt abandoned in Wolverhampton. NASS made a lot of promises that there would be support, a college course, friends, social groups, but there was nothing, so he left the one choice of accommodation and at this time, in 2004, he was living on a £30 a week support package only, with no accommodation, and sleeping on friends' floors.

Another young man was dispersed to Stoke-on-Trent when he reached his 18th birthday. He was also given a dispersal letter with a train ticket. Two of the Dreamers staff went to visit him, to follow up the dispersal. They eventually tracked him down. He was living in a house with BNP graffiti daubed on the walls. It was supposed to be a 'safe house'. NASS promised school, college, safety. Dreamers lost touch with this young man.

Another young man's (Iraqi Kurd) application for asylum was refused by the Home Office. His solicitor, based in London, told him he could not help him any longer. He is currently trying to find another solicitor. He likes to study English and work. He was dispersed to Wolverhampton on his 18th birthday. He said,

> 'When I go out in Wolverhampton it is a problem, I like to come here [Loughborough] to see my friends, I feel safe here.... It is no better in Iraq now, in my city there are many problems.'

The young man's family were wealthy but both parents died. The young man worked in one of his father's (13) shops. Here in the UK he works in a factory because he came before the ruling (2002) that took away asylum seekers' right to work:

> 'I like working in a factory and then maybe a shop when my language is better.... I helped in my father's shop ... in secondary school I liked design but cannot do this at Loughborough.... I would like my own place and to work.'

Group members talked about going out together to prevent risk of assault but this could lead to perceptions of them being a gang. Racist bullying was experienced at school, at work, at college and on the streets of Charnwood and Leicester:

> 'I cannot express my feelings – imagine you are foreign and people do not like you, how would you feel?'

> 'British citizens need to be educated in the background of new arrivals.'

Many young people are coping with the trauma that led them to flee, the loss of family and friends, the loss of history and culture and social networks. The additional stress of dislocation and transition to life in the UK, negotiating agencies, learning the language and dealing with racism and bullying is hard.

The majority of young men have solicitors in London. On seeking an appeal to a negative decision one young person was asked for £800 by his solicitor. Limited legal aid provides insufficient time for complex lives to be communicated to solicitors; other problems included solicitors losing paperwork and young people having to travel to London with little or no money to meet with solicitors. Temporary status means that they are in a state of limbo, which is stressful. The fear of return, of deportation, hangs over them. 'What is a refugee? You are no-one in this country and you have no-one' (Ryan et al, 2004, p 28). Moreover, dispersal at 18 (or deportation) means that attempts at settlement are disrupted, important networks and friendships are broken and siblings/cousins can become separated.

Research recommendations

Across both Loughborough and Leicester the research identified a lack of overall coordination between agencies, gaps in understanding the issues and needs of new arrivals, lack of comprehensive data and access to data that would inform policy making, and an absence of communities' voices and concerns in reports and policy making. The research also documented the agencies that were supporting new arrivals and the associational, distributive and recognitive processes set in motion by partnerships between Dreamers, Charnwood Arts, the local college and Connexions.

Our report (O'Neill et al, 2003) stressed that in fostering links across the horizontal and vertical processes of social inclusion the following needed to be taken into account: community formation and the development of micro-communities who are transnational; understanding what citizenship means in a more holistic sense; delivery of appropriate services; and the impact of government policy and the ways it is interpreted and represented at local level, in the mass media too, as this has an important bearing on the reception and welcome (or not) for new arrivals at all levels. The research and the publication created by Charnwood Arts (Ryan et al, 2004) as a result of the research gave Dreamers an opportunity to tell their stories and to share these with many other people. As Andrew Lake writes, 'Such expression is a celebration of freedom, something Dreamers members value greatly' (2008, p 19).

A range of recommendations were made, by O'Neill et al (2003) and Ryan et al (2004), including: the development of a high-profile, high-priority strategic lead on new arrivals in Leicester and Loughborough; developing a strategy for inclusion; development of a partnership to steer coordination of information, services and research; reflection on progression and implementation; regular participation across horizontal and vertical agencies as partners to share and enable creative use of resources; better communication and coordination of information with a map of routes new arrivals might take to accessing services and the development of a resource to provide a coordinated welcome; and ensuring participation and inclusion of voices of new arrivals, communities and stakeholders to be heard and listened to, and taken seriously that includes provision of safe spaces for dialogue.

Young people themselves wish the asylum system could be speeded up and that their needs could be taken seriously; they want to feel a sense of belonging. They want job search and access to training and employment that matches skills and training; some would like to set up businesses or gain employment that improves life chances; some want guidance on laws and regulations, on accessing information; some want unity of provision, with respect to housing and support to education; some want help with racism and incivilities, isolation and loss of status; and some want skills training.

The research recommendations helped Dreamers to develop supported housing, and supported their plans to develop a more holistic support package for young people and better partnership working with other agencies, including Jobcentre Plus, social services and foster parents.

Hidden voices

In 2006, Dreamers attended the launch of the Making the Connections regional network, were actively involved over the two years of the programme and hosted a workshop/seminar for the region and beyond to share their work and experiences, and most importantly, to raise greater awareness about the issues facing unaccompanied asylum-seeking young people.

The workshop, 'Making connections: helping asylum seekers through arts inclusion', was led by young people at Dreamers supported by Andrew Lake, youth workers and Charnwood Arts at a day-long event, held at the Dreamers drop-in centre. It involved presentations by Andrew and the young people involved in making *Hidden voices*, a publication written by Andrew Lake about the development of the group and his experiences in supporting the group.

There were exercises for participants to learn something about each other and the issues affecting young people, presentations from young people about their lives and experiences and evaluation sessions where they planned what would happen next.

At the workshop young people shared their experiences of war, bombing and shelling; destruction of their homes; violent deaths of families and friends; being separated from family; being injured; being arrested and detained; being tortured; being forced to join armies and militias; sexual assault and abuse; shortage of food and water; fear of arrest and discovery; hostility and racism; deprivation; being with people who did not understand or know about the violence they had experienced; and isolation.

Figure 37 Participants in 'Hidden voices'

'I lost my mother, father and sister. They are alive, I have to have that hope. We were on the same journey but somehow got separated'. (young person aged 17)

'Sadam's people killed my brother and sister. Now the British and Americans have killed my Mother and Father with their bombs. I just want to be with them.' (Iraqi young person aged 16)

'I looked back from the hilltop. I could see my house was on fire.' (young person aged 16) (all quoted in Lake, 2008, p 22)

In his publication, Lake (2008) writes about the significant mental and emotional difficulties experienced by the young people, with some saying, "I feel I only want to die. Everyday I feel like killing myself" (Iranian, aged 17); "I cut myself. I burn myself with cigarettes" (young Kurdish person, aged 19); "I hear prison. I hear my torturers. I can't leave them behind in my past" (young Kurdish person, aged 16); "I feel violent when I remember what those men did to me" (young Kurdish man, aged 15). Andrew writes that young people struggle to try and rebuild themselves and their lives against such dreadful experiences. Isolation is increased by racism and the feeling from the young people that they are on the margins of society and communities who do not care about them and resent their presence.

Figure 38: Participants in 'Hidden voices'

Moreover, their stories are often not believed by immigration officers, and they must tell their stories again and again. Andrew writes about the suffering he has witnessed as a consequence of this, when the telling and re-telling of their stories, 'the opening of wounds', in this experience, hurts (Lake, 2008, p 22). The human stories behind the journeys young people take are missing in the mainstream press, where the focus is on the mode of transport and the subsequent activity to strengthen borders to prevent people arriving by air, lorry, whether inside or in the undercarriage.

Their journeys are hard, dangerous and long, and some do not survive:

> 'My sister was only little. I think she was 4 or 5. She didn't make the journey. She died. We had to bury her. My Mum was so sad. She is still very sad.' (Kosovan, aged 11) (quoted in Lake, 2008, p 28)

> 'The worst thing I ever saw was when I became a refugee for the first time fleeing Saddam's regime. I have had to flee twice in my life. The first time I was only 9 years old and we had to flee across the mountains in winter. It was so cold, snow was falling, and we had no food. I was so hungry. There were hundreds of us walking. I saw a man holding his baby under the water of a stream. It was ice cold water.

He was drowning his baby. He could not face seeing his baby suffer any more.' (Kurdish young person) (quoted in Lake, 2008, p 42)

Figure 39: Participants in 'Hidden voices'

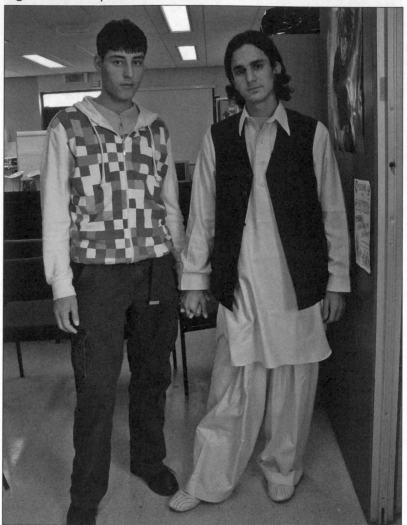

Some young people have experienced torture and are lucky to be alive – they are all survivors:

'They brought the gun down on my eye. I am blind in one eye. I see nothing in it and I hate the scars.' (aged 16)

'They hit me with a pistol on my windpipe which is why
I now need an operation.' (aged 17)

'The police tied me upside down and fastened me to a metal
bar that spanned the room. They sent electricity through
my body. I thought I was going to die.'

'The police used surgical instruments on me. I was very
young perhaps 14 years old. They used a scalpel to scar me.
I was very afraid. I thought I was going to die.' (all quoted
in Lake, 2008, p 31)

'I helped my uncle hand out leaflets that spoke against the
government. They took me to prison. For six months, every
day I was beaten and tortured. It never stopped. I hear the
voices of those men in my head now. I can't get them out
of my head. All that shouting and noise is still inside me.'
(Iranian young person, aged 18) (quoted in Lake, 2008, p 34)

Dreamers youth workers learn about the history and culture of the
young people to help build relationships, recognise and respect their
cultural belongings and to '"appreciate, acknowledge and value the
young people.... To recognise and celebrate difference is critical in
helping young the people keep some semblance of cultural identity"
(youth worker)' (quoted in Lake, 2008, p 37). And the youth workers
say that learning about culture and history helps them to offer better
guidance and support to young people, for example around sex and
drinking alcohol, differences in sexuality and sexual identity, as well as
expressing political views:

'We are afraid to be together talking about politics. In our
country some of us would disappear for talking like this. We
find this freedom very difficult and unbelievable.' (quoted
in Lake, 2008, p 40)

'The Serbians stopped us having a voice. That is why they
took our education first. Now I can go to college. I can
learn. Education is now going to be my weapon. I am going
to try to be a human rights lawyer so I can fight injustice.'
(young person, aged 18) (quoted in Lake, 2008, p 40)

Figure 40: Participants in 'Hidden voices'

Dreamers also contributed to the conference in July 2008 and were one of the four groups involved in the 'Towards a sense of belonging' project in 2008-09, leading guided walks around Loughborough, producing a play for the launch of the exhibition and having their stories and experiences exhibited through the work of Paul Gent.

The Dreamers group is an example of a recognitive community, where cultural citizenship can thrive, be supported, where difference is respected, where the sense of community articulated by Nancy is operationalised; being-together, being-in-common and being-with. And importantly, where principles of social justice and cultural citizenship[6] are offered to and fostered in the young people who are lucky enough to find their way to the community centre. I argue that the group, the dynamics, the principles and the practices, are an example of radical democratic pluralism in action.

Dreamers is a place where young people are welcomed, with generosity, with warmth, where young people are connected, supported and linked to other groups. Andrew Lake writes that Dreamers

> gives them a sense of belonging that helps them to cope with separation from family and other friends ... the fact that young people travel right across the country to reach the group stands as testament to this.... Being part of the group helps them to deal with discrimination and to feel

more positive about their identity as young refugees.... Dreamers youth workers actively encourage the use of first languages and the celebration of cultural and traditional art forms such as dance and song....This enriches the life of the group and the wider community. (Lake, 2008, p 45)

Andrew reflects on a conversation between two young people:

'How can you understand me? You have never had all your family executed and killed in war" (young Kurd to a youth worker). In response a young Albanian aged 17 said "NO, he can't understand you, but I can, my family are all dead. I can understand what you feel.'

A father of two young Albanians said:

'I am so pleased that my sons are going to a group where they can talk Albanian and mix with other Albanian children. I know you let them play Albanian music and let them sing. Thank you so much for showing such respect.' (quoted in Lake, 2008, p 46)

The young people are incredibly resilient and mature. They are multilingual, highly motivated and hardworking. As Bloch et al (2009) state, migration is a formative experience.

The group are also active in raising awareness about experiences of young and unaccompanied asylum seekers, lobbying MPs, interacting and communicating with lots of agencies to reach young people scattered across the region. As Andrew's visits to a school, a local college and a local university show, there is much misinformation, prejudice and acceptance of media myths in the general population. He states, 'there were virtually no views offered by the young people that were based around compassion, care and moral responsibility' (Lake, 2008, p 49).

Myths and stereotypes were common, such as refugees receiving lots of benefits and swamping the country. Some believed Britain was supporting between 4 and 10 million refugees; they did not know the difference between an asylum seeker and a refugee and believed that economic migrants from Eastern Europe such as Polish migrants were refugees; they had little understanding of the impact of war and poverty and little understanding of the contribution refugees make to our lives, businesses or hospitals.

Andrew ends his publication *Hidden voices* with a quote from Kofi Annan, and I borrow it in closing this chapter. The message is important for our future in a globalised world: 'Young people should be at the forefront of global change and innovation. They can be key agents for development and peace. If they are left on societies' margins, all of us will be impoverished' (Lake, 2008, p 65).

Notes

[1] The Children's Legal Centre document that around 3,000 unaccompanied children a year enter the UK to seek asylum.

[2] A former teacher, and an educational policy adviser to the Refugee Council between1988 and 2001.

[3] And the report also urges the government to repeal section 55 of the Nationality, Immigration and Asylum Act 2002, which withdraws support from in-country applicants.

[4] NASS is no longer in operation; the UKBA is now looking after the practicalities of the asylum process.

[5] Soft Touch Arts worked with us and the young people, and facilitated the young people making their own film. The film was shown at the launch and had a very powerful impact on policy makers, including the director of education.

[6] As the right to presence and visibility, not marginalisation; the right to dignity and maintenance of lifestyle, not assimilation to the dominant culture; the right to dignifying representation, not stigmatisation. Social justice is understood as involving the absence of exploitation, economic marginalisation and deprivation/destitution; associational justice includes networks of support that enable people to fully participate in decision making and governance; and cultural justice includes the absence of cultural domination, non-recognition or mis-recognition and disrespect.

SEVEN

Women refugees and asylum seekers

A headline in the *New Statesman* 29 October 2009 reads: 'Home is where the heartbreak is. Asylum-seeking women are especially vulnerable to persecution, but the British immigration system does little to help':

> 'Maybe I should just go back and die,' says Esther. 'It happens all the time. People go to sleep and just don't wake up.' If she returns to her native Kenya, Esther will be under threat of murder and rape. But the UK has refused her asylum. Her situation is typical of the plight of vulnerable female refugees, trapped in a system that does not recognise their needs. (Shackle, 2009)

As Sales (2007) states, knowledge about the feminisation of migration grew largely out of feminist work that explored migration and changing migration flows from a gendered perspective. Contradicting the mainstream view of chain migration (the man would migrate and then be joined by his wife, family and others in his social network), feminist analysis explored women's lives and women's experiences of migration (Phizaklea, 1983; Gray, 2000; Koffman et al, 2000). Research on women who migrate into domestic service (Anderson, 1993) or who migrate to work in the sex industry (Aoyama, 2005; Agustin, 2007; Mai, 2009) show the agency and complex lives of the women involved, contesting simplistic notions of the migrant domestic service worker or sex worker as victim. Women may experience victimisation on the journeys and in their working roles, but this research shows the intersecting oppressions and structural forces that create conditions where pragmatic choices are made to seek a better life and for many to send remittances home to enable families living in absolute poverty to survive.

The people and families seeking refuge as asylum seekers have undergone the most traumatic and life-changing events one could imagine. As discussed in previous chapters research shows that there are multiple reasons for mobility within the context of globalisation (linked to modernity and humiliation), global inequalities and a combination of honour codes and human rights, leading to an increase in cross-border flows of people from South and East to North and West (see Bloch, 2002a, 2002b; Castles, 2003; Marfleet, 2006; Sales, 2007; Castles and Miller, 2009).

What we know about the lives and experiences of women seeking asylum in the UK is based on a relatively small amount of research. Available research shows that asylum policy in the West is gender-biased and statistical data on women is limited.[1] Women refugees and asylum seekers suffer particular problems and inequalities as a consequence of gender-biased asylum policies and there is a dearth of research on refugee women and their families:

> There has been a gradual shift in the realization that there needs to be specific research on immigrant women and children if we are to understand the gendered, cultural and class experiences of immigrant women and girls. Migrant women are especially vulnerable to various forms of discrimination in all walks of life and this has serious policy implications. (Castles et al, 2002, p 147)

The needs of women refugees, asylum seekers and their children are clearly a major gap and an important focus for improving asylum policy that is based on equitable and transparent policy making for women, their families and children (some of whom are left behind in their home country). The legal context provides important benchmarks for social policy (Crawley, 2001). Clearly the legal context in the UK falls short of supporting women asylum seekers, largely because women's needs are not enshrined in law and dominant discourses operate in such a way to reproduce the myth that women asylum seekers are mostly dependants or 'followers' of men.

Castles et al (2002) conducted a Home Office-funded mapping exercise documenting research conducted between 1996 and 2001 on refugees and asylum seekers. The research team highlight only six publications relating to refugee women concentrating on: the legal status of refugee women (for example, Crawley, 1999, 2001); a gender-sensitive approach to migration (Sweetman, 1998); and experiences of exile of refugee women from specific ethnic backgrounds in one locality (Sales and Gregory, 1999). Although a considerable amount of more general research had been conducted during the five-year period on matters of integration, the available research was described as *uneven*, with good coverage of some areas and little or none of others ... *poorly co-ordinated*, and is not based on any systematic attempt to cover all relevant topics or to prioritise work on policy-relevant topics. Existing research is therefore not adequate for evidence-based policy-making with regard to integration of immigrants and refugees. (Castles et al, 2002, p 195)

To fully grasp and respond to the changing face of our cities and communities we need research that seeks to understand the asylum-migration nexus as well as its impact with and for women at local, regional, national and international levels. This is vitally important for the production and implementation of evidence-based policy making.

Women claiming asylum

Women claim asylum for the same reasons as men. They flee to escape persecution for their political activities, for supporting rights to freedom and free speech, for hiding people, passing messages, providing community services and providing food and shelter. They seek asylum out of fear, because they do not conform to social norms and expectations; as a response to humiliation, inhumane and degrading treatment; and to seek better lives for themselves, their families and their children. However, because their political activity is often deemed at a lower level than that of men, they are perceived as being at less risk and so it is harder to prove a well-founded fear of persecution, especially when the risk of violence is from family members such as in domestic violence, genital mutilation or 'honour crimes'. As Shackle (2009) documents, the problem is often concerned with evidencing their claims:

> Political persecution is one thing, but how can a raped woman prove that her family will murder her because of the shame she will bring? A good lawyer can argue that a woman is part of a certain social group with unchangeable characteristics – a divorced woman, for example, will be a social outcast in many countries – but this is the legal point on which women's cases often fail. (Shackle, 2009)

Shackle states that the Home Office in these circumstances recommend 'internal flight'. In the case of Esther (above) this would mean 'returning to another part of Kenya. To do so she will have to pass through Nairobi.

"They will hack me" she says, fearing death by machete at the hands of her persecutors' (Shackle, 2009). Meena Patel, of Southall Black Sisters, points out the danger for women in the approach taken by the Home Office:

> The Home Office now quite consistently says that a woman can't return to her particular area but can return to another part of her country. But women such as these in countries throughout Asia and Africa will struggle to survive. They will be targeted, vulnerable and ostracised. It will be very difficult to get jobs, especially if they are single, leading to poverty and destitution. It doesn't matter if you're from the Punjab and you go back to Gujarat – you are a single woman, therefore you may be seen as a loose woman or a prostitute. There are no systems in place to protect lone women from the risks they face. (Shackle, 2009)

Gender-biased asylum policy

Available research shows that asylum policy in the West is gender-biased and statistical data on women is limited: statistics using gender as a category were not gathered until 2001 (Dumper, 2004).[2] Moreover, there are no reliable national statistics on the number of women asylum seekers/refugees in the UK. Dumper (2004) found that there is no information published on the sex of those arriving as dependants of asylum seekers after the initial decision stage (that is, during the appeals process), and removals are not yet disaggregated by sex. However, 'the annual statistics also now disaggregate data on the dependants of asylum seekers by age and sex, and provide a breakdown of initial decisions outcomes by sex and nationality' (Dumper, 2004, p 36).

A number of national and regional initiatives have been developed in response to this gap and concerns with the needs of refugee women. These include: Asylum Aid's *Women's charter*, Refugee Action's 'Standing up for Women's Safety' campaign and *Is it safe here?* (Dumper, 2002) as well as the regional Making the Connections Network's seminar and manifesto on 'Women and migration: art, politics and policy' (O'Neill and Cohen, 2008). These are discussed below.

Research on women refugees and asylum seekers

In 2002, research conducted by Refugee Action, *Is it safe here?* (Dumper, 2002), subsequently formed the basis for Refugee Action's campaign

'Standing up for Women's Safety'. The research documents that 83 per cent of women interviewed feel so unsafe that they live under self-imposed curfew, locking themselves indoors after seven o'clock at night. A third of those interviewed had been spat on or shouted at in the street. One in two women felt so depressed and anxious they were not able to sleep at night. The research also found that women asylum seekers were facing a number of problems under the then NASS system. As a result of the campaign, NASS agreed to fund places in women's refuges for those fleeing domestic violence as common practice; to offer all women single-sex accommodation if preferred; and to set up a working group, led by Refugee Action and consisting of relevant NASS staff and colleagues from the other agencies, to look specifically at the needs of women refugees and asylum seekers.

In research published in 2005 by the Refugee Council, *Making women visible* (Dumper, 2005), Dumper continues to stress the need for a gender-sensitive system of protection based on women's specific gender-based experiences of persecution that may include conforming to social expectations, sexual violence, trafficking, forced marriage, honour killings and female genital mutilation (FGM). The research also documents the many barriers that make it difficult for a woman to pursue a claim for asylum in her own right. Women do claim asylum in the UK in their own right, as well as through family reunion and as dependants.

Making women visible (Dumper, 2005) develops a strategy for women that is aimed at those who work with refugee women as well as the women themselves, and it uses the category of 'refugee' to accommodate refugees, asylum seekers and those with leave to remain. This study found that the issues faced by women seeking protection in the UK as a consequence of the impact of current asylum policy were: poverty and destitution, dispersal, accommodation, health issues, maternity issues, detention and problems accessing information.

The research also highlights that many women seeking asylum in the UK suffer gross forms of sexual abuse before arrival, and it raises the issue of the sexual abuse of women by individuals they come into contact with here in the UK. Trafficking is another issue of concern. The research documents reports of women who have been trafficked being taken away from accommodation centres by traffickers (Dumper, 2005, p 14). Moreover, girls and young women are especially vulnerable to sexual exploitation and often feel very isolated. Issues of domestic violence and sexuality are also of concern. There is a need for research in this area, particularly as government-estimated figures for trafficked women have been grossly overestimated (Kempadoo and Doezema,

1998; O'Connell Davidson, 2006; Agustin, 2007; Mai, 2009), and there is a conflation with migrant sex work and trafficking per se, which closes off enquiry into the complexity of migration and the choices people make under conditions that are not of their own choosing. In the migration-trafficking nexus the distinction between forced and economic routes into sex work are blurred.

The migration-trafficking nexus

There is an urgent need to disentangle trafficking (forced labour in the sex industry or other informal employment) from migration into the informal economy of sex work/domestic labour/agriculture/caring services. The UK appears to have minimised concern for the human rights of migrant workers to an almost singular focus on trafficking into the sex industry (defined as sexual exploitation). This individualising of the problem prevents a fuller understanding of the complex lives, journeys and choices for migrants that are often situated in the blurring of migration experiences and trafficking. Just as migrants might pay agents to smuggle them across borders to safety and a better future, women and men pay agents to get them work in the sex industry. Some of these relationships may become exploitative and lead to conditions of slavery; many do not.

We need to understand the complex social and political forces at play alongside the experiences of those involved through participatory approaches to research, and create policy accordingly. Globalisation and North–South relations as well as the 'internationalisation' and 'mainstreaming' of sex work impacts on push-pull factors. People will pay (agents) to travel for work in the informal economy of the sex industry. Forced migration is not a modern phenomenon and exists within the context of globalisation and North–South relationships. Castles (2003, p 15) states:

> The growth in people trafficking is a result of restrictive immigration policies of rich countries. The high demand for labour in the North, combined with strong barriers to entry, has created business opportunities for a new 'migration' industry. This includes 'legal' participants, such as travel agents, shipping companies and banks, as well as illegal operators.

There is an urgent need for research to challenge the myth of the numerical crisis. Operation Pentameter 1 took place in 2006 and 'rescued' 88 'victims of trafficking' (VoT) and Operation Pentameter 2 'rescued' 167 VoT between 2006-08. Operations Pentameter 1 and 2 are proactive policing operations focused on trafficking. Pentameter 1 aimed to rescue and protect victims and increase the number of arrests and prosecutions for crimes of trafficking. Pentameter 2 aimed to develop further the work undertaken by Pentameter 1 (that included all 55 forces in the UK) but also to increase knowledge and understanding about trafficking and organised crime. These official 'rescue' figures are not the thousands documented in some media representations (see O'Connell Davidson, 2006). We need quality research that supports policy making at the migration-trafficking nexus that takes account of 'negative globalisation' (Bauman, 2007) and the inter-relationships between globalisation, modernity and humiliation.

How do we define 'forced labour' and 'victims of trafficking', for these are not always clear-cut? The International Labour Organization report of 2005 (p 8) referenced in O'Connell Davidson (2006) states:

> ... forced labour in the global economy acknowledges, 'the line dividing forced labour in the strict legal sense of the term from extremely poor working conditions can at times be very difficult to distinguish'. And even if such definitional problems could be resolved, the Trafficking Protocol would remain a highly selective instrument with which to address the general problem of forced labour because, framed as it is within a Convention on transnational organised crime, the interventions that flow from the Protocol are necessarily only triggered by immigration offences and/or organised criminal activity ... this means they inevitably focus on an extremely limited and narrow part of the problem. (O'Connell Davidson, 2006, p 5)

Definitional problems create tensions in government rhetoric: between protecting human rights *and* controlling UK borders linked to discourses of national safety/security. A singular focus on trafficked people as victims of agents/criminal gangs/evil employers without examining the structural issues of immigration and informal employment is not a sound basis for policy making. What is clear from research that spans politics, economics and the social sciences is that the migration-trafficking nexus is the result of powerful market forces inextricably tied to globalisation and the mainstreaming of the sex industry. There is, therefore, an urgent need to understand sex work as a form of 'informal employment'.

A key issue to consider in current and future research on the migration–trafficking nexus is that women, men and young people working in the informal sector are vulnerable to human rights abuses. There is an urgent need to address how government policies contribute to informal employment, both in terms of the intended and unintended consequences of government policy. What are the push factors in countries of origin? Looking at the home countries of women situated in the migration–trafficking nexus, these are marked by economic and political problems, poverty being a major motivating factor. There is also a need to examine the role of global networks, not just those defined as organised crime/criminal networks.

Therefore policy measures should focus not on individualising victims of traffickers and traffickers/smugglers/networks but rather should emerge from quality research that takes more than just a snapshot to inform policy making. A human rights approach to the issues is important, taking into account the welfare and human dignity of those working in the sex industry, as well as the rights of people who migrate. A human rights approach will be much more effective than one based solely or primarily on criminal justice measures.

Methodological research undertaken in this area should be done so independently. Using PAR methods would help to avoid reproducing binaries that ultimately help to reinforce the 'othering' of women and men who sell sex, thus producing knowledge based on the inclusion, participation and evidence of key stakeholders, including the women and men who are situated in the migration–trafficking nexus. Such research might also map mobilities in the national/European and international contexts and extend work conducted by Mai (2009), Agustin (2007) and Kempadoo and Doezema (1998). This could form one strand of a more constructive policy agenda and lead to more effective policy making in this complex and emotive area.

Making women visible

In *Making women visible* Dumper (2005) calls for a focus on training and employment for women as a key area of need and concern. She also raises: the right to work for asylum seekers; the need for greater involvement of women in refugee-led community organisations; and the need for more projects led by refugee women, including supporting the capacities of refugee women themselves to develop their own services and support systems.

In 2006, in a conference held by Refugee Action the barriers to integration faced by refugee women were documented as follows:

- childcare: many refugee women do not have support systems to help with childcare duties, and it is difficult for them to balance childcare responsibilities with integration activities;
- standard of living: refugee women living in substandard accommodation in distant locations find it very difficult to get involved in integration;
- lack of knowledge about the systems in place and opportunities;
- isolation: refugee women may not have many friends or contacts to learn about opportunities;
- communication: language is a big difficulty for many refugee women;
- lack of confidence;
- managing a home, work and other commitments;
- transferring skills: it can be a long and slow process for refugees to transfer their skills and qualifications;
- non-addressed psychological issues: many refugee women have suffered mental health problems and managing these often takes priority over getting involved in integration activities;
- living with hostility;
- lack of support from other refugee men and women;
- ongoing process (status, dealing with paperwork, for example Home Office, local authorities to contact for housing issues/benefits/ education).

At this conference Jeremy Oppenheim, then Director of NASS, spoke about the work NASS is doing to improve refugee integration and services to asylum-seeking women. The problem, it seems, is not the guidelines, which are very good, but the issue of whether 16,000 staff use them properly. IND published gender guidelines a few years ago, including sections on domestic violence, forced abortion, slavery, FGM and difficulties for women in reporting gender persecution and their reluctance to talk about it. Caseworkers must follow the guidelines that call for sensitivity with women clients (Dumper, 2005, p 25).

Oppenheim documents the challenges to refugee women as follows:

- learning English (lack of knowledge is very isolating), can be difficult with regional accents and local differences;
- childcare: all women with children say lack of childcare is a key problem. Refugee women are not used to leaving children with

strangers and find existing childcare provisions unsuitable. Some local authorities have worked hard on this area while others have not;

- social isolation: suspicion of authority – the local authority can appear oppressive. Clashes in cultural background may make it hard for women in a male-dominated structure to control finances, childcare etc;
- potent stigma attached to refugees in the media, hard to get access to positive images (at this point Jeremy highly praised Refugee Action publications, which have achieved success in showing positive images of asylum seekers and refugees!);
- refugee women may be afraid to ask for help, may lack trust in authority and lack support from their own community and family.

Research with refugee and asylum-seeking women

Research conducted in 2002 and 2005 (O'Neill and Tobolewska [2002b]; O'Neill et al [2007])[3] using PAR methods further supports the findings of research by Dumper (2002, 2005) for Refugee Action. Many women spoke of their first experience of coming to the UK:

> '... when I came to this country, [it was a] completely different system. Different life. Not only the language. At the beginning it was really difficult.' (O'Neill et al, 2005, p 23)

For some the arrival experience was compounded by the attitude of immigration authorities and the general culture of disbelief surrounding the asylum process. They felt humiliated and degraded by their experiences:

> 'My experiences were disgusting and horrible. I was detained for two days and with my pregnancy. The officers knew about my pregnancy because they saw my bulge stomach. I was stripped naked because they said they were looking for drugs maybe because of suspicion ... since then it affected my reasoning and consciousness.' (O'Neill et al, 2005, p 23)

A sense of dislocation, not knowing the language and also culture shock added to feelings of fear and isolation:

'When I was coming from London and was given a house here, the only thing I was given was an agreement with lists of facilities. Because I knew nothing of anything concerning the location of the areas I was depressed.

'It is so lonely, like I stayed in the house for I think two months. Would just go and pick the money, do some shopping and come back in the house.

'I think if I can get some counselling, if I talk it out first, then I will feel more settled, a bit better. You know I think it is because I am not busy, I have been thinking about it so much [circumstances including isolation, poor housing situation and living on a limited budget] and it is getting on my nerves. And it is the thing that has even stopped me from breastfeeding my baby.' (O'Neill et al, 2005, p 24)

This woman was dispersed from Oxford and had a very bad experience of both dispersal and arrival:

'I stayed Banbury at hostel and one night they said to me you have to go to Nottingham tomorrow. And the following day they send us, they send 'erm they send the coach … they didn't explain anything that night. That night they decide to take us to Nottingham from Oxford and then they said OK. They put us in groups, little, little groups. They said through a microphone, they just said yeah this group has to come.' (O'Neill and Tobolewska, 2002, p 39)

Another couple signed papers in a house in Nottingham, but did not know what for. The woman told her husband not to sign:

'We arrive seven o'clock, we arrive Nottingham. They said us, they, I didn't know where am I going because on the list they just said this person has to come down and then they separate and then all like groups. I didn't know. I was scared really very much and I can't explain my feelings. They put us back in the auto, yeah it was the minibus and then they put us back off the bus. It was night. They took us to somewhere, it was night and through the dark places and yeah they did not know the streets and then we didn't know where we are going to. It was very narrow streets, dark and everything. They, we had to, they said that we get into house from back door not in front door and I shout why

not in front door? We don't speak any English but they try
to explain us but you know it's just you know they were
reading you know they said we have to sign this but no
language. They read us and then they said you have to sign
it but we didn't know what. And I just push my husband,
don't sign it you don't know what you are, and then they
say you have to sign this paper. I said to him, I pushed him I
said don't sign it, you don't know what you sign for and he
said we have to do something and he signed everything and
if you don't you know you can't understand them you have
no choice to ask questions because we have no language.'
(O'Neill and Tobolewska, 2002, p 40)

Women describe the fear of living in limbo, waiting to hear if the
application for leave to remain will be agreed, or not, and the fear of
return:

'We are, we are scared to go back to our country. We would
like to answer you, some people answer it, can we stay or not
and psychologically we are under pressure on this because
we don't know what our future will be. We don't know what
we have so if, we don't mind health problem and because
if we know we are going to stay in this country, if we are
going to stay if we will have a life to stay and maybe can
work on our problems but like this we don't know what
will happen to us.' (O'Neill and Tobolewska, 2002, p 41)

A woman talked about her experience of being tagged:

'The Home Office said we are going to tag you. They said
that's the rule that they have now. I did not know what the
tag meant until, you know when you are in emergency
accommodation, staying with other asylum seekers and
refugees as well, they will ask you questions like why is it
that you have a tag? You have committed a crime! It was
difficult for me and I used to cry always, and they would
say if you are not a mafia, you wouldn't have the tag. It
was not easy for me to explain to them that I am someone
who has run away from abuse.... I went to the doctor, they
sent me to a counsellor, because I was saying it is better to
kill myself. I came here to seek protection. They are giving
me a hard time.... Really, I had come to the conclusion to

end my life. Because one, my children are suffering. I can't support my children because the case is taking long! And there is no support that you get. They even haven't done anything to find out if what I am saying is true. That hurts me the most!… I have not committed any crime.' (O'Neill et al, 2005, p 42)

The constant threat of deportation when cases take a long time to be resolved also had a profound effect on some women, who spoke of the stress of waiting over a long period for any result:

'I know the government makes good things for us here like benefits and gives us a home, but I have now lived here four years with the threat of deportation. I have no family at home, I have no parents, nothing to go back to over there. Now I am so, so worried that they will send me back. I can't sleep at night. I wake up and go to the bathroom and cry and cry for myself and my children.' (O'Neill et al, 2005, p 42)

There were also concerns that asylum interviews were sometimes undertaken by people without sufficient knowledge of some of the issues, who may not be able to bring out all of the problems relevant to the case because of their sensitivity. This could impact on whether women were able to get legal support in order to appeal. According to an agency representative:

'In general what happens at the moment is that refugee women wanting to get protection have a problem. Sometimes initial interviews are done by Home Office caseworkers who do not have enough training in gender issues or refugee women's issues. If women haven't mentioned in their initial interview that they've been raped in wartime or in prison, they may lose the chance of getting protection. Sometimes at the appeal stage it is too late for women and they lose their chances because there is no access to legal aid.' (O'Neill et al, 2005, p 43)

Lack of childcare could create problems for women attending interviews at the Home Office:

'What's happening is access to childcare during interviews with the Home Office. There's no support for women with

young children. If they go for a Home Office interview
they have to take their children with them. For example,
sometimes women could be talking about a difficult
situation in their country, such as rape or torture which
can be difficult for children to hear or for women to say
in front of their children.' (agency representative) (O'Neill
et al, 2005, p 43)

For those using vouchers, they felt the humiliation of paying with
vouchers and the guilt and pain of not calculating correctly the cost
of food and goods to the full value of the vouchers, thereby losing
money when 'no change' was given.[4]

In some instances women described being too scared to go outside.
Some of the women were housed in areas where there was perceived
high levels of crime that contributed to feelings of insecurity. Some
experienced hostility and violence from other residents:

'... they don't care too much for the refugees.'

'I was pregnant. They [a group of children] threw stones at
me and my children. They hit us with sticks and we ran, and
they come after us and the broke our windows.' (O'Neill
et al, 2005, p 43)

Some women told us about being helped by local residents or people
in the street. One woman talked of a 'kind lady' she met in the street
who showed her the location of the local school.

Our interviews with a range of support agencies reinforced the
women's narratives:

'There've been a lot of emotional needs, because either it
has been the case that the women have come to this country
on their own, or they have actually suffered trauma where
they have come from, and that's in terms of not having their
own family support over here, or it could be that some of
their children are here with them and some of them they
have had to leave behind.' (project support worker)

'People come over with a lot of problems, psychological,
physical and mental. Some have been tortured or raped.
They don't tend to come with coughs or colds, but more

serious problems.' (medical professional) (O'Neill et al, 2005, p 24)

We were also told about the impact of 'removals' on the mental health of families as well as the impact on the friends and support workers/ services that had made connections and offered support to asylum seekers. In one of the group interviews those present talked about a lady (who had hepatitis) and her child who were deported:

> 'Her husband had died and she was not allowed to stay. What happened to her, is she dead, is her baby gone too? The returns are devastating.' (agency representative) (O'Neill et al, 2005, p 25)

Another agency representative had this to say:

> 'Another family were taken, deported – their flat was left with everything there – they were taken at 3am. It is desperate, their plight, their relationships, the people that are left behind.... If they are known in the community ... and are gaining skills but also they are cared for, loved, understood they are treated like human beings their dignity is upheld. To see the mothers and for the kids to see their mothers treated with dignity, to see that mum is valued and so the child is valued. In schools they are anxious to know that kids are whipped away at 3am.' (O'Neill et al, 2005, p 25)

Language problems, financial hardship, the impact of dispersal and destitution are all part of the experiences of women asylum seekers:

> 'One family had three moves in two months, they were desperate and experiencing great difficulties ... this can cause problems with the case, information goes to the wrong address and it can take a while to get it back on track.' (agency representative) (O'Neill et al, 2005, p 28)

> '... a woman from Uganda with mental health issues, the woman could not attend court because of her distress and a doctor signed a note to say so as she feared her case might be rejected on the grounds of non-compliance. The very next day she had a letter telling her she was being moved

to Hull and she had to return back to here for the court hearing – she had recently given birth to a baby.' (agency representative) (O'Neill et al, 2005, p 29)

'Destitution is the big thing with this group and there are so many gradations along that line.' (agency representative) (O'Neill et al, 2005, p 29)

The agency representative documented these gradations as: (a) asylum seekers without support due to refusal or non-compliance, or not re-registering; (b) asylum seekers of no fixed abode due to refusal to accept one choice of accommodation; or (c) documentation submitted too late to the court hearing. We were told of one case submitted to the Home office two months earlier and the person was still awaiting a reply; in the meantime the person was homeless:

'If they say your case is over, you are moved out of the NASS house, you don't have anywhere to go. Sometimes you are forced to go and stay with a friend. If you stay with that friend she may also have problems. You become like a destitute, going back to where you started. It is so difficult.' (asylum seeker) (O'Neill et al, 2005, p 28)

Sexual exploitation and vulnerability are also concerns. Women did not talk to us directly about sexual exploitation and we did not ask; however, some agency representatives were concerned:

'Occasionally a woman finds a boyfriend and he helps her in other ways but it does not always work out. In another instance one lady would not sign the deportation form she had support only for her child. Had she signed it she would have had accommodation until deportation. In these circumstances exchanging sex is a possibility to help pay solicitors fees to have the case re-opened.' (agency representative) (O'Neill et al, 2005, p 29)

The key issues women raised were basic needs such as a roof/supported housing of a reasonable quality; poverty; communication and relational needs; education and training opportunities; childcare and support; counselling; access to health and sexual health services; and some spoke of sexual exploitation, violence and vulnerability.

What is clear from our research findings is that processes and practices of integration and holistic support services that foster human dignity and counter the prejudice, humiliation and loss of dignity that many women experience (in the process of seeking a place of safety in the UK for themselves and their families) are vital when developing responses to the needs of refugee and asylum-seeking women, their families and their children. Moreover, where the horizontal (grass-roots, face-to-face work by refugee support organisations, arts and cultural organisations) and vertical processes (local and regional policy making) of social inclusion are linked, there is greater scope for the sustained social inclusion, and support of refugees/asylum seekers and their families.

Our research highlighted the impact of isolation, separation and destitution on the mental health and confidence of many women, and how such conditions may make them vulnerable to exploitation. The research also highlighted the strength and resourcefulness of these same women, the fact that everyone we interviewed wanted to contribute to society and improve language, skills and employability; as well as the commitment and energy of the individuals in services that are supporting them.

The study also considered a number of gaps in service provision and suggested potential improvements that could help to address the multiple needs of refugee and asylum-seeker women and their young children. Such service developments are only possible within the context of a wider regional and national strategy that takes into account the findings from this and other related research and ultimately needs to be tied to a more humane asylum system.

To summarise what we know about women asylum seekers and refugees: they experience particular sexual and social inequalities when seeking asylum and in the process of integration; they are relatively absent in the literature and research; they suffer from gender-biased asylum policies; and their voices go unheard in many policy debates, yet nationally ICAR reported that 43 per cent of those asylum applicants supported through NASS accommodation were female (Dumper, 2004). Women cope with the dislocation of arrival, the loss of families, loved ones and children (some of whom they have had to leave behind), the impact of violence and abuse and the impact of dispersal, and yet, as we have found, they are resilient, hopeful, want to contribute, want to work and earn a living for themselves and their children.

A gender-sensitive asylum system?

Deborah Singer, coordinator of the Refugee Women's Resource Project at Asylum Aid, highlights that in the context of the government's strategy to end violence against women and girls, launched in November 2009, there are 'at least twenty-six laws or policies on working with women victims of crime while the UK Border Agency has just two' (Singer, 2009). Singer quotes a woman who has 'had the misfortune to spend time in both prison and an asylum detention centre. When I asked the difference between them, her answer shocked me: "I'd prefer, rather than going in a detention centre ... to be in prison for the rest of my life"' (Singer, 2009). The woman talks to Singer about the male staff at Yarl's Wood immigration removal centre 'appearing unannounced, entering her room and searching through her possessions, including her underwear. Having experienced rape in the Cameroon, this was particularly frightening. In prison a search was always undertaken by a female prison officer and always after she had been warned that this would take place' (Singer, 2009).

UK prison regulations state that there should be 60 per cent or more female staff in a woman's prison. This policy does not exist in detention centres. Moreover, at Tinsley House removal centre, at Gatwick Airport, there is room for 116 men and five women.[5] Women in this situation can feel intimidated, scared and isolated (Shackle, 2009). Despite the fact that the UKBA do have gender guidelines, a recent inspection was described by Dame Anne Owers, the Chief Inspector of Prisons, in the inspection report (Owers, 2009) as 'deeply depressing' (p 6). Her last visit was in 2007 and since then arrangements for women and children had deteriorated. She wrote:

> Overall, this is a deeply depressing report. Provision across a number of areas at Tinsley House had deteriorated since our last visit. In particular, the arrangements for children and single women were now wholly unacceptable and required urgent action by G4S and UKBA.... Tinsley House has become almost an afterthought, housing some poorly cared for children and a small number of scared and isolated single women. This is more than a missed opportunity; it is a wholly unacceptable state of affairs. (Owers, 2009, p 6)

The inspection report states that:

Unnecessary force was used on children during the removal of a family, while childcare and education have got progressively worse. Children at the centre were also said to have limited access to fresh air, and the centre's male-dominated population was described as intimidating for the single women being held there....There had been no progress in childcare and child protection, and significant deterioration in some areas, with an unfocused attitude to the needs of children. The facilities for children had deteriorated, with the loss of specialist childcare staff and the absence of a teacher qualified to teach them. During the inspection, there were no qualified childcare staff at all in the family unit. Parents were anxious about having their children in a facility with adult males, and were reluctant to let them play outside in close proximity to unrelated adults. (Owers, 2009, p 10)

Prison inspectors called for urgent action, describing conditions as 'wholly unacceptable':

There is a failure to ensure even adequate treatment of and/ or conditions for detainees. Immediate remedial action is required. (Owers, 2009, p 9)

As Shackle (2009) states, the UK is one of five countries in the world that has gender guidelines linked to the asylum process. The guidelines state that, if requested, a female asylum seeker must have a female interviewer and childcare for the duration of her interview. However, only some regions can provide this, and 'caseworkers report that gender guidelines are rarely enforced' (Shackle, 2009).

While the treatment of rape victims in the criminal justice system is far from ideal (and the subject of separate campaigning), there are 16 gender-sensitive provisions. For women seeking asylum, there are just two. The lack of sufficient gender guidelines and indeed not using the few that there are 'leads not only to distress for women, but also a waste of public funds as many cases go to appeal' (Shackle, 2009).

Singer (2009) calls for a change of culture; she wants the UKBA to undergo a similar culture change to the more gender-sensitive policies that define the criminal justice system's treatment of women experiencing violence. These have been fought for by women activists, practitioners and researchers and are still not implemented consistently. The Refugee Council's Vulnerable Women's project states that 76 per cent of the women they support have been raped. The situation for women and children in these circumstances is unimaginable. The focus on removals at the cost of care and humanity is not only deeply depressing it is shameful, and it is an indictment of 'an empty and cold forgetting' (Adorno, 1998, p 98) as well as an example of the length the state will go to to police its borders.

As Paleologo (2009, p 24) states, detention centres are the result of policy that makes borders the benchmark for the guarantee of civil and social rights and prioritises perceived 'national interest' over the well-being of vulnerable people.

To counter such exclusionary processes and practices the AHRC-funded Making the Connections Network sought to make connections across the horizontal and vertical processes of inclusion, the intention being to facilitate spaces for dialogue that would provide knowledge about complexity, and connect the people who are migrants, asylum seekers and refugees, researchers, practitioners and policy makers. This participatory approach is documented in the next section.

Making the Connections manifesto: 'Women and migration: art, politics and policy'

In June 2008, the regional Making the Connections Network held a day-long seminar as part of the national refugee week activities. Participants were from a range of policy, practitioner, academic/research and (forced) migration backgrounds. The event focused on women and migration within the broader asylum/migration process.[6] What became clear in the course of the seminar was that overall the voices of migrants were usually mediated by others (journalists, advocacy groups, researchers), that women faced many barriers including a gender-biased asylum system and that through their migration experiences women often ended up feeling as if they had been rendered invisible. Keynote speakers focused on the role of law, arts and theories of citizenship. It was suggested through discussion that in this challenging and often painful context, arts and cultural activities could enable women to share experiences, facilitate connection, communication and foster cultural citizenship.[7] These activities may also open up employment possibilities.

Hardening of UK policy

The hardening of UK policy with respect to asylum and immigration issues, and in particular the increasing numbers of forced removals within the current policy context of managing migration in such a way that it is beneficial to the UK was a key area of concern (Sood,[8] 2008). The failure to recognise and support in law some of the most vulnerable members of society has meant an increase in marginalisation, insecurity and humiliation. Women who enter the UK as refugees, asylum seekers, workers, students, wives and dependants of men are frequent casualties of this increasingly rigid system (Sood, 2008).

Against this backdrop, at the seminar Sood discussed the creative ways in which legal experts seek to protect people, sometimes mobilising legislative frameworks outside of immigration and asylum (for example family law) as a way of overcoming barriers and constraints. Drawing on her own extensive experience, she provided numerous examples and raised her deep concerns about the invisibility of some people and groups in our society, and of the importance of supporting people to find their own mechanisms for speaking out.

Invisible women

The invisibility of women in much of the existing research was a key issue raised by Dumper (2008). Her research findings tell us that women face an excluding asylum process and an unwelcoming media and social environment. They are often very isolated (single, loss of family), are still not being accommodated appropriately and they do not feel safe. Although women are highly motivated to better themselves and to make a life for their children, they are held back by lack of childcare support and face many barriers to employment including language, prejudice and lack of recognition of their skills. Women also face numerous health problems. In the current policy context Dumper (2008) highlighted some issues to take forward when thinking about a manifesto for the East Midlands region. These include: destitution; a gender-(in)sensitive asylum process; access to health; and the cutting back of ESOL. Moreover, Dumper is concerned that there should be rigorous monitoring of the gender impact of the UKBA and NAM.

Refugee Action's Women's Development project 2005-08[9] has developed knowledge and understanding of the experiences of women asylum seekers and refugees and provides a range of services to support women. Speaking on behalf of Refugee Action at the seminar, Amanda Soroghan said half of the world's refugees are female (49 per cent); in 2006 7,363 women applied for asylum in the UK in their own right. The asylum experience involves loss on an enormous scale, loss of family and friends, loss of homeland and culture, loss of socioeconomic status, loss of personal belonging, loss of support networks, loss of 'way of life'. Dumper's survey for Refugee Action (2002) found that 70 per cent of women surveyed were in the UK without a spouse and 37 per cent were mothers separated from their children, and most of these had no families in the UK.

Women are faced with the possibility of detention, uncertainty about their future, culture shock, language difficulties, loss of status, financial difficulties, poor and temporary housing, difficulties in understanding how systems operate and difficulties accessing services, racist abuse and attacks and prolonged unemployment. In 2006 the refusal rate for women at initial decision was 83 per cent. Six per cent were granted refugee status and 12 per cent were granted other forms of short-term protection/leave to remain (these figures do not take account of those granted leave to remain on appeal). Women in these circumstances experience inhuman, humiliating and degrading treatment.

The Women's Development project works with the generic needs of women with special emphasis on education, healthcare and maternity provision. Helping to develop new opportunities that empower women to not only use their existing skills but to develop new skills is a key aspect of the project. The project also works in partnership with other organisations and service providers to improve women's access to services, to ensure existing services are accessible to female asylum seekers and refugees and are culturally and gender sensitive.

Women and contested citizenship

Understanding citizenship as a contested concept, which involves both formal legal status and also rights and responsibilities, also involves both who we are and what we do in relation to each other (Lister, 2007, 2008).[10] Lister states that citizenship can be viewed as both a force for inclusion and emancipation and also of exclusion and oppression. Currently, the government's emphasis on conditional citizenship, which prioritises duties over rights, can seem oppressive, especially in relation to the situation of asylum seekers and refugees. Lister discusses 'how we make good on citizenship involving an emancipatory frame while also challenging the exclusionary dimensions of citizenship' (p 6). One response would involve drawing on Naila Kabeer's work on citizenship (2005, p 6), that we consider Kabeer's four values of citizenship when focusing on women and migration: justice, recognition, self-determination and solidarity, including at the international level. Lister also argues that the concept of human rights is helpful in both the politics of poverty and with regard to the protection of people moving between nation states. In response to the question 'How might we strengthen these rights?', she suggests that we need to strengthen belonging and participation in the civic (the right to work and the right to dignity), political (rights to participate and to a political voice) and social (legal and social rights in contrast to the current policy of destitution which makes women vulnerable to sexual exploitation) spheres.

Taken together these points coalesce into an account and understanding of the importance of cultural citizenship, as the right to recognition, dignity and respect and the importance of an holistic notion of social justice.

Cultural citizenship

Cultural citizenship is supported by PAR and PA. In Chapters Three and Four I explored the value of arts and culture in facilitating processes of belonging. Cultural activity and creative expression are key to the formation of identity, both at an individual and a community level – it is vital for refugees to be able to engage in creative acts. Such participation brings benefits to them as individuals and communities and can also contribute to social inclusion.

Methodologies that incorporate the voices and images of refugees and asylum seekers through ethno-mimesis and participatory collaborative research not only serve to raise awareness about the issues for women but might also produce critical texts that may help to mobilise change. Ethno-mimesis is founded on principles of mutual recognition and seeks to speak in empathic ways with new arrivals through narrative and visual texts that counter valorising discourses and the reduction of the 'other' – the stranger – to a cipher of the oppressed, marginalised and exploited.

The work that art and cultural activities engage us in are important to culture and belonging. In this sense, art does not simply hold up a mirror to the world, but rather can be part of the process through which we come to see, understand and interact with our world/s. Meskimmon[11](2008) discussed the role art can play in contesting these definitive versions, and creating alternative modes of thinking and acting.

Taking up these three nodes, arts and culture, law and citizenship, the afternoon workshop sessions explored these themes further with the participants around themes of: media, culture, policy, employment and destitution. From these sessions a manifesto was created and agreed and distributed across the region.

The manifesto 'What women want'

Women participants wanted to ensure that women's needs identified by research and community projects[12] were met through targeted support. 'This should include support with legal representation, capacity building, networking and the opportunities to sustain our skills' (O'Neill and Cohen, 2008, p 10). The concept of Leicester as a 'city of sanctuary' was also seen as an important practically and symbolically (see www.cityofsanctuary.org/leicester). As a matter of urgency participants wanted politicians at local, regional and national levels to address discrimination and the serious problem of destitution that involves humiliation, lack of representation, poverty and extreme marginalisation. It was unanimously agreed by all that there should be fairer alternatives for refused asylum seekers and an end to destitution. Participants urged everyone to sign up to the Refugee Action campaign at www.refugee-action.org.uk/campaigns/destitution/joinourcampaign.aspx and the Strangers into Citizens campaign at http://strangersintocitizens.blogspot.com/

Media representations of women

A key focus was given to addressing the representation of asylum seekers and refugees in the mainstream media, creating a regional 'alternative news agency' to feed the 'big' media and developing a regional alternative media for/by women refugees and asylum seekers through working in participation with agencies, asylum seekers and refugees and journalists. Also discussed were the negative images portrayed of 'asylum' and the ways in which a particular 'victim' experience around seeking asylum can be fostered that leads to disempowerment, and loss of 'voice'. Participants stated that gendered stereotypes can lead to secondary victimisation and ultimately self-victimisation and they argued for media portrayals that were positive, that there was a need for alternative media that could be proactive rather than reactive. They stressed the need for the right to communicate as a fundamental human right; refugees should be enabled to express their identities and maintain communication with families and homelands; they should have the space to have a 'voice' to counter the negative images of mainstream media and to express their gendered views/aspirations; and there should be recognition and participation by the 'non-citizen' (failed and destitute asylum seekers).

Women's employment, education and training

Women seeking asylum want the right to work and to contribute through paid employment. It was recommended that people sign up to the Refugee Council and Trades Union Congress (TUC) campaign to give asylum seekers the right to work (www.refugeecouncil.org. uk/news/archive/news/2008/April/20080418).

The work conducted by NIACE on alternatives to the mainstream curriculum vitae was highly valued by participants who suggested that NIACE might develop and then roll out the concept of the 'Life CV' and encourage employers to recruit refugees linked to the life skills highlighted by the CV. The Life CV is an alternative form of curriculum vitae that values more flexible and biographical experiences and transferable skills.[13] Supported by the European Social Fund the NIACE project Asset UK was also seen as an example of good practice (although it is now no longer running due to lack of funding). It was also recommended that NIACE be supported with funding to roll out Asset UK and Progress GB to support capacity building and enable women to sustain and develop their skills (see http://archive.niace.org. uk/Research/ASR/Projects/Progress-GB.htm). Moreover, participants suggested that universities allow young asylum seekers access as home students so as to provide a legacy for the next generation.

Role of culture and the arts

Participants agreed that the arts provide a voice to communicate through creative means, and that this was important in developing cultural citizenship as well as generating dialogue between asylum seekers, refugees, new communities and mainstream arts organisations. They also agreed that the creative and cultural means of creating spaces for women's voices and informing policy makers should be encouraged, thus linking horizontal and vertical processes of inclusion through the arts and culture.

Women and destitution

Participants discussed women and destitution with a self-organised group of women who support destitute women, asylum seekers and refugees from African countries. A survey of their members had found that 95 per cent were asylum seekers without any status; three per cent had refugee status; and two per cent were immigrant workers on work permits. The majority (76 per cent) were between 31-60 years old. Twelve per cent were between 21–30 and eight per cent below 20. Members were from the Democratic Republic of the Congo (DRC), Somalia, Sudan, Zimbabwe and Malawi. Seventy-five per cent of the women had children and the majority of these were teenagers who could not access university. Twenty-five per cent of the children were under five and around 30 per cent were between the ages of 6 and 12. The women lived in areas of severe social and economic deprivation where social housing was available. All of the women who took part in the survey were educated to high school equivalent, with 60 per cent having diplomas as for example, designers and teachers; 35 per cent had degrees; and five per cent had postgraduate qualifications. Ninety-five per cent were unemployed and some of these were working in a voluntary capacity. Five per cent were in paid employment. Eighty-five per cent of the women suffered health problems including stress, blood pressure and respiratory health problems – 'diseases of poverty'. Eighty-five per cent had been in Nottingham for 6–10 years, 15 per cent for up to five years.

All of the women had hopes and aspirations – they wanted to be self-sufficient, pay their own way, be able to access services, contribute their skills and creativity and be properly integrated into wider communities. Key issues to be addressed by social policy are: the future of their young people in the British system; health and well-being; employment issues related to poverty; lack of status (and citizenship); becoming integrated; and the need to help people achieve a sense of belonging.

Women face many barriers, especially when they are refused leave to remain. Barriers for destitute women include poor representation and poor legal support and there is an urgent need for capacity building, networking and enabling women to sustain their skills. When leave to remain is given, the transition can be very be difficult. However, despite experiencing poor legal representation and inadequate support, women are incredibly resilient. Longitudinal, biographical and participatory research would enable the production, representation and 'understanding' of women's lives and experiences, which could also have some impact on policy and practice.

Women's action, practice and policy making

Finally, a point on which all participants agreed was the need to examine issues of power and empowerment – not just tokenistic ideas of sharing power and empowering women. Women spoke about the need for targeted and tailored support to facilitate their empowerment, participation and inclusion in a whole range of community-based activities including the right to a political voice as well as help in accessing arts funding and claiming a space through arts for representing themselves, and accessing training and employment.

The manifesto is an example of radical democracy in action and the event and the broader network from which the event emerged is an example of a recognitive community and practice.[14]

Notes

[1] For some helpful examples of research on and with asylum-seeking and refugee women see Crawley (2001); Castles et al (2002); Dumper (2002, 2004, 2005).

[2] Hildegard Dumper is a research consultant who has conducted much research on women's experiences as refugees and asylum seekers. Hildegard is the author of *Is it safe here?* with Refugee Action and numerous other reports.

[3] The research was commissioned by Marchbid Ltd and focused on the needs of refugee women and their children in an area of the UK.

[4] These two women were part of a focus group conducted in 2002.

[5] Group 4 Security (G4S) manage Tinsley House on behalf of the UKBA.

[6] Specifically, it explored the relationship between women's experiences as asylum seekers, refugees or migrants, and issues of culture, law, citizenship and politics. In the morning, keynote speakers from a variety of sectors discussed the important role that the arts, social policy, citizenship, the law and the media play with regard to women and migration, and particularly how they can work to ensure that women migrants have a voice. In the afternoon, participants were involved in an exciting variety of workshops led by NAWEF, NIACE, the Long Journey Home (an East Midlands organisation for artists in exile), Nottingham Trent University and Refugee Action. Delegates engaged in discussion and creative tasks to explore how the issues debated throughout the day could be taken forward practically through the creation of a regional manifesto on 'What women want'.

[7] Here cultural citizenship was expressed as the right to presence and visibility, not marginalisation, the right to dignity and maintenance of lifestyle, not assimilation to the dominant culture, and the right to dignifying representation, not stigmatisation.

[8] Usha Sood, barrister, Head of Trent Chambers, specialises in human rights, family and public law.

[9] Presented by Amanda Soraghan, Kate Wigglesworth and Santok Odedra.

[10] Ruth Lister is Professor of Social Policy in the Department of Social Sciences at Loughborough University.

[11] Marsha Meskimmon is Professor of Art History and Theory at the Loughborough University School of Art and Design.

[12] Women's needs were identified by the Refugee Action Women's Development project, Derby Open Space event, NAWEF and various research.

[13] See the special edition of the *Journal of Vocational Behaviour* on 'career and migration', edited by L. Cohen, J. Arnold and M. O'Neill (forthcoming in 2011).

[14] To see the publication from the event including the manifesto visit: www.lboro.ac.uk/departments/ss/global_refugees/reports.html

EIGHT

Refused asylum seekers, destitution, poverty and social networks

> Destitution is shaming. Both for the individual and for the society that tolerates it....Hungry and homeless people who lack any sense of purpose in their lives, who cannot, will not or fear to return to their country of origin ought not to disappear into a murky twilight on the fringe of society. It benefits no one. It has a negative impact on the economy, on public health, on community relations. These 'invisible people' need to be brought out of the shadows so that they may be both treated humanely – and enabled to contribute to our society. (Kate Adie, quoted in JRCT, 2007, p 3)

Refused and 'undocumented' migrants who do not have permission to reside in the country because they may have overstayed their visa, been refused asylum or entered the country 'illegally' are likely to experience destitution. Undocumented migrants do have rights under European and international law but the fact that their entitlement to rights is being questioned poses a threat to human rights within Europe (Geddie, 2009, p 29). It has been suggested that the government is using destitution as a mechanism to send messages about the lack of support to deter asylum seekers and to pressure those who refuse to sign up to voluntary return. See the 'Still Human Still Here' campaign at www.stillhumanstillhere.wordpress.com. For those who do sign up to voluntary return (deportation), a roof and some costs towards subsistence are provided. Because refused asylum seekers are denied access to public funds, they are outside of citizenship and the law and their status as 'undocumented', 'sans papiers', makes them incredibly vulnerable on a number of registers. Lacking in social rights they cannot access health, welfare and support services – their lives are truly lived on the margins of the margins:

> Their lack of adequate housing, education, health care and fair working conditions creates a state of extreme poverty

and destitution, belying the myth of a socially inclusive Europe. While undocumented migrants constitute a considerable proportion of Europe's migrant population, they have remained invisible to policymakers and there are few social strategies that address their needs. (Geddie, 2009, p 29)

During O'Neill et al's research conducted in 2005, an agency representative told the researcher:

> 'For example we had a woman who was a failed asylum seeker, who was thrown out on the street, because her benefits had stopped. So she came here because she had nowhere else to go. And this has happened with other people. And we just don't know what to do with them. There is no system. As soon as the Home Office decides it is a failed application, they don't have any provision. They [the Home Office] should do something! They shouldn't just leave the poor people to fend for themselves. They're thrown out on the streets, the money stops and that's it.' (agency representative, quoted in O'Neill et al, 2007)

As Geddie (2009) makes clear, the undocumented do have the right to access health and education under human rights law yet inequality and discrimination are widespread. Non-discrimination is a core enabler in the provision of human rights:

> The European Union and its Member States are obliged to uphold the human rights of those within their jurisdiction…. Under human rights law, migrants without a valid residence permit should not face limitations on their fundamental rights on the grounds of their immigration status. Any distinction made in relation to undocumented migrants seeking to realise their innate entitlement to health care, adequate housing, fair working conditions and education are thus in violation of universal principles of human rights protection. (2009, p 29)

Yet despite human rights law social and sexual inequalities are widespread. Undocumented and refused asylum seekers in the UK are supported by a range of NGOs such as faith groups and support networks, with some doctors turning a blind eye to the status of people in order to provide emergency treatment. In Europe there is a wide gulf between 'the theoretical entitlements granted by law to all and the concrete practices experienced by undocumented migrants. The current barriers implemented at the policy level have placed an enormous strain on local actors such as NGOs, health care and educational professionals, as well as local authorities, who witness firsthand the humanitarian crisis they cause' (Geddie, 2009, p 31). Moreover, the fact that so many networks and groups exist to support the rights of the destitute not only in providing a safety net of basic support such as food and blankets but in campaigning for human rights and raising awareness about the humiliating circumstances in which people are surviving is testimony to the moral outrage many feel at the reduced and humiliated circumstances of the destitute.

In France 'the Network for Education Without Boarders (Réseau Education Sans Frontiers – RESF) grew from a gathering of trade unions, parents' associations, community groups and educational institutions who were committed to the protection of non-deportation of undocumented student, at all educational levels' (Geddie, 2009, p 31).

A more temporary form of destitution can also be experienced by asylum seekers as a result of the failure of bureaucracy or the UKBA in sending or responding to documents, that is, sending documents to the wrong address. These people are without public funds until the situation is rectified:

> 'One family had three moves in two months, they were desperate and experiencing great difficulties … this can cause problems with the case, information goes to the wrong address and it can take a while to get it back on track.
>
> 'We were told of letters going to the wrong (old) address and people failing to report as a consequence and a woman who was not aware she had to register after she had had indefinite leave to remain for a year and so her support was stopped.
>
> 'A woman with two kids and a disabled aunt, they had been here for two weeks without food, money and could not speak English. Information had been posted to their old address and so they had nothing. We got on to the Refugee Council and vouchers arrived via a man on a motorbike. The constant moving around is inhuman.' (agency representative, quoted in O'Neill et al, 2007, p 29)

In 21st-century Europe we have the creation of a new underclass – people living in absolute poverty, in a liminal state, outside the framework of citizenship (Taylor, 2009). For Bauman, the existence of this group is much less the result of personal tragedy or misfortune than an inevitable byproduct of a global system that classifies some as without worth (identifying them, literally, as human waste). For Bauman (2004, p 56), 'immigrants embody – visibly, tangibly, in the flesh – the inarticulate yet hurtful and painful presentiment of their own disposability'. The failed asylum seeker is hence 'stateless, placeless, [and] functionless' (Bauman, 2004, p 76), an 'other' that delimits the boundaries of the social body. Stripped of rights, the failed asylum seeker stands on the threshold between insider/outsider, a non-citizen whose existence reminds citizens of their own precarious hold on the 'political'. Indeed, as Tyler (2006, p 186) notes, 'the figure of the asylum-seeker increasingly secures the imaginary borders of Britain today'. And, 'in contrast to the term refugee, which names a (legal) status arrived at, "asylum-seeker" invokes the non-status of a person who has not been recognized as a refugee. Asylum-seekers are literally pending recognition' (Tyler, 2006, p 189).

Tyler argues that identification of an asylum seeker is grounded in deliberate strategies of mis-recognition. In the media politics and media representation of asylum we can see many examples of this:

> Inscribing the category of asylum-seeker in British law through the enactment of a series of punitive asylum laws has enabled the British Government to manoeuvre around the rights of the refugee as prescribed by international law. While the possibility remains that some asylum-seekers will be granted refugee status under the new legislation, this possibility infinitely recedes. For example, section 55 of the Nationality, Immigration and Asylum Act 2002 reintroduced the notorious 'white list' of 'safe' countries of origin and removed in-country appeal rights from asylum claimants. The logic behind the white list is that countries on the list are safe and democratic, and therefore nobody coming from these countries can be a 'real refugee'. (Tyler, 2006, p 189)

And, as Agamben (1995) and others state, the paradox is that the figure of the refugee should embody 'the rights of man par excellence'; instead the figure of the refugee represents 'the radical crisis of the concept of rights' (Tyler, 2006, p 189).

European policy context

As identified by Tisheva and van Reisen (2009, p 4), the EU is a key player in the development and defence of human rights yet the gap between 'discourse and practice is stark'. Increasingly tighter border controls lead to greater numbers paying traffickers or agents to secure border crossings. Increasing use of detention, humiliating practices and the criminalising of people 'whose "crime" is to seek a better life or to escape from persecution find them deprived of their freedom.... The EU is outsourcing immigration controls beyond its frontiers by building detention camps in neighbouring countries often lacking any acceptable control mechanisms with respect to the adherence to fundamental human rights' (Tisheva and van Reisen, 2009, p 4). Experiences of those seeking asylum who become undocumented find that they are outside the international standards of human rights as defined in the UDHR, the Convention on the Elimination of All Forms of Discrimination against Women and the UNCRC, as well as the European Charter. And, as Verhaeghe (2009) points out, the European Pact on Immigration and Asylum 2008[1] that aims to 'create a comprehensive partnership with the countries of origin and transit and encourage the synergy between migration and development', uses 'development aid conditional on cooperation in border control' and thus as 'a tool for immigration policy' (2009, p 4).

Yet the fear and risk surrounding the penetration of fortress Europe by those seeking the benefits of Europe, a 'land of prosperity and freedom' (Tisheva and van Reisen, 2009, p 4), prevents nations of Europe from working with a more open border policy. 'The World Bank claims that a 3 per cent increase in the numbers of migrants in high-income countries would result in a $356 billion increase in global income. The EU also acknowledges that "Migration, if properly managed, can contribute to the reduction of poverty in developing countries"' (Tisheva and van Reisen, 2009, p 4). Instead the policing and protection of borders and the criminalising of some who seek entry mean that '14,7941 have died trying to reach EU borders' and 'In July 2009, 73 African migrants trying to reach Italy from Libya perished at sea after drifting for three weeks in the Mediterranean. During this time 10 ships reported their predicament, but no action was taken' (Tisheva and van Reisen, 2009, p 5). This outrageous and inhuman lack of response shows 'with painful clarity that restrictive immigration laws are indeed deadly' (Tisheva and van Reisen, 2009, p 5). 'An agency of European police for external borders, Frontex, was established in Warsaw in 2007 to co-ordinate operational co-operation of the EU's external borders' (Tisheva and van Reisen, 2009, p 5). Many more who survive the dangerous and deadly journeys face detention, destitution, mis-recognition and humiliation, for they are deemed outside the protection of nation states, and indeed, outside human rights law. Negative globalisation (Bauman) and 'assertions of territorial sovereignty' (Benhabib, 2004, p 7) lead to 'statelessness' (Arendt, 1994) and the loss of the 'right to have rights' (Benhabib, 2004, p 50).

Destitution in the UK

There is little in the way of academic research on destitution, with most research undertaken by NGOs, voluntary and faith sectors. The available research documents the experiences of refused asylum seekers and recommendations for policy and practice emerge from a grounded consideration of the conditions facing destitute asylum seekers in the UK today.

The Joseph Rowntree Foundation conducted research based on extensive networking and consultation in Leeds in 2006 (JRCT, 2007). A key conclusion was that the current system fails when measured against principles of humaneness and human decency and ultimately drives people into an underground economy where they are without rights and recourse to support. To end the shaming process of destitution the report argues for changes to ensure that:

> The asylum claims process keeps people in the system, and does not drive them from it; that asylum seekers can contribute to host communities whenever possible rather than being a burden on them; and that all asylum seekers have access to the basic necessities of life. (JRCT, 2007, p 7)

The report's recommendations seek to facilitate a shift from destitution to a system that provides opportunities for asylum seekers to make a contribution, as well as monitoring asylum seekers' whereabouts to prevent disappearances. The key message of the report is that the asylum process should be genuinely fair, fast and firm, pandering neither to the 'get tough' or 'soft hearted' lobby. Thus, once decisions are made, it is claimed they should be implemented quickly: 'No-one should be left in administrative limbo' (JRCT, 2007, p 4). The suggestion here is that the asylum process should be cost-effective and not wasteful; resources and support should be available for the host population where asylum seekers are living; decisions should be meaningful (those whose cases are still being assessed or refused should not have the same entitlements as those who have been accepted); no one should be left without access to basic resources; and the policy should be credible and benefit the country by avoiding the creation of instability.

The report's recommendations are therefore as follows: that the asylum process should be improved via NAM,[2] which would place voluntary return at the heart of the system; that asylum seekers should be given a licence to work and be able to contribute through working; and the culture of denial that includes applications being refused if there is 'any reasonable means to do so' (JRCT, 2007, p 7) needs to be ended, with the issue of asylum no longer being used as a political football. The report calls for the establishment of an independent decision-making body, separate from the Home Office, to ensure fairness. It is also recommends that the system bring those 'lost' back in. The Joseph Rowntree Charitable Trust (2007) estimates that there are now around half a million refused people 'lost to the system', and it would take between 10 and 18 years at a cost of £4.7 billion to 'return' these people. Thus it is important on moral, social and economic grounds that those living in and contributing to communities and neighbourhoods are granted leave to remain. It is also suggested (in line with human rights law) that people be granted automatic access to healthcare; that local agencies are given adequate support; that asylum myths are challenged; and that detention[3] should be used as a very last resort because detention is isolating, alienating and against the principles of human decency for people who have not committed a crime (other than trying to enter the UK). The report states very clearly that for people unable to be returned home, detention is totally unjust.[4]

A report conducted in Leicester (Jackson and Dube, 2006) details a 212 per cent increase in refused asylum seekers sleeping rough since 2004, and a 47 per cent increase in people sleeping on friends' floors. This increase in destitution is put down to the impact of government policy and lack of access to good legal support. The absolute poverty experienced by refused asylum seekers is of grave concern to the authors, Jackson and Dube. Almost all of the asylum seekers who reported destitution had had their asylum claim refused but were not prepared to sign up to voluntary return because they felt it was not safe to return. The report acknowledges that those contributing to the research were people known to agencies, and as such are the tip of the iceberg. 'Past traumatic experiences have left many asylum seekers with a lack of trust of anyone in "authority" and they therefore choose not to share their stories but seek to remain invisible' (Jackson and Dube, 2006, p 12). Recommendations suggest that destitution should not be used as a coercive tool to force people from the country and that asylum seekers should be granted the right to dignity by contributing to society through paid work while their cases are properly and fairly heard.

In a report on destitution by Refugee Action in 2006, *The destitution trap*, Sandy Buchan writes in the foreword that 'It is hard to read the quotes and the narratives in these pages without believing that there is an overwhelming moral and practical case for reform of this policy' (Refugee Action, 2006, p 2). One hundred and twenty-five destitute asylum seekers were interviewed as part of the research conducted by Refugee Action and Amnesty International (Amnesty International, 2005). Like the aforementioned reports, it argues that no refused asylum seeker in the UK should be forced into destitution. Similarly it is argued that the provision of support to refused asylum seekers should be separated from any requirement to return, so that those receiving asylum support (including those with refused asylum claims) can work so as to reduce the cost to the state. Recommendations are directed to the Home Office as well as to other government departments and public bodies, spelling out the desperation of many who have fallen through the 'tattered support net' (Refugee Action, 2006, p 2) documented below in quotations from all three of the aforementioned research reports:

> 'We're here. We need to live, survive. The government has to give jobs. If, mentally, people are busy it will help them. If not they lose their minds.' (refused asylum seeker, cited in JRTC, 2007, p 8)

> 'I am being forced into prostitution. What else can I do? I have to sell my body to survive.' (quoted in Jackson and Dube, 2006, p 9)

> 'I was involved in politics as part of my research. One day they searched my taxi and found me with a political card. I was kept in prison.... They hit my family members like they were dogs. When they detained me the last time, they had recognised me on a protest march. They took me to jail where I was raped by two policemen. I was handcuffed and they beat my feet.' (37-year-old woman from Cameroon, cited in Refugee Action, 2006, p 43)

> 'I worked for a trade union – I was supporting the lowest paid people in the company and I was politically active....

I was arrested due to my activity against the government.'
(48-year-old man from the DRC, cited in Refugee Action,
2006, p 43)

'I worked with my father on a farm. He had cows and I
had to help him so I didn't go to school. Then soldiers
came, and they killed my father, mother and sister.... I ran
away, and then they told me that they had demolished the
village.' (27-year-old man from Sudan, cited in Refugee
Action, 2006, p 44)

'Government soldiers came to my house before we could
leave. They raped my sisters, broke my brother's arm and
hit me with a rifle. They even raped my daughter – she was
only three and she died.' (30-year-old man from the DRC,
cited in Refugee Action, 2006, p 47)

'There is a civil war. We are from a minority clan. I was
abused, I can't describe what happened. My father was killed
in front of me. My sister was raped. I fled to the Kenyan
border. There the police were raping the girls. I went back
to Somalia, but there we are considered non-Somalis and
seen as Arabs. They attacked me and they destroyed my
manhood.' (31-year-old man from Somalia, cited in Refugee
Action, 2006, p 44)

'I worked for a human rights organisation, and the
organisation and I had many problems ... was arrested and
tortured a lot.' (27-year-old woman from the DRC, cited
in Refugee Action, 2006, p 46)

In each of the above cases these individuals had exhausted the right
to appeal and had their claims refused. A shortage of legal support and
changes in the legal aid system (including restrictions on the funding
for legal assistance and an inability to challenge poor decisions due
to lack of funding) made it increasingly difficult to get legal support
and to mount appeals. Jackson and Dube (2006) argue that, given that
we know 20 per cent of cases are granted on appeal, the flaws in the
decision-making process are hiding a much larger figure of potential
successful applicants, suggesting there is an urgent need to review
this process. Consequently, many people with a well-founded fear of
persecution are undoubtedly falling through the net.

Given this evidence, what is clear is that the destitution of refused asylum seekers is primarily due to the asylum system. Moreover, the way the refused asylum seeker is figured as deviant, criminal, illegal, a non-person, is not only deeply humiliating but reduced in Agamben's terms (1995) to 'bare life'. Narratives documenting the impacts of the asylum process on people's self-worth and dignity tell similar stories across the three reports cited above:

> 'I used to be a respectable teacher back home, owning my own house and a car. But now I am a beggar – I can't believe it.' (cited in Jackson and Dube, 2006, p 11)

> 'When I see the TV or the news [in Iraq], I say, 'thank God I'm here'. But am I staying here? Are they considering me? What's going on? I really don't know. Everything is foggy in the future. I cannot see through. I don't know what's going on; what's going to happen.' (cited in Refugee Survival Trust, 2005, p 15)

> 'Where to go? Where to sleep? Where to eat? I even feel shy to eat at my closest friends' houses. If I visit, I think people will think I am here to scrounge.' (cited in Refugee Survival Trust, 2005, p 15)

The latter quote stresses the anxieties caused by the uncertainty around the asylum processing system, not least the statement of evidence form and the initial interview (whose importance cannot be overstated). Refugee Action research revealed differing experiences of the process and some people did not know what stage they were at or what was expected of them. Some were given an initial screening interview (that included photographs being taken, fingerprints and basic details) and yet some went straight into the main interview:

> 'One of the officers at my interview was very emotional and got angry. He would say, "No, I'm not asking you that question," when I wanted to elucidate on various points and kept saying "just one word answers". He would get angry for no apparent reason. He was the one completing my SEF [statement of evidence form].' (woman from Zimbabwe, cited in Refugee Action, 2006, p 54)

Anything omitted from this interview may be considered as inadmissible at a later stage or held as evidence that the asylum seeker is fabricating his or her claim (Refugee Action, 2006, p 54). The authors state that a bad interview at this stage, especially when combined with poor legal representation later, can make it difficult for an individual to regain their credibility within the asylum process. This flawed process may have increased the refusal and return rate for asylum seekers, but the pay-off is a system that is inconsistent and unjust.

Common across the reports and research documented in this section is the importance of the right to work, not only with respect to being able to satisfy basic needs through paid work but also in the dignifying and relational processes involved. The right of access to healthcare and legal advice is also stressed. It is further recommended that the Department of Health publish guidance in different community languages about the health and social services available to those 'refused' in different community languages, with 'legacy cases' given support. The Joseph Rowntree report (JRCT, 2007) calls for legacy cases to be given automatic leave to remain, not simply healthcare support. The report also recommends that minor incidents of crime such as working illegally or stealing food should not be taken into account when granting leave to remain. Preventing destitution means granting the right to work, vastly improving access to and quality of legal advice, as well as continuing and developing partnership working between agencies and organisations across the statutory and voluntary sector.

Refusal and return

Those making arrangements for assisted voluntary return are entitled to section 4 ('hard case') support, which consists of bed and breakfast accommodation plus £35 in voucher support (in 2009). The numbers unable to return home for medical or safety reasons who have been in receipt of section 4 support has risen rapidly, from some 300 in 2003 to nearly 11,655 by the close of 2009. Yet the majority of failed asylum seekers do not register for voluntary assisted return because of fear of persecution: 'often there is no safe passage or authorities in the country of origin refuse to provide the necessary paperwork' (JRCT, 2007, p 6). Many others have their support revoked when the authorities decide they are not taking steps to return voluntarily. Estimates suggest that as many as 110,000 who failed their asylum claim between 1994 and 2004 remain in the UK but without support (NAO, 2005). Many who apply for support find their claim is subject to delays. As such, there are many failed asylum seekers who receive no support from the state, and are forced to rely on charity handouts, the goodwill of local communities and kinship/friendship networks or drift into the informal economy. Such scenarios are also likely for those who receive section 4 support long term, with 28 per cent on such support for more than one year (with reports of one individual in 2005 on such support for over six years). Given voucher support is seen to be inadequate and inflexible (for example supermarket vouchers are not ideal for those wishing to buy halal meat), those receiving section 4 support are not just destitute and dependent, they are often depressed, distressed and desperate (Martin, 2006).

The reality is that networks of voluntary agencies, including faith groups, refugee organisations and micro-communities, are the safety net for those people living in destitution. Inevitably some people can slip through this net. Refused and destitute asylum seekers constitute a new underclass. Under section 55 of the Nationality, Immigration and Asylum Act 2002, if people do not claim asylum at the point of arrival (within 72 hours) they will receive no support. On 23 May 2004, a small gain was won. The Court of Appeal in London upheld an earlier ruling that section 55 as part of the 2002 law is in breach of Article 3 of the ECHR, which guarantees shelter as a 'basic amenity', and states that no one should be subjected to 'inhuman or degrading treatment':

> The case was brought by three asylum-seekers, Wayoka Limbuela, Binyam Tefera Tesema and Yusif Adam. They had their applications refused and were denied benefits and housing after falling out of the three-day limit for claiming asylum. Mr Adam had to sleep in a car park for a month after his application was refused, and Mr Limbeula spent two nights without food or shelter outside a police station until 'interim relief' was provided. Adam Sampson, director of the homeless charity Shelter, said 'This ruling is a victory for vulnerable people who are in desperate need'. (Casciani, 2004)

The Refugee Council has conducted a survey investigating the real impact of section 55 one year after its implementation (Refugee Council, 2004). The report reveals that section 55 is forcing many asylum seekers into destitution and placing an unsustainable burden on the voluntary sector and refugee community.

> 'I just want to say that section 55 leads people to despair, loneliness, and theft, as what are you supposed to do when

you are sleeping rough and do not have the right to work? NASS seems to think I have hidden people able to help me should things go wrong, but I have no one, nothing, nowhere.' 26 year old male from Somalia – awaiting section 55 decision. (Refugee Action, 2004, p 1)

More research in this area is clearly needed to get a comprehensive national picture. This research should be undertaken by academics in partnership with the NGO sector and refused asylum seekers.

Refugees, asylum seekers and refused asylum seekers often occupy marginal positions and experience varied forms of exclusion within the UK. Refused asylum seekers are non-citizens, denied basic human rights that render them destitute. Revealing their stories of migration and discourses of dislocation, and representing the complexity of their lived experiences is a vital step in creating a more compassionate society and policy. However, what is needed ultimately is for European countries: to cease the practice of using destitution as a tool of immigration control; to cease treating people in such inhuman and degrading ways via the operation of law and the policies of border control and restrictions on entry: and to recognise and remedy the fact that migration is a result of inequalities between countries of the North and South. Criminalising those who seek safety and a better life is counter-productive. For, ultimately:

> The European Union will remain a magnet for people seeking a better life, regardless of the risks they face, until the differences in opportunity at home and in Europe become more equal. Any attempt to halt irregular migration will fail and be harmful as long as the people in question are not offered valid and legal alternatives for the development of themselves and their families, either in their country of origin or in the destination country. In consequence, development policy is inextricably linked with approaches to migration. (Tisheva and van Reisen, 2009, p 5)

Notes

[1] The European Pact on Immigration and Asylum was first approved by the Justice and Home Affairs Council on 25 September 2008. With the adoption of the Pact, the Council made five basic commitments: (1) To organise legal immigration to take account of the priorities, needs and reception capacities determined by each member state, and to encourage integration. (2) To

control illegal immigration by ensuring that illegal immigrants return to their countries of origin or to a country of transit. (3) To make border controls more effective. (4) To construct a Europe of asylum (to create a single European asylum procedure by 2012). (5) To create a comprehensive partnership with the countries of origin and of transit in order to encourage synergy between migration and development (Verhaeghe, 2009, p 9).

[2] The model has three distinct features: (1) segmentation of claims; (2) fast-track processing; and (3) single case ownership. Concerns have been expressed by refugee organisations that 'segmentation will result in claims being pre-determined before they have been given substantive consideration', and fast tracking may not allow enough time for the claimant to seek legal advice, prepare their claim properly nor provide enough time 'for decision makers to consider the claim adequately' (Ward, 2003, p 16).

[3] Yet as ICAR's recently published briefing notes, 'The use of detention is an integral part of the Home Office's strategy to facilitate the removal of asylum seekers with unfounded claims. This is illustrated most notably in the name change from "detention centres" to "Immigration Removal Centres" (IRCs) introduced under the Nationality Immigration and Asylum Act 2002 and in the government's commitment to increasing the capacity of the detention/removal estate' (ICAR, 2007, p 12).

[4] See also Amnesty International's report *Seeking asylum is not a crime*, published in June 2005. The report highlights the fact that despite the Home Office claim that 'detention would only be used as a last resort', there is evidence of the increased use of detention under immigration powers. 'Amnesty believes that many thousands were detained in 2004, some languishing in detention for many months in grim prison-like conditions. Others were detained for the duration of the asylum process.' (p 8)

NINE

Human dignity, humiliation and social justice: beyond borders – re-imagining the asylum-migration-community nexus

This chapter highlights the profound importance of 'understanding' experiences of humiliation and mis-recognition experienced by those in the asylum-migration nexus and the importance of fostering human dignity and social justice globally and locally. Given the research documented and discussed in previous chapters, the following questions need to be addressed. How can we address the processes of 'othering', humiliation and subjugation experienced by people situated in the asylum-migration nexus? How can we foster processes of social justice that include mutual recognition, dignity and egalization in our institutions, policies and practices towards people seeking safety and refuge? The work of the HDHS global network offers a way forward towards the promotion of social justice and cultural citizenship for all. HDHS is an example of a recognitive community, working towards a radical democratic imaginary. Moreover, using participatory research constituted by recognition and respect for people seeking asylum, refuge, belonging are key to answering the aforementioned questions.

Participatory action research and the HDHS network

Since 1989 my work has been rooted in PAR methodologies, working with communities to achieve change. Whose knowledge counts is an important dimension of this work in that PAR facilitates a loosening of the power/knowledge axis involved in 'expertness' and values the knowledge/experience of people in communities. There is a commitment to fostering spaces for dialogue through the principles of PAR. For me PAR is a combination of critical theory and praxis. This is an interpretive, hermeneutic action-oriented theory that is influenced by my readings in the critical theory of the Frankfurt School, feminisms, critical and cultural criminology, ethnography and experimental ways of understanding and representing lived experience such as ethno-mimesis. Praxis (as purposeful knowledge) may take many forms; at every stage of the PAR process there is the possibility for change (Askins and Pain, 2009; Pain, 2009).

PAR, as defined in Chapter Three, is interventionist, action-oriented and interpretive and based on principles of inclusion, participation, valuing all voices, mutual recognition and links to social justice, which in turn may foster recognition and 'understanding'.

The HDHS network explores the dynamics of humiliation and human dignity through what is called an appreciative 'frame' for enquiry that places importance on 'it is not just the work that we do together that is important, it is how we work together that strengthens our shared efforts' (Hartling, 2005, p 1). Thus, 'within this frame, participants are invited to co-create a context of mutual openness, mutual empathy, and curiosity' (Hartling, 2005, p 1). The process is relational and mutual recognition is fostered in workshops and conferences where 'open space' principles are embedded. Hartling suggests that growth fostering relating is characterised by 'mutuality, authentic engagement and communication, zest, mutual empathy, mutual empowerment, leading to greater knowledge and clarity, greater sense of worth and a desire for more connection' (2005, p 3).[1] The HDHS global network recognises the fact that global interdependence forces humankind to face its global challenges, both ecological and social, as a shared responsibility that has to be shouldered jointly. This is reflected in the principles and practices of the network itself. Scholars from around the globe are representative of a worldly engagement where 'recognition' and 'understanding' in the senses discussed earlier in this book are practised. The network is founded on deep respect for the forms in which scholarship and enquiry takes place, and this is as important as what we study. Hence appreciative enquiry (developed by David Cooperrider at Case Western Reserve University, Cleveland, Ohio) is encouraged. Academics, researchers and practitioners make up the membership of the network, which grew out of Lindner's (2006) work, vision and her relationship with Hartling (who until recently was director of the Jean Baker Miller Training Institute).

Diaspora, humiliation and belonging

> Humiliation is about *putting down* and *holding down*. (Lindner, 2006, p 3)

The following narrative (an excerpt from an interview conducted in 2000)[2] gives a sense of the humiliation, loss of dignity and respect experienced by an asylum seeker, Leyla, which must be contextualised in her experiences of forced migration, dislocation and the temporary nature of being an asylum seeker, as well as the lack of care and communication provided by the officers who were responsible for her 'dispersal' from London to the East Midlands.

Leyla's brother was killed and she was forced to flee because of a well-founded fear of persecution that included possible death at the hands of the authorities. She arrived in Britain using a visa and claimed asylum when the visa expired. She was dispersed to a city outside of London:

> 'They didn't explain anything that night. That night they decide to take us to X from X. That night they just took us in the bus and then we didn't know where we had to go and then we arrived to X.... It was the middle, midday and then we arrived about night-time. There were people from somewhere else they dropped them from other towns and places. The one important thing is that the main thing is that they didn't explain us where we had to go.... And then they separate everybody and we just see women left because they, our names weren't on the list, our names weren't on the list and other people they had accommodation ... we are speaking very little English and then I ask them why, where I am going for. And I tried to hit the person because my temperature was over and then I called my sister on the phone.... I forced a person to call my sister to communicate....' (Leyla, quoted in O'Neill, 2007, p 76)

She describes being very scared and humiliated by this experience. Her asylum claim took one-and-a-half years to be processed and her application was refused. She appealed against the decision and at the time of the interview was awaiting news of the appeal. During this time she tried to kill herself twice. In her home country Leyla was a journalist writing for a Kurdish women's newspaper. She said:

> 'We are scared to go back to our country ... can we stay or not and psychologically we are under pressure on this because we don't know what our future will be ... we don't know what will happen to us.' (O'Neill, 2007, pp 76-7)

In response to processes and practices of humiliation the aims of the HDHS network are to 'stimulate systemic change, globally and locally, to open space for mutual respect' and to break cycles of humiliation throughout the world. The network also seeks to counter the negative impact of globalisation that Bauman defines with a focus on the need for growth fostering social communities and relationships to interrupt pathways of violence, to build egalization and human dignity, and to counter negative social forces such as the impact of authoritarianism, humiliation, instrumental reason, racism, sexism and identity thinking (see www.humiliationstudies.org).

Linda Hartling, currently director of the HDHS network, articulates her position:

> For me, rather than thinking of human dignity as an individual, internal phenomenon, I like to think of human dignity as a co-created experience. It is an experience developed through respectful connection (interpersonal, social, international, etc) in which people feel known and valued, they feel that they matter.... It is our responsibility to participate in the construction of this relational experience for all people. (www.humiliationstudies.org/whoweare/annualmeetings.php#quotes)

The network is founded on the importance of emotions on conflict as well as the need to influence public policy. It is grounded in academic work and the relationship between theory and practice. Since 2004 a two-day annual workshop has been held at Teachers College, Columbia University, that brings together scholars from the social sciences, humanities, international relations and politics, practitioners, mediators, teachers and counsellors 'to probe the role of the notion of humiliation from the two different angles of conflict and emotion'.

The workshops are developed on 'open space' principles; they are interactive and highly participatory and humiliation is discussed in an

> atmosphere of openness and respectful inquiry.... We believe that notions such as dignity and respect for equal dignity are important not only for conflict resolution, but also for conferences such as our workshops. The name Human Dignity and Humiliation Studies attempts to express this. We wish to strive for consistency between what we think are important values for conflict resolution, and the way we conduct our work and our conferences (www.humiliationstudies.org/whoweare/annualmeeting14.php).

Within the context of the workshops participants are encouraged to co-create in the context of mutual openness, recognition and empathy and curiosity. I suggest, rather like the space between art and ethnography in the concept of ethno-mimesis, the network events also provide 'potential space' in Winnicott's terms (1982). Potential space is a relational and dialogic space that feels safe enough to support an ongoing process of relaxed self-realisation and depends for its existence on living experiences.

> In the spirit of our vision, we, the HDHS network, wish to foster an atmosphere of common ground and mutually caring connections as a space for the safe expression of even the deepest differences and disagreements, and the toughest questions of humiliation, trauma, and injustice. This means practicing radical respect for differences and being open to a variety of perspectives and engaging others without contempt or rankism. As we have seen in many fields, contempt and rankism drain energy away from the important work that needs to be done. Most people only know 'conflict' as a form of war within a win/lose frame. 'Waging good conflict', (Jean Baker-Miller) on the other side, is about being empathic and respectful, making room for authenticity, creating clarity. (www.humiliationstudies. org/whoweare/whoweare.php#organization)

The workshops and conferences seek to 'foster an atmosphere of common ground and mutually caring connections as a space for the safe expression of even the deepest differences and disagreements, and the toughest questions of humiliation, trauma, and injustice' (www. humiliationstudies.org/whoweare/index1.php).

Primarily grounded in academic work, the HDHS network seeks to bring this into 'real life'. Professor Shibley Telhami's comment underpins this connection, for he advocates the following:

> I have always believed that good scholarship can be relevant and consequential for public policy. It is possible to affect public policy without being an advocate; to be passionate about peace without losing analytical rigor; to be moved by what is just while conceding that no one has a monopoly on justice. (http://humiliationstudies.org/whoweare/ whoweare.php#introduction)

A core concept is the notion of unity in diversity. This is a fundamental principle for the network. The HDHS as a network and organisation is built on a threefold vision:

1. *Research* that increases understanding of the nature of the humiliation dynamic, destructive outcomes resulting from humiliating strategies and tactics and factors contributing to its use in international affairs.
2. *Education* of both children and adults that both increase understanding of the negative consequences of humiliation and generate support of alternative approaches that promote human dignity.
3. *Interventions* that promote the use of appreciative and affirming approaches in interpersonal, intergroup and not least in international relations, so as to promote an increased sense of global community.

Importance of humiliation

Lindner (2002, p 1) writes that in the events of 9/11 2001 terrorists acted as

> the ultimate humiliators. Taking down the World Trade Centre's Twin Towers was a cruel message of humiliation. History offers numerous other examples of atrocious outcomes of cycles of humiliation. It is common knowledge to assume that World War II was triggered, at least partly, by the humiliation that the Versailles Treaties inflicted on Germany after the First World War. The urge to redress and avert humiliation powered Hitler and provided him with followers. War and Holocaust were the result. (pp 3–4)

Moreover, processes of globalisation are central to 'newly emerging feelings of humiliation'. As people become more interdependent and indeed dependent:

> As people move closer to each other, expectations rise and disappointments are bound to occur. Human rights ideals with their notion of dignity and respect are equally deeply interlinked with the concept of humiliation. The first sentence in Article 1 of the Universal Declaration of Human Rights reads 'All human beings are born free and equal in dignity and rights'. Thus, the central human rights message stipulates that every human being has an inner core of dignity that ought not to be humiliated. (2006, p xiv)

Lindner continues:

> Wherever the human rights message is heard and accepted
> by people around the globe, people feel that their humanity
> is being humiliated whenever their dignity is violated or
> soiled. Human rights ideals squarely oppose hierarchical
> rankings of human worthiness that once were regarded as
> 'normal' – and still are 'normal' in many parts of the world.
> In the cross-fire between both paradigms, particularly hot
> feelings of humiliation emerge. (2006, p xiv)

For Lindner (2006, p xiii) humiliation is the 'nuclear bomb of emotions'
and 'humiliated hearts and minds are the only "real" weapons of mass
destruction, particularly in a globalized and interdependent world that
embraces the human rights ideals of equal dignity for all'. Hence, for
Lindner, 'the phenomenon of humiliation should be studied, prevented,
mitigated and healed in the context of globalization and human rights,
culture differences and inter-group conflict, cooperation and violence,
competition and negotiation, and power and trust' (2006, p xiii).

Lindner (2006) not only calls for a moratorium on humiliation
to be included into new public policy planning, but also for new
decent institutions and leadership to heal and prevent the dynamics
of humiliation, othering, de-humanisation and an examination of
governance both nationally and globally.

Dennis Smith (2006) agrees, and he also writes about the dynamics of
humiliation in relation to globalisation and the regulation of modernity:

> ... globalization is a major cause of humiliation for many
> people, and the codes of modernity (the honour code, the
> human rights code or some mixture of the two) have a
> great influence on the ways in which this humiliation is
> experienced and understood. (2006, p 9)

For Smith, globalisation (the imperial impulse, the logic of the market
and the cosmopolitan condition), humiliation (conquest, relegation
and exclusion leading to responses of escape, acceptance, rejection
and potentially triggering cycles of fear, victimisation, revenge), the
regulation of modernity (through the honour code, the human rights
code or a mixture of the two) are deeply interrelated via the concept
of the 'triple helix' and are 'shaping globalization's hidden agenda'
(2006, p 9).

Smith (2006) seeks transformation of humiliating cycles and he pins his hope on the EU, defining 'transformation' as a kind of collective renewal with humiliation gradually removed (or decommissioned) through an emancipation cycle that involves: truce, dialogue, a new language of peace seeking as a shared enterprise and the gradual creation of a new set of joint interests. Poverty must be eliminated and humiliation has to diminish radically (Smith, 2006, p 197). '[W]e need to build strong institutions of governance at global –regional and global level that can codify and enforce those rights.... The EU has made good start' (Smith, 2006, p 199). 'Decent democracy' for Smith has 'at its heart the following proposition: The implementation of the human rights code by states and citizens has the object of making sure that everyone gets decent life insofar as it is possible' (Smith, 2006, p 201).

As we saw in the last chapter, the ambiguity at the heart of EU policies, especially in relation to those seeking asylum and the treatment of refused, destitute and detained asylum seekers, is deeply ambiguous and does not appear to usher in much hope. Instead, the digging that Bauman speaks of as a consequence of negative globalisation is apparent. However, I argue that fostering decent democracy (or rather radical democracy) is a good start. As a space of radical democracy in action, the HDHS network provides a potential space, a creative space that is both the medium and the outcome of collaborative work based on a global network of people committed to working for change, against the grain and in ways that are premised on the awareness of our relational connectedness.

The experiencing of feeling

The process of collaborating within the appreciative frame of enquiry does not compel but allows participants to 'tap into the rich diversity of knowledge and experience that each person brings to the meeting' (Hartling, 2005, p 1). For Klein this also includes the potential to 'avoid wasting energy on distracting thoughts, including the fear of humiliation' (Klein, 2004, p 4, quoted in Hartling, 2005, p 2).

The appreciative framework at the centre of the work of the HDHS and the principles of PAR are, for me, related. One can re-imagine the asylum–migration–community nexus by 'understanding' experiences of humiliation, mis-recognition and lack of respect through PAR that is underpinned by principles and practice that are committed to fostering human dignity and social justice locally and globally. In Bourdieu's sense of the word:

'Understanding' involves attempting to situate oneself in the place the interviewee occupies in the social space in order to understand them as necessarily what they are.... [T]o take their part ... is not to effect that 'projection of oneself into the other' of which the phenomenologists speak.... It is to give oneself a *general and genetic comprehension* of who the person is, based on the (theoretical or practical) command of the social conditions of existence and the social mechanisms which exert their effects on the whole ensemble of the category to which the person belongs ... and a command of the psychological and social, both associated with a particular position and a particular trajectory in social space. Against the old Diltheyan distinction, it must be accepted that *understanding and explaining are one*. (Bourdieu, 1996, pp 22-3)

The reflexive sociologist can 'provide the felicific conditions which will facilitate open and frank communication' (Fowler, 1996, p 14).

Therefore, 'understanding' emerges from methodological immersion in a subject–subject relationship. In this respect the commitment and 'understanding' facilitates the site of a 'democratization of the hermeneutic' (Fowler, 1996, p 15). The texts, objects and images that can emerge from PAR and PA (ethno-mimesis, see Chapter Five) have the potential to enable us to experience and re-imagine the intersecting and embodied experience of exile, displacement and belonging.

The process of 'understanding' is of course dependent on connection and 'attunement' through listening as well as sensuous knowing. In the process of conducting sensitive ethnographic work, or PAR, or entering the dialogic space created at HDHS network events using principles of 'open space', we 'attune' ourselves to the 'other' through 'immersion, identification, followed by critical distancing and reflexivity involved in interpretation, commentary and criticism' (O'Neill, 2002, p 80; 2008, p 32).[3] It is also a similar process to what Witkin (1974, 2002) calls 'subjective–reflexive feeling'.

Witkin writes that social being is configured in the feelings experienced by individuals who are party to relatedness: 'In the pure subjective–reflexive relationship, the identities of the parties are reflexively improvised in and through relatedness. Identities are not brought to the relationship they are lived out in the process of relating' (p 182). Following Buber, Witkin calls these I–thou (ich–du) relations, or, 'as Victor Turner uses it "being present to one another", which can be said to constitute social being' (Witkin, 1974, p 182).

I–thou relations are not you and me or we; I–thou stresses mutuality, relatedness and recognition. Witkin states that 'to create an I–thou relationship one must be open to it as a concept rather than actually pursue it – to generate an I–thou relationship the qualities associated with it must be created' (Witkin, 1974, p 182). This can also be expressed through Lindner's (2006) gesture of openness to the other: 'we recognise that all human beings share fundamental existential similarities, among them the need for validation and recognition. We extend our hand' (Lindner, 2006, p 150).

In contrast are the I–it (ich–es) relations, the I confronts the other as an object. One can recognise this in the treatment of asylum seekers left to sink in the Mediterranean, in the de-humanising of refused asylum seekers,[4] in the withdrawal of the means of survival to refused asylum seekers, in the way those seeking asylum are treated as social junk, as objects, to be tagged, contained, deported. To a lesser degree the 'ich–es' relation is reflected in the way that agencies mediate the voice of asylum seekers and refugees, speaking for the other as victim. As Tyler (2006) says, this generates compassion, but in objectifying and homogenising the other, the opposite is achieved. In a similar sense one can see 'I–it' relations in the way that the (communitarian) New Labour and Conservative Parties in the UK define and treat what they call the 'underclass', 'the disproportionately non-white impoverished peoples of the inner cities' (Smith, 1998, p 196). Not only are they blamed for their own 'impoverishment and constructed as sub-humans, they are punished by the withdrawal of welfare support and contained through inner city policing leading to the view that they are, in fact, a disposable population, who are structurally excluded from participation' (Smith, 1998, p 197).

Related to participatory methodologies and indeed arts-based methodologies (discussed in Chapters Three and Five), Jones (2006) argues that traditional methodologies do not deal well with the sensory, emotional and kinaesthetic aspects of lived experience, and in considering these aspects in research, interviews could be the locus not for gathering information but for producing performance texts and performance ethnographies. Collaborating across disciplines, 'finding co-producers for our presentations ... pushing the limits of dissemination ... involving research participants in the production and dissemination of their own stories' is, for Jones (2006, p74), a way of overcoming practical obstacles of knowledge transfer. This also involves 'relational aesthetics' drawing on the work of Bourriard (1998): 'Central to its (*relational aesthetics*) principles are intersubjectivity, being-together, the encounter and the collective elaboration of meaning, based in models of sociability, meetings, events, collaborations, games, festivals and places of conviviality' (Jones, 2006, p 74). Jones writes, 'it is in these moments of shared, extended reality that we connect to what it means to be human and, therefore, reached [sic] a higher plane of understanding and a blurring of individual differences' (Jones, 2006, p 83). The approach Jones takes to social research through performative means is similar to the operation of ethno-mimesis and appreciative enquiry; what they share is a focus on the imaginary, a focus on the utter relationality of our encounters with each other, a focus on recognition and on the possibilities for radical democracy.

Radical democratic imaginary

For Cornell (1995) the imaginary domain is a moral and psychic space that is necessary in order to keep open and rework the repressed elements of the imaginary. I argue that such a space is also necessary to open and keep open critical discourse, that works against the grain, that 'wages good conflict' towards a radical democratic imaginary. Laclau and Mouffe's 'radical democratic pluralism' represents

> the image of the democratic revolution as a subversive force that can be spread throughout the social in the form of an infinite number of contingent recitations. From this perspective, democratisation is understood not as a set of superficial reforms, but as the struggle to institutionalise a radical democratic pluralist imaginary. (Smith, 1998, p 5)

A radical democratic imaginary is important in articulating a recognitive theory of community (Yar, 2003) that might transgress the current regressive discourses and practices by states towards asylum seekers, refugees and migrants and towards possibilities for open borders. Radical democracy reinforces the need for:

1) The circulation, radicalisation and institutionalisation of democratic discourse (Smith, 1998, p 7). Political activists need to engage in what Laclau and Mouffe call a retrieval project, 'a hegemonic struggle to bring more democratic moments ... to the fore in both liberal and socialist traditions' (that is, socialism can be democratic and undemocratic – but 'it is the democratic moment that holds promise for radical theory') (Smith, 1998, p 15). By way of an example social democratic policies impoverished the notion of democracy as they intensified state control over the lives of the poor, such that

welfare programs in the US have institutionalised a feminisation of poverty and 'disempowered single women with children', leaving them 'exposed to the moralistic demonizations of the right' (Smith, 1998, p 15).

2) The space for democratic contestation must be preserved within democratic struggle, against the forces of authoritarianism and identity thinking.

3) 'Equal access to material resources necessary for self development and meaningful participation in social, cultural, political and economic decision making' (Smith, 1998, p 31).

4) Anti-essentialism is crucial to the construction of radical democratic pluralism: what Adorno called non-identity thinking.

5) Radical democratic pluralism that resists all forms of domination and 'disciplinary normalisation'. For example, 'a top down leadership that imposes disciplinary normalisation upon a variety of progressive struggles according to its own abstract program would not benefit from the contextually-specific wisdom that the locally-situated groups have developed' (Smith, 1998, p 35).

6) Participatory processes and practices and arts-based research are embedded in a radical democratic project towards a radical democratic imaginary.

As stated in chapter three, critical and cultural analysis using participatory methods could help to access a richer understanding of the complexities of forced migration, develop knowledge and analysis that might foster a more radically democratic imaginary that challenges exclusionary discourses and connects to more relational ways of promoting social justice and egalization. Certainly, the methodological approach of combining ethnography/biographical research and art/mimesis involves the creation of a 'potential space' (Winnicott, 1982) a reflective space (between art and ethnography) for dialogue, narratives and images to emerge (O'Neill, 2008, 2010).

Beyond borders: making connections

In the introduction I began this book by situating myself as an interdisciplinary scholar working across the borders of sociology, criminology and critical theory with a strong interest in arts and cultural analysis. My research activity in the area of forced migration uses PAR methodologies including biographical sociology, arts practice and the production of praxis (knowledge), which addresses and intervenes in public policy. I have argued during the course of this book that participatory and arts-based methodologies have a vital role in conducting research with people and groups situated in the asylum-migration-community nexus. Through critical theory in practice (as praxis) sociologists and criminologists can better understand the socio-cultural-political (macro) relations and interrelations, and the multiple (micro) 'realities' we might want to transform. Accessing and documenting lived experiences in a reflexive, critically aware way can lead us to a better understanding of psychic processes and sociocultural structures and processes. This knowledge can in turn help us to develop transformative possibilities through conducting PAR. My concept of 'ethno-mimesis' is defined through a combination of PAR and PA informed by the work of Adorno and Benjamin. Ethno-mimesis draws on 'feeling forms' such as photography, art, performance art and life story narratives, and engages dialectically with lived experience through critical interpretation, towards social change. Examples of ethno-mimesis have been introduced and discussed in various chapters as critical theory in practice.

PAR seeks to understand the world from the perspective of the participants. Fals-Borda quotes what Agnes Heller termed 'symmetric reciprocity' as a key tension in PAR, in order to arrive at a 'subject–subject horizontal or symmetric relationship' (Fals-Borda, 1996, p 13). Additionally, recognising this symmetry involves developing what Gramsci called 'good sense' (p 13) and, achieving authentic 'participation'. A key aspect is praxis as purposeful knowledge involving interpretation, action and transformation. At every phase of the PAR model there is the possibility for change. PAR can validate the experiences of the participants and also of grass-roots knowledge. In the process of involving participants as co-researchers, this validation is transformed into constructive and creative responses with them and their communities. Outcomes of participatory research can inform, educate, remind, challenge and empower both those involved and the audiences of the research outcomes. Outcomes can be print-based or performance-based, or art/exhibition-based. The combination of popular knowledge and academic knowledge can create change. Fals-Borda tells us that 'popular knowledge has always been a source of formal learning. Academic accumulation, plus people's wisdom, became an important rule for our movement' (1996, p 7).

The interrelationship between research and praxis is fraught with tensions, and PAR is not, of course, a panacea. Renewed methodologies that incorporate the voices of citizens through scholarly/civic research as participatory research not only serve to enlighten and raise our awareness of certain issues but can also produce critical reflexive texts that may help to mobilise social change. Ethno-mimesis as critical praxis seeks to speak in empathic ways with the participants in the research, represented through the performance text in ways that counter valorising discourses and the reduction of the 'other' to a cipher of the oppressed/marginalised/exploited.

Such methodological approaches are important for creating spaces for dialogue and 'understanding' what Buber (2004) calls I–thou relations and Witkin (1974) subjective–reflexive relationships. Such methodologies, and I include appreciative enquiry, are vital for more integrated horizontal and vertical processes of inclusion, for opening and keeping open spaces for critical discourse, for facilitating a politics of inclusion, a radical democratic pluralism and a radical democratic imaginary. Central to this project is the importance of the relational and psychosocial dimensions of our research and practice, the sensuous, performative dynamics of praxis, the importance of innovative and interdisciplinary methodologies.

In identifying the asylum-migration-community nexus I focused attention on a more phenomenological meaning of community, away from simple associations with geography and place towards concepts of communitas, being-together, being-in-common, being-with, in the sense of Buber's I–thou relations and Witkin's subjective–reflexive relations.

This text has engaged with literature in refugee and migration studies to show the treatment of migrants who seek safety in the UK and Europe from war, danger, poverty and unfreedom, who are defined as risky and dangerous, as outsiders and disposable. This constitutes what Adorno (1984, 1998) would define as identitarian thinking accompanied by an empty and cold forgetting of the circumstances that led to the 1951 Refugee Convention, and the development of international human rights.

Asylum seekers and especially refused asylum seekers are constituted as deviant objects, and the state's response is to treat them as deviant bodies through law and order policies that seek to prevent access to the nation in the first place by strengthening borders, increasing legislation to make it harder and harder to gain refugee status – the right to remain. Some people are under continued surveillance and containment in the extreme margins of the society (under circumstances of what Agamben [1995] calls 'bare life') in holding centres, prisons, detention centres and camps, and eventually those who are refused access will be deported – 'returned'.

Asylum seekers, especially the refused, become a 'disposable population' (Lowman, 2000), their very disposability created through the discourses of abjection. Defined as outsiders, not welcome, marked by stigma and prejudice, where possible they are kept marginalised, beyond citizenship and inclusion. Regressive refugee policy and laws that instantiate ever tighter border controls distances states from their involvement in the production of refugees and it is instead the asylum seeker or the refused asylum seeker who has broken the law and who bears responsibility for their 'deviance' in seeking a place of safety in the first place.

We need 'community' more than ever and analysis that deals with the relational dynamics between asylum-migration and community. Beyond neoliberalism and communitarian discourses I suggest that we need critical theory more than ever, including radical democratic pluralism underpinned by a recognitive theory of community and a notion of cultural citizenship (drawing on Yar, Lister and Pakulski, among others). A recognitive notion of community resonates with the methodological process of ethno-mimesis and performative praxis as well as claims for mutual recognition, dialogue and subjective–reflexive relations that can be instantiated through PAR and PA.

Concepts of diaspora, hybridity and cosmopolitanism are all connected to the broader concept of 'community' and have both transformative and regressive elements, but they articulate the possibilities of being-together, being-with and being-in-common (Nancy, 1991, 2000).

I suggested that global networks such as HDHS are an example of a movement for radical democracy and for a radical democratic imaginary, beyond borders and boundaries – prioritising human dignity and human rights – facilitating processes of mutual recognition and dialogue, that may be contested, but will also be creative. The importance of engaging with the concept of humiliation and human rights cannot be overstated in facilitating space for transformation in our social and cultural life worlds. The impact of globalisation and humiliation on the mobilities of people and migration/forced migration on the development of transnational communities is, I hope, made clear in these pages.

As Smith (2006), Linder (2006) and a vast amount of empirical research has shown, the processes of dislocation, of forced displacement, are deeply humiliating, told in the fragments of narratives from those who experienced expulsion or who were compelled to make the difficult and arduous journeys in search of safety, peace and freedom. Holocaust survivor Rabbi Hugo Gryn stated just before his death in 1996 that historians 'will call the twentieth century not only the century of great wars, but also the century of the refugee. Almost nobody at the end of the century is where they were at the beginning. It has been an extraordinary period of movement and upheavals' (quoted in Kushner and Knox, 1999, p 1). Moreover, for Gryn,

> asylum issues are an index of our spiritual and moral civilization.... I always think that the real offenders at the half way point of the century were the bystanders, all those people who let things happen because it didn't affect them directly. I believe that the line our society will take on this matter on how you are to people whom you owe nothing is a signal. (quoted in Kushner and Knox, 1999, p 416)

Matarasso (2006) writes that 'Democracy should not be mistaken for a natural outcome of development. It needs to be created, supported and protected.' And, 'given its function as a creator of meanings and a carrier of values, culture is a powerful force within any strong democracy' (2006 , p 4). The cultural arena is a crucial component of democratic life and every citizen has the right to participate. And as Matarasso states, cultural diversity is the norm of human experience. I have argued that cultural citizenship, rights, recognition and redistribution are centrally implicated in the radical imagining of 'decent democracy' that seeks to foster processes of dignity and egalization in the institutions, policies and practices towards people seeking safety, people located in the asylum-migration-community nexus. Moreover, our task as researchers is to take responsibility for catalysing what Bauman (1995, p 242) describes as the need for 'dialogic understanding in the general public, to opening up and keeping open spaces for what has been called "critical discourse"'.

Currently the UK and Europe are on the road to becoming 'committed to asylum without the possibility for entry' and in the words of Kushner and Knox (1999, p 417) it is vital that 'by facing our global responsibilities towards the displaced, we begin the process of changing for the better a world which creates the misery of growing refugee movements'.

Notes

[1] 'Our aim is therefore to invite academics around the world to work together and carry a joint responsibility to lead the world away from deepening divides that might cost us our survival in times when only global cooperation can address the global problems that we have. Why is there not a World University dedicated to the human rights ideal that all humans deserve to live dignified lives? Such a World University should exist, and, ideally, connect all national universities. Academic freedom ought to be exercised globally and not

harnessed into national interests' (www.humiliationstudies.org/research/research.php).

[2] The interview was conducted as part of an AHRC-funded research project examining experiences of exile and integration led by O'Neill and Tobolewska (2002b).

[3] This describes Adorno's writings (1984, 1997) on coming to know the work of art.

[4] There are parallels here with Marcuse's *One-dimensional man* (1964).

Bibliography

Abdi, M. (2006) 'Refugees, gender-based violence and resistance: a case study of Somali refugee women in Kenya', in E. Tastsoglou and A. Dobrowlesky (eds) *Women, migration and citizenship: Making local, national and transnational connections*, Aldershot: Ashgate Publishing.

Adelman, H. (1999) 'Modernity, globalization, refugees and displacement', in A. Ager (ed) *Refugees: Perspectives on the experience of enforced migration*, London: Continuum, pp 83-110.

Adorno, T.W. (1973) *Negative dialectics*, (trans. E.B. Aston) London: Routledge & Kegan Paul.

Adorno, T.W. (1978) *Minima moralia: Reflections from a damaged life* (translated by E.F.N. Jephcott), London: Verso.

Adorno, T.W. (1984) *Aesthetic theory* (edited by G. Adorno and R. Tiedemann, translated by C. Lendhart), London: Routledge.

Adorno, T.W. (1997) *Aesthetic theory* (translated by R. Hullot-Kentor), Minneapolis, MN: University of Minnesota Press.

Adorno, T.W. (1998) 'The meaning of working through the past', in T. Adorno *Critical models: Interventions and catchwords*, New York, NY: Columbia University Press.

Adorno, T.W. and Horkheimer, M. (1995) *Dialectic of enlightenment* (trans. John Cumming) London: Verso.

Agamben, G. (1995) *Homo sacer: Sovereign power and bare life*, Stanford, CA: Stanford University Press.

Agustin, L. (2007) *Sex at the margins: Migration, labour markets and the rescue industry*, London: Zed Books.

Ahmed, S. (2003) 'Collective feelings or, the impressions left by others', *Theory, Culture and Society*, vol 21, no 2, pp 25-42.

Ahmed, S. (2004) *The cultural politics of emotion*, Edinburgh: Edinburgh University Press.

Ahmed, S. and Fortier, A.-M. (2003) 'Re-imagining communities', *International Journal of Cultural Studies*, vol 6, no 3, pp 251-9.

Amnesty International (2004) *Get it right: How Home Office decision making fails refugees*, London: Amnesty International.

Amnesty International (2005) *Seeking asylum is not a crime: Detention of people who have sought asylum*, London: Amnesty International.

Anderson, B. (1983) *Imagined communities: Reflections on the growth and spread of nationalism*, London: Verso.

Anderson, B. (1991) *Imagined communities: Reflections on the growth and spread of nationalism*, London: Verso.

Anderson, B. (1993) *Britain's secret slaves*, London: Anti-slavery International.

Anderson, B. (2001) 'Different roots in common ground: transnationalism and migrant domestic workers in London', *Journal of Ethnic and Migration Studies*, vol 27, issue 4, pp 673-83.

Anthias, F. (1998) 'Evaluating "diaspora": beyond ethnicity?', *Sociology*, vol 32, no 3, pp 557-80.

Aoyama, K. (2005) 'Becoming someone else: Thai migrant sex workers from modernisation to globalisation', PhD thesis, University of Essex.

Applebaum, B (2004) 'Social justice education, moral agency, and the subject of resistance', *Educational Theory*, vol 54, no 1, pp 1-1(1).

Arendt, H. (1958) *The human condition*, Chicago, IL: University of Chicago Press.

Arendt, H. (1970) *On violence*, New York, NY: Harcourt Brace.

Arendt, H. (1973) *The Origins of Totalitarianism*, New York, NY: Harcourt Publishers Ltd.

Arieli, S., Friedman, V. J and Agbaria, K. (2009) 'The paradox of participation in action research', *Action Research*, no 7, pp 263-90.

Askins, K. and Pain, R. (2009) *Contact zones: Participation, materiality and the messiness of interaction*, unpublished paper, from personal communication with the authors.

Asylum Destitution and Working Group (2008) *Asylum matters: Restoring trust in the UK asylum system*, London: The Centre for Social Justice.

Bailey, O. (2007) Workshop Report on 'Destitution and the role of ethnic minority media in representing asylum-seekers' as part of the Making the Connections: Arts, Migration and Diaspora series (www.lboro.ac.uk/departments/ss/global_refugees/reports.html).

Bailey, O. and Harindranath, R. (2005) 'Racialised "othering": the representation of asylum seekers in the news media', in S. Allan (ed) *Journalism: Critical issues*, Maidenhead and New York, NY: Open University Press, pp 274-87.

Bailey, O., Georgiou, M. and Harindranath, R. (2007) *Transnational lives and the media: Reimagining diasporas*, Basingstoke and New York, NY: Palgrave Macmillan.

Bauman, Z. (1989) *Legislators and interpreters: On modernity, post-modernity, and intellectuals*, Cambridge: Polity Press.

Bauman, Z. (1992) *Intimations of postmodernity*, London: Routledge.

Bauman, Z. (1995) *Life in fragments: Essays in postmodern morality*, Oxford: Blackwell.

Bauman, Z. (1998) *Culture as praxis*, London: Sage Publications.

Bauman, Z. (1998) *Globalization: The human consequences*, Cambridge: Polity.

Bauman, Z. (2000a) *Globalization: The human consequences*, Cambridge: Polity Press.

Bauman, Z. (2000b) 'On writing sociology', *Theory Culture and Society*, vol 17, no 1, pp 79-90.

Bauman, Z. (2001) *Community*, Cambridge: Polity Press.

Bauman, Z. (2004) *Wasted lives: Modernity and its outcasts*, Cambridge: Polity Press.

Bauman, Z. (2007) *Liquid times: Living in an age of uncertainty*, Cambridge: Polity Press.

Beck, U. (1998) *Democracy without enemies*, Cambridge: Polity Press.

Benhabib, S. (1992) *Situating the self*, Cambridge: Polity Press.

Benhabib, S. (2002) *The claims of culture: Equality and diversity in the global era*, Princeton, NJ: Princeton University Press.

Benhabib, S. (2004) *The rights of others: Aliens, residents, and citizens*, Cambridge: Cambridge University Press.

Benjamin, W. (1985) *One-way street and other writings* (translated by E. Jephcott and K. Shorter), London: Verso.

Benjamin, W. (1992) 'The storyteller', in W. Benjamin, *Illuminations*, London: Fontana Press, pp 83-107.

Benjamin, J. (1993) *The bonds of love: Psychoanalysis, feminism, and the problem of domination*, London, Virago Press.

Benson, M. and O'Reilly, K. (eds) (2009) *Lifestyle migration: Escaping to the good life?*, London: Ashgate Publishing.

Bianchini, F. and Santacatterina, L.G. (1997) *Culture and neighbourhoods: A comparative report*, Council of Europe Press.

Black, R. (1998) *Refugees, environment and development*, New York, NY: Addison Wesley Longman Ltd.

Black, R. (2001) 'Fifty years of refugee studies: from theory to policy', *International Migration Review*, vol 35, no 1, pp 57-78. Bloch, A. (2002a) *The migration and settlement of refugees in Britain*, London: Palgrave.

Bloch, A. (2002b) *Refugees, opportunities and barriers in employment and training*, DWP Research Report 179, Leeds: Department for Work and Pensions.

Bloch, A. (2005) *The development potential of Zimbabweans in the diaspora: A survey of Zimbabweans living in the UK and South Africa*, Migration Research Series 17, Geneva: International Organization for Migration.

Bloch, A. (2007) 'Methodological challenges for national and multi-sited comparative survey research', *Journal of Refugee Studies*, vol 20, no 2, pp 230-47.

Bloch, A. and Levy, C. (eds) (1999) *Refugees, citizenship and social policy in Europe*, Basingstoke: Macmillan.

Bloch, A., Sigona, N. and Zetter, R. (2009) *'No Right to Dream': The social and economic lives of young undocumented migrants in Britain*, London: Paul Hamlyn Foundation.

Bourdieu, P. (1996) 'Understanding', *Theory, Culture and Society*, vol 13, no 2, pp 17-39.

Brah, A. (1996) *Cartographies of the diaspora: Contesting identities*, London and New York, NY: Routledge.

Bromley, R. (2000) 'Between a world of need and a world of excess: Globalized people, migration and cinematic narrative', unpublished paper from personal communication with the author.

Bromley, R. (2001) *Narratives for a new belonging: Diasporic cultural fictions*, Edinburgh: Edinburgh University Press.

Bromley, R. (2005) 'Between a world of need and a world of excess: globalized people, migration and cinematic narrative', Unpublished paper [personal communication with the author].

Bromley, R. (2007) 'Lives not worthy of life', Immigration, Exclusion and National Identity paper given to the AHRC-funded Making the Connections: Arts Migration and Diaspora workshop on 'Destitution and the role of alternative ethnic media in representing asylum-seekers', Nottingham Trent University, 27 April.

Buber, M. (2004) *I and Thou*, London: Continuum International Publishing Group Ltd.

Buchanan, S., Grillo, B. and Treadgold, T. (2003) *What's the story? Results from research into media coverage of refugees and asylum seekers in the UK*, London: Article 19 (www.article19.org/).

Burawoy, M. and van Antwerpen, J. (2001) *Berkeley sociology: Past, present and future*, Berkeley, CA: University of California.

Byrne, L. (2009) 'Communitarian politics for Britain's poorest places', Fabian Speech, Washington, DC: The Communitarian Network (www.gwu.edu/~icps/Communitarian%20Ideas%20Bryne%20Fabian.html).

Cantle, T. (2002) *Community cohesion: A report of the Independent Review Team*, London: HMSO.

Cantwell, R. (1993) *Ethnomimesis: Folklife and the representation of culture*, Chapel Hill, NC: University of North Carolina Press.

Carey-Wood, J. (1997) *Meeting refugees' needs in Britain: The role of refugee-specific initiatives*, London: Home Office Publications Ltd.

Casciani, D. (2004) 'Asylum seekers to be housed' BBC News online http://news.bbc.co.uk/1/hi/uk_politics/3840439.stm

Castles, S. (2003) 'Towards a sociology of forced migration and social transformation', *Sociology*, vol 37, no 1, February, pp 13-34.

Castles, S. and Miller, M.J. (2009) *The age of migration*, (4th edn) Basingstoke: Palgrave Macmillan.

Castles, S., Korac, M., Vasta, E. and Vertovec, S. (2002) *Integration: Mapping the field*, Report of a project carried out by the University of Oxford Centre for Migration and Policy Research and Refugee Studies Centre, Online Report 28/03, contracted by the Home Office Immigration Research and Statistics Service (IRSS), London: Home Office.

Cernea, M.M. and Mcdowell, C. (2000) *Risks and reconstruction: Experiences of resettlers and refugees*, Washington DC: The World Bank.

Chamberlayne, P., Bornat, J. and Wengraf, T. (eds) (2000) *The turn to biographical methods in social science*, London: Routledge.

Chatty, D. (2007) 'Researching refugee youth in the Middle East: reflections on the importance of comparative research', *Journal of Refugee Studies*, vol 20, no 2, pp 265-80.

Clarke, J. (2004) *Changing welfare, changing states: New directions in social policy*, London: Sage Publications.

Cohen, L., Arnold, J. and O'Neill, M. (eds) (2011: forthcoming) 'Career and migration', Special edition, *Journal of Vocational Behaviour*.

Cohen, R. (1997) *Global diasporas: An introduction*, London: Routledge.

Cohen, S. (1985) *Visions of social control: Crime, punishment and classification*, Cambridge: Polity Press.

Cohen, S. (2001) *States of denial: Knowing about atrocities and suffering*, Cambridge: Polity Press.

Communitarian Network, The (nd) 'The communitarian vision', Washington, DC: The Communitarian Network (www.gwu.edu/~icps/About%20Com2.html).

Communitarian Network, The (1995) 'Nation in need of community values', *The London Times*, 20 February, Washington, DC: The Communitarian Network (www.gwu.edu/~ccps/etzioni/B262.html).

Coole, C. (2002) 'A warm welcome', *Media, Culture and Society*, vol 14, no 6, pp 839-52.

Cornell, D. (1995) *The imaginary domain*, London: Routledge.

Craib, I. (2003) 'The unhealthy underside of narratives', in C. Horrocks, N. Kelly, B. Roberts and D. Robinson (eds) *Narrative, memory and health*, Huddersfield: University of Huddersfield Press, pp 1-11.

Crawley, H. (1997) *Women as asylum seekers: A legal handbook*, London: Refugee Action.

Crawley, H. (1999) 'Women and refugee status in the UK', in D. Indra (ed) *Engendering forced migration: Theory and practice*, New York, NY: Berghahn Books, pp 308-30.

Crawley, H. (2001) *Refugee and gender: Law and processes*, Bristol: Jordan Publishing. ribb, A. and Gewirtz, S. (2003) 'Towards a sociology of just practices: an analysis of plural conceptions of justice', in C. Vincent (ed) *Social justice, education and identity*, London: Routledge/Falmer, pp 15-30.

Cruikshank, B. (1994) 'The will to empower: technologies of citizenship and the war on poverty', *Socialist Review*, vol 23, pp 29-55.

Darke, C. (2003) 'The underside of globalisation: on Michael Winterbottom's *In this world*' (www.opendemocracy.net/arts-Film/article_1120.jsp).

de la Fuente, E. (2007) 'The "new sociology of art": putting art back into social sciences', *Cultural Sociology*, vol 1, no 3, pp 409-25.

Dennis, J. (2002) *A case for change: How refugee children in England are missing out*, First findings from the Monitoring Project of the Refugee Children's Consortium, London: Refugee Council, The Children's Society and Save the Children.

Deutsch, M. (2006) 'Foreword by Morton Deutsch', in E. Lindner (2006) *Making enemies: Humiliation and international conflict*, Westport, CT and London: Praeger Security, pp vii-viii.

de Tocqueville, A. (1994) *Democracy in America*, London: Fontana Press.

DfES (2004) *Aiming high: Guidance on supporting the education of asylum seeking and refugee children*, London: The Stationery Office.

DfES (Department for Education and Skills) (2003) *Every Child Matters*, London: The Stationery Office.

DfES (2004) *Aiming high: Guidance on supporting the education of asylum seeking and refugee children*, London: The Stationery Office.

DfES (2006) *Youth matters: Next steps*, London: The Stationery Office.

Dona, G. (2007) 'The microphysics of participation in refugee research', *Journal of Refugee Studies*, vol 20, no 2, pp 211-29. du Bois, W.E.B (1897) 'Strivings of the Negro people', *Atlantic Atlantic Monthly*, no 80, pp 194-8.

Du Bois, W.E.B. (1903) *The souls of Black folk: Essays and sketches*, Chicago, IL: AC McClurg.

Dumper, H. (2002) *Is it safe here? Refuge women's experiences in the UK*, London: Refugee Action.

Dumper, H. (2004) *Women refugees and asylum seekers in the UK*, ICAR Navigation Guide, London: Information Centre about Asylum and Refugees (www.icar.org.uk/9568/navigation-guides/women.html).

Dumper, H. (2005) *Making women visible*, London: Refugee Council.

Dumper, H. (2008) 'Women and migration', in M.O'Neill and L. Cohen (eds) *Women and migration: Art, politics and policy*, report of the Women and Migration AHRC Funded Network, Loughborough: Loughborough University.

Dunkereley, D., Hodgson, L., Konopacki, S., Spybey, T. and Thompson, A. (2002) *Changing Europe: Identities, nations and citizens*, London: Routledge.

Dutton, D.G., Boyanowsky, E.O. and Harris Bond, M. (2005) 'Extreme mass homicide: From military massacre to genocide', *Aggression and Violent Behavior*, vol 10, no 4, pp 437-73.

Duvell, F. and Jordan.B. (2002) 'Immigration, asylum and welfare: the European context', *Critical Social Policy*, no 22, p 498.

Eastmond, M. (2007) 'Stories as lived experience: narratives in forced migration research', *Journal of Refugee Studies*, vol 20, no 2, pp 248-64.

Elias, N. and Scotson, J. (1994) *The established and the outsiders: A sociological enquiry into community problems*, London: Sage Publications.

Fals-Borda, O. (1988) *Knowledge and people's power: Lessons with peasants in Nicaragua, Mexico and Columbia*, New York, NY: New Horizons Press.

Fals-Borda, O. (1995) 'Research for social justice: some North-South convergences' (http://comm-org.wisc.edu/si/falsborda.htm).

Fals-Borda, O. (1996) 'A north-south convergence on the quest for meaning', *Collaborative Inquiry*, vol 2, no 1, pp 76-87.

Fals Borda, O. (1999) *The origins and challenges of participatory action research*, MA: Center for International Education, University of Massachusetts at Amherst.

Fangen, K. (2006) 'Humiliation experienced by Somali refugees in Norway', *Journal of Refugee Studies*, vol 19, no 1, pp 69-93.

Feingold, H. (1970) *The politics of rescue: the Roosevelt Administration and the Holocaust 1938–45*, New Brunswick: Rutgers University Press.

Finney, N. (2003a) *Asylum seeker dispersal: Public attitudes and press portrayals around the UK*, Summary of Research Project, Department of Geography, University of Wales, Swansea.

Finney, N. (2003b) *The challenge of reporting refugees and asylum seekers*, Bristol: Information Centre about Asylum and Refugees and the Presswise Trust.

Flum, H. (1998) 'Embedded identity: the case of young high-achieving Ethiopian Jewish immigrants in Israel', *Journal of Youth Studies*, vol 1, no 2, pp 143-61.

Fowler, B. (1996) 'An introduction to Pierre Bourdieu's *Understanding*', *Theory, Culture and Society*, vol 13, no 2, pp 1-17.

Fraser, N. (1997) *Justice interruptus: Critical reflections on the 'post-socialist' condition*, London and New York, NY: Routledge.

Fraser, N. (2000) 'Rethinking recognition', *New Left Review*, May/June .

Fraser, N. (2004) 'Recognition as justice? A proposal for avoiding philosophical schizophrenia', in S. Cheng (ed) *Law, justice and power between reason and will*, Palo Alto, CA: Stanford University Press.

Garland, D. (2001) *The culture of control*, Oxford: Oxford University Press.

Geddie, E. (2009) '"Undocumented migrants" right to health and education in Europe: protection needs vs immigration control', in European Social Watch Report, *Migrants in Europe as development actors: Between hope and vulnerability*, Brussels: Eurostep.

Geertz, C. (1973) 'Thick description: toward an interpretive theory of culture', in *The interpretation of cultures: Selected essays*, New York, NY: Basic Books, pp 3-30.

Giddens, A. (1984) *The constitution of society*, Cambridge, Polity.

Giddens, A. (1991) *Modernity and self-identity: Self and society in the late modern age*, Cambridge: Polity.

Giddens, A. (1994) *Beyond left and right: The future of radical politics*, Cambridge: Polity Press.

Gilroy, P. (1993) *The black Atlantic: Modernity and double consciousness*, London: Verso.

Gilroy, P. (2000) *Against race: Imagining political culture beyond the color line*, Cambridge, MA: Harvard University Press.

GLA (Greater London Authority) (2004) *Offering more than they borrow: Refugee children in London*, London: GLA.

Goddard, C. (2009) 'Children's authors join campaign to end immigrant detention', *Children and Young People Daily Bulletin*, 11 December (www.cypnow.co.uk/bulletins/Daily-Bulletin/news/973705/?DCMP=EMC-DailyBulletin).

Goldsmith, Lord (2007) *Citizenship: Our common bond* (www.justice.gov.uk/reviews/docs/citizenship-report-full.pdf)

Gray, A. (1997) 'Learning from experience: cultural studies and feminism', in J. McGuigan (ed) *Cultural methodologies*, London: Sage Publications.

Gray, B. (2000) 'Gendering the Irish diaspora: questions of enrichment, hybridization and return', *Women's Studies International Forum*, vol 23, no 2, March–April, pp 167-85.

Greenslade, R. (2005) *Seeking scapegoats: The coverage of asylum in the UK press*, London: Institute for Public Policy Research.

Griffiths, D.J. (2002) *Somali and Kurdish refugees in London: New identities in the diaspora*, Aldershot: Ashgate.

Griffiths, D.J., Sigona, N. and Zetter, R. (2005) *Refugee community organisations and dispersal: Networks, resources and social capital*, Bristol: The Policy Press.

Haggerty, K.D. (2004) 'Displaced expertise: three constraints on the policy relevance of criminological thought', *Theoretical Criminology*, vol 8, no 2, pp 211-31.

Hall, S. (2002) 'Political belonging in a world of multiple identities,' in S. Vertovec and R. Cohen (eds) *Conceiving cosmopolitanism: Theory, context, and practice*, Oxford: Oxford University Press.

Harindranath, R. (2007) 'Refugee communities and the politics of cultural identity', in O. Bailey, M. Georgiou and R. Harindranath (eds) *Transnational lives and the media*, Basingstoke and New York, NY: Palgrave Macmillan.

Harrell-Bond, B. (1999) 'Refugees' experiences as aid recipients', in A. Ager (ed) *Refugees: Perspectives on the experience of enforced migration*, London: Continuum, pp 136-68.

Harrell-Bond, B. and Voutira, E. (2007) 'In search of "invisible" actors: barriers to access in refugee research', *Journal of Refugee Studies*, vol 20, no 2, pp 281-98.

Hartling, L. (2005) *An appreciative frame: Beginning a dialogue on human dignity and humiliation*, www.humiliationstudies.org/documents/hartling/HartlingAppreciativeFrame.pdf

Hayter, T. (2001) 'Open borders: the case against immigration controls', *Capital & Class*, no 25, pp 149-56.

Heller, A. (1984) *Everyday life*, London: Routledge and Kegan Paul.

Heynon, H. (1999) 'Mimesis, dwelling and architecture: Adorno's relevance for a feminist theory of architecture', in M. O'Neill (ed) *Adorno, culture and feminism*, London: Sage Publications.

Hillis Miller, J. (1992) *Illustration*, London: Reaktion Books.

Home Office (2004) *National refugee integration strategy*, London: The Stationery Office.

Home Office (2006) *RDS asylum statistics, fourth quarter, 2006*, London: The Stationery Office.

Home Office (2008) *Better outcomes: The way forward. Improving the care of unaccompanied asylum seeking children*, London: The Stationery Office.

Home Office (2009) 'Border security and immigration issues', Press release, 17 October, London: Home Office (http://press.homeoffice.gov.uk/Speeches/IB-immigration.html).

Honneth, A. (1996) *The struggle for recognition*, Cambridge: Polity.

Horrocks, C., Kelly, N., Roberts, B. and Robinson, D. (eds) (2003) *Narrative, memory and health*, Huddersfield: University of Huddersfield Press.

Hubbard, P. (2005) 'Accommodating otherness: anti-asylum centre protest and the maintenance of white privilege', *Transactions, Institute of British Geographers*, vol 30, no 1, pp 52-65.

Humphrey, R. (2005) 'Life stories and social careers: ageing and social life in an ex-mining town', in D. Mathew (ed) *Case study research. 4 Volumes*, London and New York, NY: Sage Publications.

Hussain, A et al (2003) *Integrated cities*, Leicester: SICUL, University of Leicester.

ICAR (Information Centre about Asylum and Refugees) (2007) *Removals: Thematic briefing prepared for the Independent Asylum Commission*, London: ICAR.

Jackson, G. and Dube, D. (2006) *What am I living for? Living on the streets of Leicester, A report on destitute asylum seekers and refugees*, Leicester: The Diocese of Leicester.

Jeffreys, J.B. (1948) *Labour's formative years*, London: Lawrence and Wishart.

Jones, K. (2006) 'A biographic researcher in pursuit of an aesthetic: the use of arts-based (re)presentations in "performative" dissemination of life stories', *Qualitative Sociology Review*, vol 2, no 1, pp 66-85.

JRCT (Joseph Rowntree Charitable Trust) (2007) *Moving on from destitution to contribution*, York: JRCT.

Kabeer, N. (2005) 'The search for inclusive citizenship: meanings and expressions in an interconnected world,' in N. Kabeer (ed) *Inclusive citizenship*, London: Zed Books.

Kaldor, M. (2003) *Global civil society: An answer to war*, Cambridge: Polity.

Kalra, V.S., Kaur, R. and Hutnyk, J. (2005) *Diaspora and hybridity*, London: Sage Publications.

Kearon, T. (2005) 'We have never been liberal – bourgeois identity and the criminal(ized) other', *Social Justice*, vol 32, no 1, pp 5-19.

Kelly, L. (2003) 'Bosnian refugees in Britain: questioning community', *Sociology*, vol 37, no 1, February, pp 35-49.

Kempadoo, K. and Doezema, J. (1998) *Global sex workers: Rights, resistance and redefinition*, New York, NY: Routledge.

Kester, G. (2004) *Conversation pieces: Community and communication in modern art*, Berkeley, CA and London: University of California Press.

Knott, K. (2005) 'Towards a history and politics of diasporas and migration: a grounded spatial approach', Paper presented at 'Flows and Spaces', the Annual Conference of the Royal Geographical Society/Institute of British Geographers, London, 30 August-2 September.

Koffman, E., Phizaklea, A., Raghuram, P. and Sales, R. (2000) *Gender and migration in Europe*, London: Routledge.

Koffman, E. Raghuram, P. and Merefield, M. (2005) *Gendered migrations: Towards a gender sensitive policies in the UK*, Working Paper 5, IPPR Asylum and Migration Series, London: IPPR.

Korac, M. (2001) 'Integration and how we facilitate it: a comparative study of the settlement experiences of refugees in Italy and the Netherlands', *Sociology*, vol 37, no 1, February, pp 51-68.

Kuhn, A. (2000) 'A journey through memory', in S. Radstone (ed) *Memory and methodology*, Oxford: Berg, pp 179-96.

Kushner, T. and Knox, K. (1999) *Refugees in an age of genocide*, London: Frank Cass.

Kuzmics, H. (1994) 'Power and work: the development of work as a civilising process in examples of fictional literature', *Sociological Perspectives*, vol 37, no 1, pp 119-54.

Laclau, E. and Mouffe, C. (1990) 'Post-Marxism without apologies', in E. Laclau (ed) *New reflections on the revolution of our time*, London:Verso.

Lake, A. (2008) *Hidden voices: Work with young refugees and asylum seekers*, Loughborough: Dreamers and Charnwood Arts Publication (www. thejitty.com/uploads/254a118ae7906a9627665867.pdf).

Langer, J. (ed) (1997) *The bend in the road: Refugees writing*, Nottingham: Five Leaves Press.

Laws, S., Harper, C. and Marcus, R. (2003) *Research for development: A practical guide*, London: Save the Children and Sage Publications.

Lay, M. and Papadopoulos, I. (2009) 'Sexual maltreatment of unaccompanied asylum-seeking minors from the Horn of Africa: a mixed method study focusing on vulnerability and prevention', *Child Abuse and Neglect*, vol 33, no 10, pp 728-38.

Lazare, A. (1987) 'Shame and humiliation in the medical encounter', *Archives of Internal Medicine*, vol 147, no 9, pp 1653-8.

Ledwith, M. and Springett, J. (2010) *Participatory practice: Community-based action for transformative change*, Bristol: The Policy Press.

Lee, D. and Newby, H. (1983) *The problem of sociology: An introduction to the discipline*, London: Unwin Hyman.

Lewis, G. (2004) 'Citizenship: rights, belongings and practices of the everyday', in G. Lewis (ed) *Citizenship: Personal lives and social policy*, Milton Keynes: Open University Press.

Lindner, E. (2001) 'Humiliation and the human condition: mapping a minefield', *Human Rights Review*, vol 2, no 2, pp 46-63.

Lindner, E. (2002) 'Healing the cycles of humiliation: how to attend to the emotional aspects of "unsolvable" conflicts and the use of "humiliation entrepreneurship"', *Peace and Conflict: Journal of Peace Psychology*, vol 8, no 2, pp 125-38.

Lindner, E. (2002) *Peace? Not as long as humiliation reigns!* (www. humiliationstudies.org/documents/evelin/PeaceICCR.pdf).

Lindner, E. (2004) 'Humiliation in a globalizing world: does humiliation become the most disruptive force?', Paper prepared for the Workshop on Humiliation and Violent Conflict, 18-19 November, Columbia University, New York.

Lindner, E. (2006) *Making enemies: Humiliation and international conflict*, Westport, CT and London: Praeger Security.

Lister, R. (2004) *Poverty*, Cambridge: Polity Press.

Lister, R. (2007) 'Inclusive citizenship: realizing the potential', *Citizenship Studies*, vol 11, no 1, pp 49-61, February.

Lister, R. (2008) 'Women and citizenship', in M. O'Neill and L. Cohen (eds) *Women and migration: Art, politics and policy*, Report of the Women and Migration AHRC funded network, Loughborough: Loughborough University.

Loizos, P. (2007) '"Generations" in forced migration: towards greater clarity', *Journal of Refugee Studies*, vol 20, no 2, pp 193-209.

Lorek, A. et al (2009) 'The mental and physical health difficulties of children held within a British immigration detention centre: a pilot study', *Child Abuse and Neglect*, vol 33, no 9, pp 573-85.

Lowman, J. (2000) 'Violence and the outlaw status of (street) prostitution in Canada', *Violence Against Women*, vol 6, no 9, pp 987-1011.

Mai, N. (2009) *Migrants in the UK sex industry*, London: London Metropolitan University (www.londonmet.ac.uk/research-units/iset/projects/esrc-migrant-workers.cfm).

Marcuse, H. (1964) *One-dimensional man: Studies in the ideology of advanced industrial society*, Boston, MA: Beacon.

Marfleet, P. (2006) *Refugees in a global era*, Basingstoke: Palgrave Macmillan.

Margalit, A. (1996) *The decent society*, Cambridge, MA: Harvard University Press.

Marinetto, M. (2003) 'Who wants to be an active citizen? The politics and practice of community involvement', *Sociology*, vol 37, no 1, pp 103-20.

Martin, S. (2006) *The impact of Section 4 support*, Glasgow: Asylum Support Programme Inter-agency Programme.

Matarasso, F. (2005) 'Many voices: the importance of cultural diversity in democratic society', Unpublished lecture given at Vara Konserthus, Sweden, 25 September.

Mayor of London (2004) *Offering more than they borrow: Refugee children in London*, London: Greater London Authority.

Merrill, B. and West, L. (2009) *Using biographical methods in social research*, London and New York, NY: Sage Publications.

Meskimmon, M. (2008) 'Women and art', in M. O'Neill and L. Cohen (eds) *Women and migration: Art, politics and policy*, Report of the Women and Migration AHRC funded network, Loughborough: Loughborough University.

Mestrovic, S. (1997) *Postemotional society*, London and New York, NY: Sage Publications.

Miller, R.L. (1999) *Researching life stories and family histories*, London: Sage Publications.

Miller, R.L. (2005) *Biographical research methods*, four volumes, London and New York, NY: Sage Publications.

Miller, R.L., Humphrey, R. and Zdravomyslova, E. (eds) (2003) *Biographical research in Eastern Europe*, Aldershot: Ashgate.

Minh-ha, T. (1989) *Women, native, other: Writing, post-colonialism and feminism*, Bloomington, IN: Indiana University Press.

Minh-ha, T. (1991) *When the moon waxes red*, London: Routledge.

Mollard, C. (2001) *Asylum: The truth behind the headlines*, Oxford: Oxfam.

Mouffe, C. (1992) 'Feminism, citizenship and radical democratic politics', in J. Butler and J.W. Scott (eds) *Feminists theorize the political*, New York, NY:/London: Routledge.

Myers, M. (2007) Homing Place (www.homingplace.org) and Way From Home (www.wayfromhome.org).

Myers, M. (2007) 'Along the way: situation-responsive participation and education', *The International Journal of the Arts In Society*, vol 1, no 2, pp 1-6.

Myers, M. (2008) 'Situations for living: performing emplacement', *Research in Drama Education*, vol 13, no 2, pp 171-80.

Myers, M. (2010) '"Walk with me, talk with me": the art of conversive wayfinding', *Visual Studies*, vol 25, no 1, pp 59-68.

Nancy, J.-L. (1991) *The inoperative community*, Minnesota, MN and London: University of Minnesota Press.

Nancy, J.-L. (2000) *Being singular plural*, Stanford, CA: Stanford University Press.

Nancy, J.-L. (2003) 'The confronted community', *Postcolonial Studies*, vol 6, no 1, pp 23-36.

National Audit Office (2005) *Returning failed asylum applicants*, London: The Stationary Office.

Newman, J. (2003) 'New Labour, governance and the politics of diversity', in J. Barry, M. Dent and M. O'Neill (eds) *Gender and the public sector: Professionals and managerial change*, London: Routledge, pp 15-27.

Nicholsen, S. (1993) 'Walter Benjamin and the aftermath of the aura: notes on the aesthetics of photography', in *Antioch Community Record*, 12 February 1993 – personal communication from the author.

Nicholsen, S. (1999) 'Adorno, Benjamin and the aura: an Aesthetics for photography', in M. O'Neill *Adorno, culture and feminism*, London: Sage Publications.

Nicholsen, S. (1997) *Exact imagination late work*, Cambridge, MA: MIT Press.

Nicholsen, S. (2002) *Adorno's minima moralia: On passion, psychoanalysis and the postemotional dilemma* (from personal communication with the author).

Nussbaum, M. (2006) *Frontiers of justice: Disability, nationality, species membership*, Cambridge, MA: Belknap Press.

O'Connell Davidson, J. (2006) 'Will the real sex slave please stand up?', *Feminist Review*, vol 83, no 1, pp 4-22.

O'Malley, P. (1996) 'Risk and responsibility', in A. Barry, T. Osbourne and N. Rose (eds) *Foucault and the political reason: Liberalism, neo liberalism and the rationalities of government*, London: UCL Press.

O'Neill, M. (1999) (ed) *Adorno, culture and feminism*, London: Sage Publications.

O'Neill, M. in association with S. Giddens, P. Breatnach, C. Bagley, D. Bourne and T. Judge (2002) 'Renewed methodologies for social research: ethno-mimesis as performative praxis', *Sociological Review*, vol 50, no 1, pp 69-88.

O'Neill, M. (2004) 'Global refugees: citizenship, power and the law', in S. Cheng (ed) *Law, justice, and power: An impossible but necessary relationship*, Stanford, CA: Stanford University Press.

O'Neill, M. (2007) 'Re-imagining diaspora through ethno-mimesis: humiliation, human dignity and belonging', in O. Bailey, M. Georgiou and R. Harindranath (eds) *Reimagining diasporas: Transnational lives and the media*, London: Palgrave.

O'Neill, M. (2008) 'Transnational refugees: the transformative role of art?', *Forum: Qualitative Sozialforschung/Qualitative Social Research*, vol 9, no 2, Article 59 (www.qualitative-research.net/index.php/fqs/article/viewArticle/403).

O'Neill, M. (2009) 'Making connections: ethno-mimesis, migration and diaspora', *Journal of Psychoanalysis, Culture and Society*, vol 14, no 3, pp 289-302.

O'Neill, M. (2010) 'Making connections: biography, art, affect and politics', in M. Svasek (ed) *Moving subjects, moving objects: Transnationalism, cultural production and emotions*, Oxford and New York, NY: Berghahn.

O'Neill, M. with F. Galli and F. Aldridge (2004) *New arrivals: Access to training, employment and social enterprise in Leicester and Charnwood*, Commissioned by the Government Office for East Midlands (GOEM), Stoke-on-Trent: Staffordshire University/Charnwood Arts.

O'Neill, M. and Webster, M. (2005) *Creativity, community and change: Creative approaches to community consultation*, unpublished paper, Staffordshire University.

O'Neill, M. and Cohen, L. (2008) *Women and migration: A manifesto on art, politics and policy*, Loughborough: Loughborough University.

O'Neill, M. and Giddens, S. (2001) 'Not all the time ... but mostly ...: renewed methodologies for cultural analysis: a visual essay for a special edition on 'Sex work re-assessed', *Feminist Review*, no 67, pp 109-10.

O'Neill, M. and Harindranath, R. (2006) 'Theorising narratives of exile and belonging: the importance of biography and ethno-mimesis in "understanding" asylum', *Qualitative Sociological Review*, vol 11, no 1, pp 39-53.

O'Neill, M. and Hubbard, P. (2009) *Trans-national communities: Towards a sense of belonging*, Report to the Arts and Humanities Research Council (AHRC), Loughborough: Loughborough University.

O'Neill, M. and Hubbard, P. (2010) 'Walking, sensing, belonging: ethno-mimesis as performative praxis', *Visual Studies*, vol 25, no 1, pp 46-58.

O'Neill, M. and Tobolewska, B. (2002a) *Global refugees: Exile, displacement and belonging: Afghans in London*, Exhibition booklet, Nottingham and Stoke-on-Trent: Staffordshire University and Nottingham City Arts, Exiled Writers Ink and Waterman's Multi-Media Centre.

O'Neill, M. and Tobolewska, B. (2002b) *Towards a cultural strategy for working with refugees and persons seeking asylum in the East Midlands*, Nottingham and Stoke-on-Trent: Staffordshire University and Nottingham City Arts.

O'Neill, M., Woods, P.A. and Webster, M. (2005) 'New arrivals: participatory action research, imagined communities and social justice', *Social Justice*, vol 31, no 1, pp 75-88.

O'Neill, M., Pitcher, J. and Krah, M. (2007) *What about me? A report on the findings of a research project on the service needs of asylum seeker or refugee women with children aged 0-5*, Loughborough University and Marchbid Ltd.

O'Neill, M., Woods, P.A. and Webster, M. (2003) *New arrivals: Report of research on effective inclusion of newly arrived families and pupils to Leicester City education*, Commissioned by Leicester Local Education Authority and Government Office for the East Midlands (GOEM), Stoke-on-Trent: Staffordshire University.

O'Neill, M., Woods, P.A. and Webster, M. (2005) 'New arrivals: participatory action research, imagined communities and social justice', *Social Justice*, vol 31, no 1, pp 75-88.

O'Reilly, K. (2000) *The British on the Costa del Sol: Transnational identities and local communities*, London: Routledge.

Ospina, S., Dodge, J., Godsoe, B., Minieri, M., Reza, J. and Schall, E. (2004) 'From consent to mutual inquiry: balancing democracy and authority in action research', *Action Research*, no 11, pp 7–70.

Owers, A. (2009) *Report on an unannounced short follow-up inspection of Tinsley House Immigration Removal Centre*, London: Her Majesty's Inspectorate of Prisons.

Pain, R. (2004) 'Social geography: participatory research', *Progress in Human Geography* vol 28, pp 652-63.

Pain, R. (2009) 'Globalized fear towards an emotional geopolitics', *Progress in Human Geography*, vol 33, no 4, pp 466-86.

Pain, R. and Francis, P. (2003) 'Reflections on participatory research', *Area*, vol 35, no 1, pp 46-54.

Pakulski, J. (1997) 'Cultural citizenship', *Citizenship Studies*, vol 1, no 1, pp 73-86.

Paleologo, F.V. (2009) 'Detention centres: an unjust and ineffective policy', in European Social Watch Report, *Migrants in Europe as development actors: Between hope and vulnerability*, Brussels: Eurostep.

Phizaklea, A. (1983) *One-way ticket*, London: Routledge.

Piccone, P. (1993) 'Beyond pseudo-culture? Reconstituting fundamental political concepts', *Telos*, No 95, Spring. Pickering, S. (2005) *Refugees and state crime*, Annandale, Australia: The Federation Press.

Pink, S., Hubbard, P., O'Neill, M. and Radley, A. (2010) 'Walking across disciplines: from ethnography to arts practice', Guest editors introduction', *Visual Studies*, vol 25, no 1, pp 1-7.

RCGP (Royal College of General Practitioners), RCPCH (Royal College of Paediatrics and Child Health), RCP (Royal College of Psychiatrists) and the UK Faculty of Public Health (2009) *Significant harm: The effects of administrative detention on the health of children, young people and their families*, Intercollegiate briefing paper (www.rcpch. ac.uk/doc.aspx?id_Resource=5829).

Refugee Action (2006) *The destitution trap*, London: Refugee Action and Amnesty International.

Refugee Council (2002) *A case for change: How refugee children in England are missing out*, London: Refugee Council.

Refugee Council (2004) *The impact of section 55 on the Inter-Agency Partnership and the asylum seekers it supports*, London: Refugee Council.

Refugee Council (2009) 'Borders, Citizenship and Immigration Act 2009', Briefing, August (www.refugeecouncil.org.uk/Resources/Refugee%20Council/downloads/briefings/BCI%20Act%20Revised%20Brief%20Sept%2009.pdf).

Refugee Survival Trust (2005) *What's going on: A study into destitution faced by refugees and asylum seekers in Scotland*, Edinburgh: Oxfam/Refugee Survival Trust.

Rieff, D. (2002) *A bed for the night: Humanitarianism in crisis*, London: Vintage.

Roberts, B. (2002) *Biographical research*, Buckingham: Open University Press.

Roberts, B. (2003) 'Narrative, memory, health and recurrence: conceptual notes', in C. Horrocks, N. Kelly, B. Roberts and D. Robinson (eds) *Narrative, memory and health*, Huddersfield: University of Huddersfield Press, pp 13-28.

Roberts, B. (2006) *Micro social theory*, London: Palgrave Macmillan.

Rogaly, B. and Taylor, B. (2009) *Moving histories of class and community*, London: Palgrave.

Rogoff, I. (2000) *Terra infirma – Geography's visual culture*, London and New York, NY: Routledge.

Rose, N. (1996) 'The death of the social? Re-figuring the territory of government', *Economy and Society*, vol 25, no 3, pp 327-56.

Rose, N. (1999) *Powers of freedom: Reframing political thought*, Cambridge: Cambridge University Press.

Rotas, A. (2004) 'Is "refugee art" possible?', *Third Text*, vol 18, no 1, pp 51-60.

Rutter, J. (2006) *Refugee children in the UK*, Buckingham: Open University Press.

Rutter, J., Cooley, L., Reynolds, S. and Sheldon, R. (2007) *From refugee to citizen: 'Standing on my own two feet', A research report on integration, 'Britishness' and citizenship*, London: Metropolitan Support Trust and the Institute for Public Policy Research (www.refugeecouncil.org.uk/policy/external_reports/reports_other_2007/refugee_citizen.htm).

Ryan, K., O'Neill, M., Gent, P., Bedford, G. and Goodwin, C. (2004) *Land of dreams: New arrivals in Charnwood*, Loughborough: Charnwood Arts.

Saeed, A. (2007) 'Northern racism: a pilot study of racism in Sunderland', in C. Ehland (ed) *Thinking northern: Textures of identities in the north of England*, Volume 2, Spatial practices: An interdisciplinary series in cultural history, geography and literature, Amsterdam: Rodopi (www.rodopi.nl/).

Sales, R. (2000) 'The deserving and the undeserving? Refugees, asylum seekers and welfare in Britain', *Critical Social Policy*, vol 22, no 3, pp 456-62.

Sales, R. (2007) *Understanding immigration and refugee policy: Contradictions and continuities*, Bristol: The Policy Press.

Sales, R. and Gregory, J. (1999) 'Immigration, ethnicity and exclusion: implications of European integration', in J. Gregory, R. Sales and A. Hegewisch (eds) *Women, work and equality: The challenge to equal pay in a deregulated market*, London: Macmillan.

Salverson, J. (2001) 'Change on whose terms? Testimony and an erotics of injury', *Theater*, vol 31, no 3, pp 119-25.

Save the Children (2001) *Cold comfort: Young separated refugees in the West Midlands*, London: Save the Children.

Scheff, T. (2006) 'Silence and mobilization: emotional/relational dynamics' (www.humiliationstudies.org/documents/ScheffSilenceandMobilization.pdf).

Schoene, B. (2009) *The cosmopolitan novel*, Edinburgh: Edinburgh University Press.

Schuster, L. (2003) *The use and abuse of political asylum in Britain and Germany*, London: Routledge

Schuster, L. (2005) *The realities of a new asylum paradigm*, Centre on Migration, Policy and Society Working Paper No 20, Oxford: University of Oxford.

Schuster, L. and Solomos, J. (1999) 'The politics of refugee and asylum policies in Britain: historical patterns and contemporary realities', in A. Bloch and C. Levy (eds) *Refugees, citizenship and social policy in Europe*, Basingstoke: Macmillan.

Sen, A. (1999) *The idea of justice*, London: Penguin.

Singer, P. (2004) *One World: the ethics of globalization,* New Haven: Yale University Press.

Shackle, S. (2009) 'Home is where the heartbreak is', *New Statesman*, 29 October (www.newstatesman.com/society/2009/11/women-asylum-woman-persecution).

Singer, D. (2009) 'We need a gender-sensitive asylum system', *The Guardian*, 30 November.

Smith, A.M. (1998) *Laclau and Mouffe: The radical democratic imaginary*, London: Routledge.

Smith, D. (2006) *Globalization: The hidden agenda*, Cambridge: Polity Press.

Smith, M.K. (2001) *Community in the encyclopaedia of informal education* (infed) www.infed.org/index.htm

Solomos, J. (2003) *Race and racism in Britain*, Basingstoke: Macmillan.

Sood, U. (2008) 'UK policy with respect to asylum and immigration issues', in M. O'Neill and L. Cohen (eds) *Women and migration: Art, politics and policy*, Report of the Women and Migration AHRC funded network, Loughborough: Loughborough University.

Soysal, Y.N. (1994) *Limits of citizenship: Migrants and postnational membership in Europe*, Chicago: Chicago University Press.

Spybey, T. (1995) *Globalization and world society*, Cambridge: Polity Press.

Stanley, K. (2001) *Cold comfort: Young separated refugees in England*, London: Save the Children.

Sterland, L. (2009) '"I don't want to sit and complain..."An exploration of refugee community workers' skills, role, motivations and aspirations and related development needs', MA thesis, European Centre for the Study of Migration and Social Care, School of Social Policy, Sociology and Social Research, University of Kent.

Stevenson, N. (2003) *Cultural citizenship*, Maidenhead: Open University Press.

Stubbs, P. (1999*) Displaced promises: Forced migration, refuge and return in Croatia and Bosnia-Herzegovina*, Uppsala: Life and Peace Institute.

Svašek, M. (2007) *Anthropology, art and cultural production*, London: Pluto Press.

Svensson, B. (1997) 'The power of biography: criminal policy, prison life and the formulation of criminal identities in the Swedish welfare state', in D. Reed Danahay (ed) *Auto/ethnography: Rewriting the self and the social*, Oxford and New York, NY: Berg, pp 71–107.

Sweetman, C. (ed) (1998) *Gender and migration*, Oxford: Oxfam.

Tastsoglou, E. and Dobrowlesky A. (2006) (eds) *Women, migration and citizenship: Making local, national and transnational connections*, Aldershot: Ashgate Publishing.

Taussig, M. (1993) *Mimesis and alterity*, London: Sage.

Taylor, C. (1994) 'The politics of recognition', in A. Guttman (ed) *Multi-culturalism: Examining the politics of recognition*, Princeton, NJ: Princeton University Press.

Taylor, D. (2009) *Underground lives. An investigation into the living conditions and survival strategies of destitute asylum seekers in the UK*, Leeds: Positive Action for Refugees and Asylum Seekers.

Temple, B. and Moran, R. (2006) *Doing research with refugees: Issues and guidelines*, Bristol: The Policy Press.

Tester, K. (1992) *The inhuman condition*, London: Routledge.

Tisheva, G. and van Reisen, M. (2009) 'Europe, a continent of migrations', Executive summary, in European Social Watch, *Migrants in Europe as development actors: Between hope and vulnerability*, Brussels: Eurostep.

Tyler, I. (2006) '"Welcome to Britain": the cultural politics of asylum', *Cultural Studies*, vol 9, no 2, pp 185-202.

UNHCR (United Nations High Commissioner for Refugees) (2007) *Convention and protocol relating to the status of refugees*, Geneva: UNHCR (www.unhcr.org/protect/PROTECTION/3b66c2aa10.pdf).

UNHCR (2009) 'Iraqis, Afghans and Somalis top list of asylum seekers in industrialized world', Press release, 21 October, Geneva: UNHCR (www.unhcr.org/4adf24079.html).

Urry, J. (2007) *Mobilities*, Cambridge: Polity Press.

Verhaeghe, P. (2009) 'Coherence between migration and development policies', in European Social Watch, *Migrants in Europe as development actors: Between hope and vulnerability*, Brussels: Eurostep.

Vertovec, S. (1999) 'Conceiving and researching transnationalism', *Ethnic and Racial Studies*, vol 22, no 2, pp 445-62.

Vertovec, S. (2001) 'Transnationalism and identity', *Ethnic and Migration Studies*, vol 27, no 4, pp 573-82.

Voutira, E. and Doná, G. (2007) 'Refugee research methodologies: consolidation and transformation of a field journal', *Journal of Refugee Studies*, vol 20, no 2, pp 163-71.

Wallace, C. (2002) 'Opening and Closing Borders: migration and mobility in East-Central Europe' in *Journal of Ethnic and Migration Studies*, vol 28, no 4, pp 603-25.

Ward, K. (2003) *UK asylum law and process*, ICAR Navigation Guide, London: Information Centre about Asylum and Refugees.

Watt, N. (2009) 'Ministers warn of poll boost for BNP after Question Time', *The Guardian*, 23 October (www.guardian.co.uk/politics/2009/oct/23/bnp-poll-boost-question-time).

Watters, C. (2007a) 'Refugees at Europe's borders: the moral economy of care', *Transcultural Psychiatry*, vol 44, no 3, pp 394-417.

Watters, C. (2007b) 'Editorial' in *International Journal of Migration, Health and Social Care*, vol 3, no 1, pp 1-3.

Webster, M. (1997) *Finding voices making choices*, Nottingham: Educational Heretics Press.

Webster, M. (2005) *Finding voices making choices*, 2nd revised edn, Nottingham: Educational Heretics Press.

Whyte, W.F. (1989) 'Advancing scientific knowledge through participatory action research', *Sociological Forum*, vol 4, no 3, pp 367-85.

Williams, R. (1985) *Keywords: A vocabulary of culture and society*, Oxford: Oxford University Press.

Willmott, P. (1989) *Community initiatives patterns and prospects*, London: Policy Studies Institute.

Wilson, R. (2001) *Dispersed*, York: Joseph Rowntree Foundation.

Winnicott, D.W. (1982) *Playing and reality*, London: Routledge.

Winter, J. and Sivan, E. (1999) 'Setting the framework', in J. Winter and E. Sivan (eds) *War and remembrance in the twentieth century*, Cambridge: Cambridge University Press, pp 6-39.

Witkin, R. (1974) *The intelligence of feeling*, London: Heineman.

Witkin, R. (1995) *Art and social structure*, Cambridge: Polity Press.

Witkin, R. (2002) *Adorno on popular culture*, London: Routledge.

Wolff, J. (1981) *The social production of art*, London: Macmillan.

Woods, P.A. (2003) 'Building on Weber to understand governance: exploring the links between identity, democracy and "inner distance"', *Sociology*, vol 37, no 1, pp 143-63.

Yar, M. (2003) 'Honneth and the communitarians: towards a recognitive critical theory of community', *Res Publica*, vol 9, no 2, pp 101-25.

Young, I.M. (1990) *Justice and the politics of difference*, Princeton, NJ: Princeton University Press.

Yuval-Davis, N. (1999) 'Institutional racism, cultural diversity and citizenship: some reflections on reading the Stephen Lawrence Inquiry report', *Sociological Research Online*, vol 4, no 1 (www.socresonline. org.uk/4/lawrence/yuval-davis.html).

Zetter, R. and Pearl, M. (2000) 'The minority within the minority: refugee community-based organisations in the UK and the impact of restrictionism on asylum-seekers', *Journal of Ethnic and Migration Studies*, vol 26, no 4, pp 675-97.

Zetter, R. (2007) 'More labels, fewer refugees: remaking the refugee label in an era of globalization', *Journal of Refugee Studies*, vol 20, no 2, pp 172-92.

Zetter, R., Griffiths, D., Feretti, S. and Pearl, M. (2003) *An assessment of the impact of asylum policies in Europe 1990-2000*, Home Office Research Study 259 (http://rds.homeoffice.gov.uk/rds/pdfs2/hors259.pdf)

Ziller, A. (2004) 'The community is not a place and why it matters. Case study: Green Square', *Urban Policy and Research*, vol 22, no 4, pp 465-79, December.

Index